STEFONN Q PINKSTON

RICH AFTER WORK

*The Architect's Blueprint for Deleting the Time Clock
and Manifesting Generational Wealth*

Copyright © 2026 by STEFONN Q PINKSTON

All rights reserved. No part of this publication may be reproduced, stored, or transmitted in any form or by any means, electronic, mechanical, photocopying, recording, scanning, or otherwise without written permission from the publisher. It is illegal to copy this book, post it to a website, or distribute it by any other means without permission.

This novel is entirely a work of fiction. The names, characters, and incidents portrayed in it are the work of the author's imagination. Any resemblance to actual persons, living or dead, events, or localities is entirely coincidental.

STEFONN Q PINKSTON asserts the moral right to be identified as the author of this work.

STEFONN Q PINKSTON has no responsibility for the persistence or accuracy of URLs for external or third-party Internet Websites referred to in this publication and does not guarantee that any content on such Websites is, or will remain, accurate or appropriate.

Designations used by companies to distinguish their products are often claimed as trademarks. All brand names and product names used in this book and on its cover are trade names, service marks, trademarks, and registered trademarks of their respective owners. The publishers and the book are not associated with any product or vendor mentioned in this book. None of the companies referenced within the book have endorsed the book.

NON-COMPLIANCE NOTICE:

The unauthorized reproduction of this "Design" is a violation of the Sovereign's Creed. This work is protected by the Bloodline Shield. Any attempt by the "Matrix Profit Center" or its "Bots" to redistribute this knowledge without authorization will be met with the full weight of the Architect's legal and financial defenses.

DISCLAIMER:

The strategies contained within—including the Broom & Shovel Engines, the Omega Protocol, and the Forensic Audit—are for informational and educational purposes only. The Author is not a "Financial Bot" for the World-Cell. The application of these protocols requires individual discernment. Sovereignty is a personal responsibility; the Architect assumes no liability for the "Escape Velocity" achieved by the reader.

JURISDICTION: UNDER THE LAWS OF THE SOURCE.

PRINTED IN THE REALM OF THE SOVEREIGN.

First edition

ISBN (paperback): 979-8-9946656-1-9
ISBN (hardcover): 979-8-9946656-2-6
ISBN (digital): 979-8-9946656-4-0

This book was professionally typeset on Reedsy.
Find out more at reedsy.com

To the Bloodline:

To those before me, whose "Super Powers" where Used to build Kingdoms that they couldn't enter. This work settles the debts that the system owes our name.

To the Architect's Seed:

To my children and the unborn: You are the reason for the Private Vaults and Bloodline Shields. May you never know "The Hum" of the Frequency Traps or the Ceremony of the Time Clocks. This is your map and your sovereignty. You were born free. Stay that way. The debt is settled. The Kingdom is yours!

THE ANCESTRAL DECREE TRESPASSERS: I AM the Great Rupture, shielded by The Father and My Ancestors. To any entity seeking to siphon my life: KNOW YOUR RUIN. My lineage will reap havoc upon your existence until you are erased. I am the Un-hackable code. I AM ALL THAT I AM AND ALL THAT I EVER WILL BE. Any interference triggers immediate spiritual foreclosure. Touch Me or My work and be consumed by the Fire of the Sovereign. I AM GODS FAVOR, THE SOVEREIGN IS AWAKE.

-STEFONN Q PINKSTON

Contents

Foreword — vi
Preface — viii
Acknowledgments — xi
Title Page — xiii
Prologue — 1
Introduction — 4
CHAPTER 0: THE AWAKENING (PART 1) — 7
CHAPTER 0: THE AWAKENING (PART 2) — 11
CHAPTER 0: THE AWAKENING (PART 3) — 14
CHAPTER 0: THE AWAKENING (PART 4) — 17
CHAPTER 0: THE AWAKENING (PART 5) — 21
CHAPTER 0: THE AWAKENING (PART 6) — 25
CHAPTER 1: THE FORENSIC AUDIT (PART 1) — 28
CHAPTER 1: THE FORENSIC AUDIT (PART 2) — 32
CHAPTER 1: THE FORENSIC AUDIT (PART 3) — 36
CHAPTER 1: THE FORENSIC AUDIT (PART 4) — 40
CHAPTER 1: (PART 5)— THE ANCESTRAL AUDIT (THE HIDDEN... — 43
CHAPTER 2: THE DESIGN (PART 1) — 45
CHAPTER 2: THE DESIGN (PART 2) — 47

CHAPTER 2: THE DESIGN (PART 3)	51
CHAPTER 2: THE DESIGN (PART 4)	55
CHAPTER 3: THE TIME (PART 1)	60
CHAPTER 3: THE TIME (PART 2)	63
CHAPTER 3: THE TIME (PART 3)	67
CHAPTER 3: THE TIME (PART 4)	71
CHAPTER 4: THE BROOM & SHOVEL ENGINES (PART 1)	76
CHAPTER 4: THE BROOM & SHOVEL ENGINES (PART 2)	78
CHAPTER 4: THE BROOM & SHOVEL ENGINES (PART 3)	82
CHAPTER 4: THE BROOM & SHOVEL ENGINES (PART 4)	85
CHAPTER 5: THE PRIVATE VAULT (PART 1)	90
CHAPTER 5: THE PRIVATE VAULT (PART 2)	92
CHAPTER 5: THE PRIVATE VAULT (PART 3)	96
CHAPTER 5: THE PRIVATE VAULT (PART 4)	100
CHAPTER 6: THE BLOODLINE SHIELD (PART 1)	102
CHAPTER 6: THE BLOODLINE SHIELD (PART 2)	106
CHAPTER 6: THE BLOODLINE SHIELD (PART 3)	110
CHAPTER 7: THE EXIT (PART 1)	113
CHAPTER 7: THE EXIT (PART 2)	116

CHAPTER 7: PART 2 — THE RITES OF EXTRACTION (THE ALCHEMY OF...	120
CHAPTER 8: THE KINGDOM (PART 1)	122
CHAPTER 8: THE KINGDOM (PART 2)	123
CHAPTER 8: PART 2 — THE SOVEREIGN JURISDICTION (THE ANCIENT...	127
CHAPTER 9: THE MULTI-GENERATIONAL BUILD (PART 1)	129
CHAPTER 9: THE MULTI-GENERATIONAL BUILD (PART 2)	133
CHAPTER 9: THE MULTI-GENERATIONAL BUILD (PART 3)	136
CHAPTER 10: THE SOVEREIGN'S CREED	142
CHAPTER 10: THE FINAL COMMAND	145
CHAPTER 10: THE CREED — THE "ADMIN ACCESS" TO REALITY	147
CHAPTER 11: THE OMEGA PROTOCOL — THE SOVEREIGN'S FINAL...	149
CHAPTER 11: THE OMEGA PROTOCOL — THE RITUALS OF POWER	156
CHAPTER 11: THE PSYCHOLOGICAL SIEGE — THE WAR AFTER 5:00 PM	159
CHAPTER 12: THE SPIRITUAL SIEGE — NAVIGATING THE HARVEST AND...	162
CHAPTER 12: THE SPIRITUAL SIEGE — BREAKING THE ANCESTRAL...	166
CHAPTER 12: THE ASTRAL BREACH	171
CHAPTER 13: THE AKASHIC PROTOCOL(PART 1) — THE UNVEILING OF...	176
CHAPTER 13: THE AKASHIC PROTOCOL (PART 2)— THE UNPRINTED...	185

CHAPTER 13: THE AKASHIC PROTOCOL (PART 3)— THE BIOLOGY OF...	193
CHAPTER 13: THE AKASHIC PROTOCOL (PART 4)— THE CRYSTALLINE...	197
CHAPTER 13: THE AKASHIC PROTOCOL (PART 5)— THE BEDROCK...	201
CHAPTER 13: THE AKASHIC PROTOCOL (PART 6)— THE GOLD-SOUL...	205
CHAPTER 13 (PART 7): THE BIO-ORGANIC CURRENCY & THE NEURAL...	209
CHAPTER 13 (PART 8): THE ARCHITECTURE OF THE "INVISIBLE...	212
CHAPTER 13 (PART 9): THE "GHOST-LABOR" OF THE AETHER	214
CHAPTER 13 (PART 10): THE SUN-EATER PROTOCOL — THE...	216
CHAPTER 13 (PART 11): THE BLOOD-LEDGER — THE BIOLOGICAL...	219
CHAPTER 13 (PART 12): THE COSMOLOGY OF THE SOVEREIGN —...	224
CHAPTER 13 (PART 13): THE FINAL EXIT-PROTOCOL — THE...	238
EPILOGUE	286
THE SOVEREIGN MANIFESTO	287
THE 30-DAY SIEGE INITIATIVE: CHECKLIST	289
THE ADDITIONAL RICHES	291
THE FORBIDDEN APPENDICES	295
TECHNICAL APPENDIX	316
THE ARCHITECT'S ENCYCLOPEDIA	318
THE SOVEREIGN INDEX:	333
THE FORBIDDEN INDEX	336

| *Book Description* | 340 |
| *About the Author* | 342 |

Foreword

THE ARCHITECT'S SHADOW

There are books written to entertain, and there are books written to inform. Then, there are rare, tectonic documents—manuscripts written to **re-order reality**.

I have watched the author of this work, the **Master Architect**, move through the "Laboratory" environments he describes. I have seen him navigate the sterile corridors of the **Matrix Profit Center** with a terrifyingly quiet clarity. While the "Bots" were focused on the next promotion, he was mapping the ventilation shafts. While the executives were obsessed with the quarterly Harvest, he was calculating the **Escape Velocity** of his own soul.

What you are holding is not a "Financial Guide." It is a **Structural Assessment of a Prison**.

To understand the weight of this work, you must first accept a disturbing truth: the world you inhabit is a **Designed Environment**. The 9-to-5 ritual is not an economic necessity; it is a **Frequency Trap**. It is a system optimized to keep you in a "Battery State"—producing just enough energy to keep the gears of the world-cell turning, but never enough to build a Kingdom of your own.

The author has spent years decoding the **Siphon**. He has

identified the precise moment when a human being ceases to be a Sovereign Spirit and becomes a "Human Resource." He has documented the **Status Tax** and the **Spiritual Ceremony of the Clock** with the cold, surgical precision of a forensic scientist.

But he didn't stop at the diagnosis.

In the pages that follow, the Architect provides the **Broom & Shovel Engines**—the mechanical protocols required to sweep away the debris of compliance and dig a foundation that can withstand the coming **Harvest**. He reveals the **Bloodline Shield**, a legal and spiritual fortress designed to protect your legacy from the prying eyes of the MPC.

This work is "Heavy." It carries the density of truth that the modern world is designed to ignore. It is written with a "World-Class" linguistic authority that does not ask for your agreement—it demands your **Awakening**.

If you are looking for a gentle transition, put this book down. This is an **Omega Protocol**. It is for those who are ready to perform the **Final Extraction** and walk away from the Laboratory forever. It is for those who realize that the only way to be **Rich After Work** is to dismantle the very concept of "Work" as the system has defined it.

The spell is cast. The blueprint is open. The Architect is waiting.

Read carefully. Your time is no longer for sale.

Preface

THE TWO-YEAR RUPTURE

Most men need forty years to realize they are being buried alive. It took me two.

I didn't need a decade of "climbing the ladder" to see that the ladder was leaning against a hollow wall. Within twenty-four months of entering a Federal Laboratory, I felt the **Terminal Friction**. I walked into those sterile corridors, sat under those flickering lights, and realized that I was surrounded by "walking ghosts"—men and women who had traded their prime electricity for a cubicle and a title that would be deleted before their obituary was even printed.

I saw the trap immediately.

I watched the "Bots" around me celebrate the 3% raises and the "Benefits" packages, while their eyes grew dimmer with every morning commute. I felt the **Siphon** pulling at my own soul, trying to groom me into a "Human Resource." They wanted My Prime Years, they wanted my intelligence. They wanted to buy my best years in exchange for the promise of a "comfortable" exhaustion at sixty-five.

I refused the trade.

I spent those two years as a mole in the machine. While my peers were learning how to "synergize" and "collaborate,"

I was performing a forensic study of my own confinement. I spent every lunch hour mapping the exits. I spent every "after work" session building my way out because I knew that if I didn't reach **Escape Velocity** fast, the "Low Vibrational Hum" of the office would eventually become my own heart rate.

This book is the result of that two-year fever dream. It is the tactical data of a man who saw the bars and refused to wait for the door to be unlocked.

I wrote this because I realized that "time served" is not a prerequisite for Sovereignty. You don't need a twenty-year career to earn the right to be free; you only need the **Will** to look at the system and say *No.* I saw the **Status Tax** for the bribe it was. I saw the **Spiritual Ceremony of the Clock** for the occult submission it was. And I decided that my life was worth more than a bi-weekly deposit from a Matrix Profit Center.

What you hold in your hands is the record of a **Rupture**.

It's not a memoir of long-term suffering; it's a manual for immediate liberation. It is for the person who feels the nausea *now*. For the person who has been in the job for six months or six years and already knows that they are standing in a graveyard of potential.

I didn't stay until I was broken. I left while I was still dangerous.

I have built the **Private Vault**. I have secured the **Bloodline Shield**. I have seen the "Cold Radiance" of a life where I am the sole Architect of my Tuesday mornings. This is the blueprint of how I did it, and how I did it before the system could even finish its first "extraction" of my soul.

The exit is right in front of you. Don't let them have

another year.

Acknowledgments

ACKNOWLEDGEMENTS: THE SETTLEMENT OF DEBTS

This work was not produced in a vacuum. It was forged in the friction between the **Laboratory** and the **Kingdom**. To those who facilitated its creation—directly or inadvertently—the debt is now acknowledged.

To the Adversaries:

To the "Matrix Profit Centers" that attempted to buy my time and the managers who tried to groom me into a "Human Resource." Thank you for the years of clarity. Without the suffocation of your cubicles and the hollow vibration of your "Low Frequencies," I may never have developed the desperation required to find the **Exit**. You provided the resistance necessary to build the muscle of my **Will**.

To the Bloodline:

To my family, who watched me descend into the "Broom & Shovel" work while the rest of the world was sleeping. Thank you for holding the line while I mapped the **Architecture of the Cage**. This blueprint is as much yours as it is mine; it is the physical manifestation of our **Bloodline Shield**.

To the Catalysts:

To the few Sovereigns I met in the trenches—those who

whispered the first codes of "The Awakening" to me when I was still a "Battery." You know who you are. Your refusal to be sedated by the "Status Tax" gave me the permission to be dangerous.

To the Source:

To THE GRAND ARCHITECT of the Universe, who provided the **Super Powers** and the original "Internal Frequency" that the system tried, and failed, to overwrite. Thank you for the Discipline, the Discernment and the will that you instilled within me that allowed me to see the world for what it truly is.

To the Reader:

By holding this manuscript, you have entered into a contract with your own potential. Your attention is the final ingredient in this **Design**. Acknowledgement is due to you for having the courage to look at the **Forensic Audit** of your own life with optimism, an open mind and the heart to understand that the Real Truth within these pages may go against everything that you think you know.

The ledger is balanced. The debts are settled. The Kingdom begins.

Title Page

RICH AFTER WORK
The Architect's Blueprint for Deleting the Time Clock and Manifesting Generational Wealth
By:
Stefonn Q Pinkston

Prologue

THE GEOMETRY OF THE UNSEEN

The most successful lie ever told was not that the Cage exists, but that you chose to enter it.

As you stand at the precipice of this work, you must understand that you are not merely holding a book; you are grasping a **vibrational disruptor**. For decades, a sophisticated, silent war has been waged against your sovereignty. It is a war of attrition, fought not with steel, but with **Frequency, Space, and Time**. It is a war designed to harvest the very essence of your humanity and convert it into the cold, digital liquid of the **Matrix Profit Center**.

Most men live and die in the **Laboratory**, never realizing that the air they breathe has been de-ionized to dull their rebellion, and the light they work under has been tuned to a frequency that induces a permanent "Beta-wave" trance. They are the **Bots**—the biological batteries of an industrial complex that views a human soul as nothing more than a "Resource" to be mined, depleted, and discarded.

They have taught you to trade your **Sunlight** for their **Fluorescence**. They have taught you to trade your **Legacy** for their **Status Tax**. And they have done it so subtly that you have mistaken your exhaustion for "purpose."

I am here to tell you that your exhaustion is the sound of your life-force being siphoned.

This Prologue is the final moment of silence before the demolition begins. As a world-class architect of your own destiny, you know that you cannot build a **Kingdom** on top of a **Cage**. You must first achieve The **Rupture**. You must look at the "Spiritual Ceremony of the Clock" and see it for the occult submission that it is. You must look at your salary and see it as the "Stay-Quiet" money it has become.

What follows is a high-density **Extraction Protocol**. It is written for the elite—for those whose spirits are too large for a cubicle and whose visions are too vast for a performance review. We are going to deconstruct the **Architecture of the Cage** brick by brick. We are going to ignite the **Broom & Shovel Engines** to clear the debris of your former life. We are going to reach **Escape Velocity**, where the gravity of the world-cell can no longer touch your assets, your family, or your mind.

This is a **Sovereign Mandate**.

The words on these pages carry a weight that the "Bot" cannot bear. This book will haunt you in the quiet hours of the "Laboratory." It will make the "Hum" of the office sound like a scream. It will make the "Benefits" feel like shackles. It is a spell of **Awakening** that, once cast, cannot be broken.

You are being called to move from the **Battery State** to the **Master Architect State**. You are being called to reclaim the **Bloodline Ledger** and build a **Private Vault** that the "Harvest" cannot reach.

Do not read this looking for "tips." Read this looking for **The Exit**. The world you knew is already dead; it just hasn't stopped moving yet. The world you are about to build starts

with the first strike of the Architect's hammer.
The frequency is locked. The Decree is signed.
Welcome to the Great Unveiling.

Introduction

THE OPENING RITE: THE ARCHITECT'S INCANTATION

You are not reading this by accident. You are reading this because the System has failed to sedate you.

Somewhere, deep beneath the layers of "professionalism," "career milestones," and the rhythmic, soul-crushing ceremony of the morning commute, a primal alarm is screaming. You have felt it in the hollow ache of your chest as you stare at the flickering 4100K fluorescent Lab Lights. You have felt it in the frantic, phantom vibration of a phone that demands your attention but offers no life. You are a **Sovereign Spirit** being forced to perform the functions of a **Biological Machine**, and the friction is burning your soul to ash.

Welcome to the **Laboratory**.

The world calls it an office. The Architect calls it an **Extraction Node**. Look around you. Notice the geometry of your confinement: the right-angled cubicles designed to collapse your **Heart-Torus**, the open-floor plans engineered for the "Panopticon Effect" where surveillance is constant and privacy is a myth. This is not a place of creation; it is a **Siphon**. It is a space where your "Super Powers"—your divine creative spark and your finite, non-renewable **Time**—are systematically harvested to fuel a **Matrix Profit Center** that does not know your name and would replace your "Battery" within forty-eight hours of your expiration.

You have been lured into the **Spiritual Ceremony of Clocking In and Clocking Out**. Every day, you perform a ritual of submission, trading the golden hours of your life for a currency designed to melt in your hands. You are then coerced into paying the **Status Tax**—buying the luxury car to sit in the traffic that leads to the job you hate; buying the designer clothes to impress the "Bots & NPCs" you don't like; buying the hollow comforts that act as a sedative for the torment of your own "Battery State."

This manuscript is the end of the sedative.

What you hold in your hands is a **Codex of Mind Altering Information**. It is a "Heavy" frequency designed to disrupt the 60Hz trance of your existence. This is not "Self-Help." Self-help is for the prisoner who wants a more comfortable cell. This is **Architecture**. This is for the prisoner who wants to level the prison and build a **Kingdom** on its ruins.

As you read these words, the **Rich After Work Spell** begins to take hold. It is a spell of **Clarity**. It is a mandate of **Will**. You will feel a cold, iron resolve settle into your marrow. The "Hum" of the Laboratory will start to sound like the screeching of a dying machine. The "Benefits" will start to look like ball & chains. The "Salary" will start to look like a ransom payment for a life you haven't lived yet.

You are mandated to read this beginning to end. Then, you will read it a second time to catch the **Geometric Codes** you missed. By the third reading, you will no longer be a "Bot." You will be a **Master Architect** in a world of "Batteries."

The torment of the 9-to-5 is a spiritual siege. They want

your attention because your attention is the only thing that creates reality. They want your energy because they have none of their own. They want your Time because Time is the only currency the Universe recognizes.

We are taking it all back.

The Audit of who you really are is going to be brutal. The **Broom & Shovel Engines** will be exhausting. The **Omega Protocol** will be terrifying. But on the other side of this Blueprint lies **Escape Velocity**—a state of being where you no longer ask for permission to exist.

The spell is cast. The frequency is locked. Your soul has already recognized the truth: You were never meant to be a "Human Resource." You were meant to be a **God of your own Domain**.

Turn the page. The **Final Extraction** has already begun.

CHAPTER 0: THE AWAKENING (PART 1)

The Architecture of the Cage

The hum is the first thing you notice when the silence finally finds you. It is a low-frequency vibration, a mechanical drone that emanates from the fluorescent ballasts in the ceiling of every Federal Laboratory, every corporate cubicle, and every industrial warehouse in the modernized world. For the average man, this sound is invisible. It has been tuned into the background of his life since he was five years old, sitting at a wooden desk in a state-run classroom, waiting for a bell to tell him when he was allowed to eat, when he was allowed to speak, and when he was allowed to relieve himself.

By the time that boy becomes a man and walks into the Laboratory of the 9-to-5, the hum is no longer an external noise; it is an internal frequency. It is the sound of "Compliance."

For two years, I sat in that lab. I sat there as a man who had "made it" by the Matrix's standards. I had the title. I had the steady deposit. I had the benefits package that promised to take care of my carcass once I was too old to be useful to the machine. But as I sat there, day after day, watching the blue light of the monitor reflect in the dead eyes of my colleagues, I began to see the "Bots."

I call them Bots not out of malice, but out of a tragic observation of their programming. These are men and women who have been systematically lobotomized by the 9-to-5 ritual. They arrive at 8:55 AM, not because they are inspired, but because they are afraid. They eat the same processed "fuel" at the same designated lunch hour, staring at their phones, scrolling through digital hallucinations of other people's lives. They are financing a slow-motion death, trading their most precious commodity—time—for a currency that is being devalued by the second by the very people who own the Laboratory.

The Extraction Protocol

I began to realize that the laboratory wasn't just a place of work; it was a place of extraction. Every person in that room was a battery. Their life essence—their "Super Powers"—were being siphoned off to power a system (the Matrix Profit Center, or MPC) that gave them back just enough "currency" to buy a car to get back to the lab and a house to sleep in so they could recover for the next shift.

It is a closed loop. A perfect circuit of enslavement that requires no chains, only the illusion of necessity. The Architect of the Matrix knows that if you keep a man busy enough, he will never have the energy to realize he is in a cage. If you keep him worried about "Performance Reviews" and "Cost of Living Adjustments," he will never look up at the stars and remember that he was designed for Dominion.

I watched a man in the cubicle next to me. He had been there for twenty-two years. He had a picture of a sailboat on his desk—a dream he had deferred so long it had become a taunt. Every day he checked the "Stock Market," watching numbers move on a screen that represented the crumbs of the wealth he was actually creating for the shareholders. He was grateful for a 3% raise. He didn't realize that inflation was 7%. He was literally paying the company for the privilege of working there, and he was smiling while he did it. That is the power of the hum.

The Spiritual Ceremony of the Clock

When you punch that time clock, you aren't just recording your arrival for HR. You are performing a spiritual ceremony of submission. You are saying to the world, and more importantly, to yourself: "My time is not my own. My value is determined by the duration of my presence in this cage."

The Creator understands that time is the only non-renewable resource in the universe. To trade it for a fixed hourly rate is the highest form of blasphemy against the Father who designed you for Abundance. Time is the canvas upon which we paint our legacy. When you sell that canvas to a corporation for $40 an hour, you are telling the Universe that your legacy is worth less than a tank of gas and a fast-food meal.

I remember the day I stopped looking at the screen and started looking at the architecture of the building itself. I started asking the questions that the "Bots" are programmed to ignore:

- Who owned the land this lab sat on?
- Who owned the debt on the equipment I was using?
- Why was the temperature in the room kept exactly at 71 degrees?

The answer was always the same: Control. The environment was optimized for the machine, not the man. The lighting was designed to keep you alert but drained. The open-plan office was designed for surveillance, not collaboration. Everything was a "Siphon."

CHAPTER 0: THE AWAKENING (PART 2)

The Anatomy of the Status Tax

As I sat within the cubicle walls confined to my desk, I began to perform a psychological autopsy on my coworkers. I wanted to understand why they didn't just walk out. These were intelligent people—engineers, analysts, and scientists—yet they were paralyzed. The answer was a parasite I call the **Status Tax**.

The Matrix does not control you through physical force; it controls you through your desire to be seen as "successful" by other people who are also trapped. The Status Tax is the premium you pay to look like you aren't a slave. I watched as my colleagues competed over who had the newest smartphone, who had the most expensive lease on a German sedan, and who lived in the "best" zip code.

To pay for these things, they had to stay in the lab. They were working jobs they hated to buy things they didn't need to impress people they didn't even like.

I realized that the "Cost of Living" in the Matrix is actually the "Cost of Pretending." If you stripped away the status symbols, the average Bot only needed about 20% of their income to survive. The other 80% was being funneled directly back into the Matrix Profit Center (MPC) via interest on debt and the purchase of depreciating assets. The MPC, not to be mistaken for the NPC (Non Player Characters, Bots) creates the "lifestyle," then they sell you the "salary" to fund it. It is the ultimate "Company Store" model. You aren't earning money; you are merely circulating it back to the people who issued it.

The Birth of the Sovereign Spy

The day I realized this, I didn't quit. Quitting without a system is just a fast way to end up back in another lab. Instead, I became a **Sovereign Spy**.

I stopped being an employee the moment I decided my life belonged to me. Physically, I was still sitting at the desk. I still replied to the emails. I still sat through the "Quarterly Alignment Meetings." But mentally, I was an undercover operative. I was using the Laboratory as my primary investor.

Every paycheck was no longer "rent money"—it was **Seed Capital**. Every hour I spent on their high-speed internet was spent researching the "Broom & Shovel" industries. I used their coffee to fuel my blueprints. I used their electricity to charge the devices that would eventually lead to my liberation.

I began to look at my manager not as a "boss," but as a temporary client who was paying me a retainer while I built my own Kingdom. This shift in frequency is vital. If you act like a victim, you stay a victim. If you act like a Spy, the lab becomes a training ground. I started observing the inefficiencies of the building. I watched how the cleaning crews were managed, how the waste was disposed of, and how the logistics were handled. I was looking for the "Gaps" in the Matrix—the places where a Sovereign man could step in and provide a real service for a real profit.

The Permission Ghost

The greatest barrier I had to overcome—and the one you are likely facing right now—is the **Permission Ghost**. We have been trained by the educational system to wait for a "grade," a "pass," or a "promotion." We feel like we need someone with a title to tell us it's okay to be wealthy.

I saw this Ghost everywhere in the lab. Men would wait for months for "approval" to change a simple process that was clearly broken. They were terrified of making a move without a signature. They had outsourced their agency to a phantom.

The Architect understands that **Permission is a Lie**. The only person who can give you permission to be free is the man in the mirror. I started making decisions without asking. I started setting my own boundaries. I realized that the "rules" of the lab were mostly suggestions backed by the *threat* of disapproval. Once you stop fearing their disapproval, the Ghost vanishes. You realize that the cage door has been unlocked the entire time; you were just waiting for someone to tell you it was okay to push it open.

CHAPTER 0: THE AWAKENING (PART 3)

The Physics of the Void

Most people fear the "Void." In the context of the Laboratory, the Void is the space between your current paycheck and your future Kingdom. It is that terrifying middle ground where you have stopped believing in the Matrix, but your Broom & Shovel engine hasn't fully manifested yet.

I sat in my cubicle and felt the weight of the Void every single day. It feels like a vacuum. The Matrix abhors a vacuum, so it tries to fill that space with noise. It gives you "Urgent" tasks that aren't important. It gives you "Crisis" emails that are just bureaucratic theater. It does this because if you sit in the silence of the Void for too long, you will start to hear the voice of the Father. You will start to remember the **Design**.

The Physics of the Void dictate that whatever you focus on during this transition will expand. If you focus on the "Lack"—the fear of losing your health insurance, the fear of the mortgage, the fear of what your neighbors think—you will manifest a collapse. But if you focus on the **Architecture**, you begin to pull the future into the present. I started spending my lunch hours in my car, staring at nothing, just practicing being "Nothing" to the Matrix. I wanted to become a ghost in their machines. I realized that the less I needed their validation, the more power I had to negotiate my exit.

The First Audit of the Soul

Before you can audit your bank account (which we do in Chapter 1), you must perform a **Forensic Audit of the Soul**. I had to ask myself: *How much of "Stefonn" is actually me, and how much is a byproduct of 20 years of Laboratory conditioning?*

I looked at my habits.

- I drank the coffee they provided because it was "free," not realizing it was a chemical stimulant designed to keep me at the desk during the 2:00 PM slump.
- I wore the clothes they expected me to wear because I wanted to "fit in," not realizing that "fitting in" is the first step to being processed.
- I spoke in their jargon—"synergy," "deliverables," "bandwidth"—until I had lost the ability to speak the language of the Kingdom.

The Audit of the Soul is painful. You have to admit that you have been complicit in your own enslavement. You have to realize that you've been protecting the very cage that is killing you. I saw men in that lab defend the company's policies more fiercely than they defended their own children's future. They had developed "Stockholm Syndrome" for a corporation.

I began to strip away the false identities. I stopped using the jargon. I started drinking water instead of the "Energy Sludge." I started looking people in the eye and speaking the **Frank Truth**. This is where the shift becomes dangerous for the Matrix. When a Bot starts speaking like a Sovereign, the "Static" starts. People will tell you that you're "changing." They will tell you that you're "not a team player." They are right. You are no longer part of their team; you are the owner of your own.

The Frequency of the Exit

The "Exit" is not a physical act; it is a frequency. You do not "quit" a job; you **outgrow** a job.

I watched the frequency of the lab—it was a jagged, anxious vibration. It was the frequency of "I hope I don't get fired" and "I hope I get a bonus." I decided to occupy the frequency of **Certainty**. I knew that my Broom & Shovel strategy was mathematically sound. I knew that my Private Vault was being built. Therefore, the lab was already a memory.

When you occupy the frequency of the Exit while still sitting in the chair, the "Authorities" lose their grip. My supervisor started to become hesitant around me. He couldn't put his finger on it, but he knew I was no longer "under" him. I was a Sovereign entity who happened to be occupying a desk in his department. This is the goal of the Awakening: to reach a state of internal liberation so profound that the external world has no choice but to provide you with the door.

CHAPTER 0: THE AWAKENING (PART 4)

The Ritual of the Red Pen

Once the Soul Audit is complete, the Architect must perform a physical act of defiance. For me, it was the **Ritual of the Red Pen**. I sat down with my previous year of Laboratory "Performance Reviews." These were documents written by people who didn't know my heart, evaluating my "worth" based on metrics designed to benefit a board of directors I would never meet.

I took a red pen and I began to cross out every lie.

- Where they wrote "Needs to be more of a team player," I wrote "Refuses to be a cog in a broken machine."
- Where they wrote "Exceeds expectations in data entry," I wrote "Wasting 40 hours a week on tasks a computer should be doing."
- Where they wrote "Annual Salary: $48,000," I wrote **"Annual Ransom: $48,000."**

This ritual is essential because it breaks the "Parent-Child" relationship between the Matrix and the Man. The Laboratory wants to be your father. It wants to be your provider. It wants you to look to it for your "Allowance" (the paycheck). By taking the red pen to their documents, you are reclaiming the role of Father over your own life. You are telling the system: "You do not define me. You only lease my time, and the lease is about to expire."

I kept those red-marked papers in the top drawer of my desk. Every time I felt the "Permission Ghost" whispering in my ear, I would open that drawer and remind myself who was actually in charge of the narrative. You must have a physical anchor in the lab that reminds you of your Sovereignty. Whether it's a red pen, a specific stone in your pocket, or a digital folder named "THE EXIT," you must have a way to stay grounded in the Kingdom while your body is in the Lab.

The Sovereign's Silence

One of the most difficult "Admin Codes" to master during the Awakening is **The Sovereign's Silence**. When you first realize the walls are made of paper, your instinct is to scream it from the rooftops. You want to wake up the other Bots. You want to tell your work-wife or your cubicle-mate that they are living a lie.

Do not do this.

The Bots are not ready to be unplugged. If you try to wake them up before they have done their own Audit, they will see you as a threat. They will report you to the guards. They will "Concern-troll" you to the HR department. The Matrix uses the other inmates to keep the jailbreak from happening.

I learned to practice a deep, tactical silence. I smiled. I nodded. I performed my tasks with a robotic precision that left no room for critique, but I shared *nothing* of my internal world. My "Broom & Shovel" blueprints were encrypted. My "Private Vault" math was done on paper that I took home every night.

This silence is your power. It creates a "Private Jurisdiction" around your desk. While the other Bots are gossiping and leaking their energy, you are condensing yours. You are becoming a "Black Hole" in the company's data stream—you take in the salary, you take in the information, but you give nothing back but the bare minimum of "Compliance Theater." This silence is the first brick in the wall of your **Bloodline Shield**.

The Geography of Enslavement

As the Awakening deepened, I began to see the very geography of the world differently. I looked at the city not as a collection of buildings, but as a map of "Extraction Zones."

- The Suburbs were "Storage Units" for the Bots.
- The Highways were "Conveyor Belts" to move the batteries to the labs.
- The Malls were "Siphon Centers" designed to empty the batteries of the currency they had just earned.

I realized that to be an Architect, I had to change my relationship with geography. I started taking different routes to the lab. I stopped visiting the "Siphon Centers." I began to visit "Sovereign Sites"—local parks where I could touch the earth, libraries where I could study the laws of Trusts, and the neighborhoods where the people who *owned* the labs lived.

I was studying the "Enemy's Terrain." I wanted to see the difference between a house built on "Credit" and an estate built on "Sovereignty." The difference is visible in the architecture. A Credit-house is loud, flashy, and built with cheap materials. A Sovereign-estate is quiet, hidden, and built to last 300 years. I decided that my Kingdom would not be a loud one. It would be a quiet, unshakeable fortress. I was no longer a resident of the city; I was a Sovereign Surveyor.

CHAPTER 0: THE AWAKENING (PART 5)

The Physics of the Paycheck

In the Laboratory, the paycheck is treated as a "reward" for good behavior. The Bots wait for it with a desperate, bated breath. But the Architect sees the paycheck for what it truly is: a **Tactical Delay**.

The Matrix does not pay you to provide for your life; it pays you to stay quiet for another two weeks. If they paid you what you were actually worth—the true value of the "Super Powers" you exert to keep their systems running—you would have enough capital to leave in a month. By dripping the currency to you in bi-weekly increments, they ensure that you are always in a state of "Just Enough."

I began to study the physics of my own deposit. I realized that the moment the numbers hit my screen, they were already spoken for. The rental companies had a straw in my cup. The car loan had a straw in my cup. The utility companies, the subscription services, and the "Status Tax" merchants all had their straws in my cup. By the time I took a sip, the cup was empty.

This is not "Financial Management"; this is **Life Essence Siphoning**. I realized that the paycheck was a chain made of digital ink. To break the chain, I had to stop viewing the paycheck as "my money" and start viewing it as "the enemy's ammunition" that I had successfully intercepted. I began a practice of "Intercepting the Flow." Instead of letting the money sit in a standard checking account where the Matrix could easily track and tempt it, I moved it immediately into the **Void**—a separate, disconnected account that the "Permission Ghost" couldn't see. I wanted to see how little I could actually survive on while still maintaining the "Spy" persona. I was testing the limits of the cage.

The Midnight Blueprints

While the Bots were sleeping—recovering their bodies so they could be efficient batteries the next morning—I was awake. These were the hours of the **Midnight Blueprints**.

There is a specific kind of clarity that comes at 2:00 AM, when the "Hum" of the city has finally died down. This is when the Architect does his best work. I would sit at my kitchen table with a single lamp, mapping out the "Broom & Shovel" engines. I wasn't just thinking about "starting a business." I was architecting a **Sovereign System**.

I asked myself: *What are the things the Laboratory needs but doesn't want to do itself?* * It needs its floors scrubbed.

- It needs its data secured.
- It needs its waste removed.
- It needs its "Bots" fed.

I began to look for the "High-Need, Low-Ego" industries. The Matrix tries to trick you into wanting a "Sexy" business—a tech startup, a fashion brand, a social media agency. Why? Because sexy businesses are fragile. They rely on "Trends" and

"Likes"—both of which are controlled by the MPC. A "Broom & Shovel" business, however, is rooted in the physical reality of the earth. If the internet goes down tomorrow, the trash still needs to be picked up. If the stock market crashes, the toilets still need to be fixed.

I spent those midnight hours becoming an expert in the "Unsexy." I studied the margins of commercial landscaping. I looked at the logistics of "Last-Mile" delivery. I was looking for the **Bore-Hole**—the single point of entry where I could insert a small system that would produce a large result. These blueprints weren't just business plans; they were my **Declaration of Independence**. Every line I drew on that paper was a blow against the laboratory walls.

The Resistance of the Familiar

As you begin to awaken, you will encounter the most dangerous form of opposition: **The Resistance of the Familiar**. This doesn't come from your boss or the government; it comes from your spouse, your parents, and your best friends.

When I started talking (carefully) about Sovereignty, the people I loved most became the loudest voices of the Matrix.

"Why can't you just be happy with what you have?"

"The economy is too unstable to try something new."

"You have a great 401k, why risk it?"

They weren't trying to hurt me; they were trying to "Save" me by pulling me back into the "Safety" of the cage. They were terrified that if I left, they would have to admit that they were still inside. Your Awakening will make people uncomfortable because it shines a light on their own compliance.

I had to learn to love them without listening to them. I had to build a "Mental Firewall." I realized that you cannot discuss the "Midnight Blueprints" with people who are still operating on the "Daylight Frequency." This is why the **Sovereign's Silence** is so vital. You must build your Kingdom in the dark so that by the time it is visible in the light, it is already too strong to be torn down by the opinions of Bots.

CHAPTER 0: THE AWAKENING (PART 6)

The Geometry of the Vault

Before the "Private Vault" is a financial instrument, it is a geometric concept in the mind of the Architect. In the Laboratory, the geometry of your life is **Linear**. You move from point A (the desk) to point B (the grocery store) to point C (the bed). Your money moves in a straight line: from the Employer to You, and then immediately out to the Merchants.

The Architect's geometry is **Circular**. The Vault is a center point—a gravity well. Every ounce of "Life Essence" (capital) that is captured must be pulled toward the center. Instead of letting the currency pass through you like water through a sieve, you create a container where the water can swirl, build pressure, and eventually drive a turbine.

I began to visualize my Vault as a "Financial Dyson Sphere." I looked at every bill I paid and asked: "How can I make this money curve back toward the center?" If I paid for gas, I looked for ways to own the spread. If I paid for insurance, I looked for ways to become the underwriter. The Vault is not just a place to hide money; it is a lens that focuses your energy. The Bots see a "Savings Account" as a stagnant pool.

The Architect sees the Vault as a **High-Pressure Boiler**. The more energy you pump into it while refusing to let it leak out into the Status Tax, the more power you have to eventually blast through the Laboratory walls.

The Final Night in the Lab

There is a specific kind of ghost that haunts the Laboratory on the final night of an Architect's tenure. For me, that night was not filled with the "Rage" that the movies promise. There was no grand scene of throwing papers in the air or insulting the supervisor. Those are the fantasies of Bots who still believe the system cares about their feelings.

The Architect's exit is a **Cold Extraction**.

On my final night, I stayed late. The cleaning crews—the very "Broom & Shovel" technicians I had been studying—were the only ones left. The "Hum" was at its peak. I walked through the rows of empty cubicles, looking at the "Nesting Materials" the Bots had left behind: the "World's Best Dad" mugs, the motivational posters about "Teamwork" (which really meant "Compliance"), and the ergonomic chairs that were designed to keep them comfortable while their souls were being harvested.

I felt a profound sense of grief, not for the job, but for the people I was leaving behind. They were good people. They were fathers, mothers, and friends. But they were batteries that had forgotten they were once lightning. I realized that my departure was not just for me; it was a "Proof of Concept" for the universe. If one man could use the "Admin Codes" to walk out of this laboratory and build a Kingdom, then the system was not absolute. The Matrix only has power over those who believe the walls are solid.

I turned off my computer for the last time. I didn't "Log

CHAPTER 0: THE AWAKENING (PART 6)

Off"; I **Terminated the Connection**. I left my Federal Government Issued ID badge on the desk—a piece of plastic that had supposedly defined my "Access Level" for years. I realized as I walked toward the elevator that my access level was now **Infinite**. I was no longer a "Level II Federal Administrator" I was a Sovereign Architect.

The Physics of the Door

Walking through the lobby of the Laboratory for the last time, I noticed something strange about the physics of the door. To a Bot, the door is a barrier. It is something that is locked at 5:00 PM and monitored by security. To the Architect, the door is a **Portal**.

The moment I stepped onto the sidewalk, the air felt different. The "Hum" was gone, replaced by the chaotic, beautiful, and terrifying frequency of the **Free World**.

You must understand: the Matrix makes the "Outside" look dangerous. It tells you that without the Laboratory's "Protection" (the salary, the insurance, the structure), you will perish. It creates a "Fear-Wall" at the exit. But as I stood there, I realized that the danger was never on the outside. The danger was in the "Slow-Motion Death" I had just left behind. On the outside, there is **Risk**, but on the inside, there is **Certainty of Decay**. I chose the risk.

I sat in my car and I didn't turn on the radio. I didn't call anyone. I just sat in the **Sovereign Silence**. I was now in the "Void" I had mapped out in my Midnight Blueprints. I was 100% responsible for every breath, every dollar, and every second of my time. It was the most terrifying moment of my life. It was the first time I had been truly alive.

CHAPTER 1: THE FORENSIC AUDIT (PART 1)

The Accountant of the Soul

At the Lab, "Accounting" is something done by a department on the third floor to track the company's budget. In the Kingdom, **Accounting is a Weapon**.

Most Bots have a vague idea of their finances. They know their salary, they know their rent, and they know if they have enough left over for a steak dinner on Friday night. This "Vague Awareness" is a deliberate state of mind maintained by the Matrix. If you knew exactly how much of your life was being stolen, you would be too angry to work. The Forensic Audit is the process of turning on the high-intensity floodlights in the basement of your life.

We are not looking for "Savings"; we are looking for **Stolen Essence**. Every dollar that leaves your pocket and goes to a destination that does not build your Fortress is a piece of your life that has been murdered. If you earn $50 an hour, and you spend $50 on a dinner that you didn't even enjoy, you have effectively worked one hour as a slave for that restaurant. The Forensic Audit is the trial where we identify the thieves.

The Three Tiers of Extraction

To perform the audit, you must categorize every cent of

your outflow into the Three Tiers of Extraction.

1. **The Survival Base:** The calories, shelter, and basic transport required to keep the "Battery" (you) functioning.
2. **The Status Tax:** The premium paid for "prestige"—the brand name clothes, the oversized house, the luxury car lease, the "Premium" subscriptions.
3. **The Matrix Friction:** Interest on credit cards, bank fees, late fees, and the "Silent Tax" of inflation.

I sat at my kitchen table with six months of bank statements and three different colored highlighters.

- **Green** for Survival.
- **Yellow** for Status.
- **Red** for Friction.

By the time I was finished, my statements looked like a crime scene. The red and yellow ink dominated the pages. I realized that while I thought I was "middle class," I was actually a high-volume transit point for the Matrix. I was a "Money Mule" for the banks. I was taking the salary from the Lab and immediately handing it over to the Merchants of Status.

Calculating the Freedom Price

The most important number you will ever calculate is not your Net Worth; it is your **Freedom Price**.

The Matrix wants you to think that "Freedom" costs millions of dollars. They want you to think you need to "Retain a Wealth Manager" and have a "Diversified Portfolio" before you can stop punching the clock. This is a lie designed to keep you in the lab for 40 years.

Your Freedom Price is the **Survival Base** + the **Fortress Seed**.

When I did the math, I realized that my Survival Base—the actual cost to keep my body alive and my head sheltered—was only $2,800 a month. My "Status Tax" was another $3,000. I was working half of my life just to maintain an image for people who didn't care about me.

If I cut the Status Tax, my Freedom Price dropped to $2,800. Suddenly, the "Unreachable Dream" of leaving the lab became a tactical math problem. If I could build a "Broom & Shovel" engine that produced $3,000 a month, I was technically a free man. I didn't need a million dollars; I needed a $3,000-a-month system. This realization is the "Admin Code" that breaks the back of the Matrix. It turns the "Giant" of the Lab into a "Dwarf" that can be outmaneuvered.

The Ghost in the Ledger

As you perform this audit, you will encounter the **Ghost in the Ledger**. This is the emotional resistance you feel when you think about cutting a "Status" expense.

When I looked at my $600-a-month car payment, the Ghost whispered: *"You worked hard for this. You deserve to drive something nice. What will your coworkers think if you show up in a 10-year-old Toyota?"* The Ghost is the voice of the Matrix Profit Center. It uses your ego to protect its revenue stream. I had to realize that the "Nice Car" was actually a $600-a-month subscription to the Laboratory. It was the chain that kept me tethered to the desk. I chose to "Kill the Ghost." I sold the car, bought a reliable "Sovereign Vessel" for cash, and watched my Freedom Price drop instantly.

Every time you eliminate a Status Tax, you are buying back

a piece of your soul. You are "De-leveraging" your life from the Matrix. You are becoming "Light." A light man can run faster. A light man can jump the walls of the Lab.

CHAPTER 1: THE FORENSIC AUDIT (PART 2)

The 12 Siphons of the Lab

Identification is 90% of the battle. The theft of your life essence is not a single, massive heist; it is a "death by a thousand cuts." The Matrix uses **12 Primary Siphons** to ensure that your "cup" is always empty by the time the next paycheck arrives. To dive a bit deeper, we must name them, understand them, and shut them down.

1. **The Convenience Siphon:** This is the tax you pay because the Lab leaves you too exhausted to cook, clean, or think. It is the $15 delivery fees, the $7 lattes, and the pre-packaged "fuel."
2. **The Digital Sedative Siphon:** Subscriptions to entertainment "feeds" (Netflix, Hulu, Gaming) designed to numb the pain of the 9-to-5 so you don't revolt.
3. **The Compound Friction Siphon:** Credit card interest. This is the Laboratory's way of charging you for the privilege of spending money you haven't earned yet.
4. **The Depreciation Siphon:** Owning assets that lose value the moment you touch them (new cars, fast fashion, high-end tech).

5. **The Social Validation Siphon:** Spending capital on "outings" and "events" purely to maintain a presence in a social circle that is also trapped.
6. **The Insurance Bloat:** Paying for "Peace of Mind" products that are statistically designed to never pay out, or over-insuring against risks that are not catastrophic.
7. **The Bank Fee Siphon:** The irony of being charged money to let a bank lend your money to someone else.
8. **The Commute Tax:** The fuel, tires, and maintenance spent simply to transport the "Battery" to the "Charger."
9. **The "Upgrade" Trap:** The belief that every new version of a tool requires a purchase, regardless of the functionality of the current one.
10. **The Impulse Siphon:** One-click purchases made during the "cortisol spikes" of the workday.
11. **The Subscription Ghost:** Forgotten memberships that draw $9.99 or $19.99 monthly, unnoticed but lethal in aggregate.
12. **The Status Rent:** Living in a neighborhood beyond your "Sovereign Number" just for the zip code on the mail.

I sat in my chair and listed every one of these. I realized that my life was a leaking bucket. I was trying to "earn more" to fill the bucket, but the holes were growing faster than the flow. The Architect stops the leaks before increasing the flow.

The Debt Jubilee Protocol

In ancient times, a "Jubilee" was a year where all debts were canceled and everyone returned to their own property. In the Kingdom, you do not wait for the government to declare a Jubilee; you declare a **Personal Debt Jubilee**.

Debt is the "Admin Code" the System uses to override your free will. When you owe the bank, the bank owns your mornings. You cannot be a "Sovereign Spy" if you are a "Debt Slave." I developed a protocol to aggressively collapse the "Friction Siphon."

We do not use the "Snowball" or "Avalanche" methods taught by Laboratory financial gurus. Those take too long. We use the **Extraction Method**.

- **Step 1: Liquidity First.** We do not pay off debt until we have $1,000 in "Strike Capital." If a tire blows, we don't use the credit card; we use the Strike Capital. This breaks the cycle of dependence.
- **Step 2: The Siphon Cut.** We take the results of the Forensic Audit and cut every yellow and red expense immediately. This creates a "Surplus of Essence."
- **Step 3: The Targeted Strike.** We don't spread the surplus across all debts. We pick the one that represents the biggest "Mental Chain" and we destroy it with every spare dollar.
- **Step 4: The Vault Pivot.** Once a debt is paid, that monthly payment does not go back into the "Status Tax." It is immediately redirected into the **Private Vault**.

I remember the day I paid off my last credit card. I didn't feel "Happy"; I felt **Lethal**. I felt like a soldier who had just recovered his ammunition. I realized that the $400 a month I had been paying in interest was now $400 a month I could use to fund my "Broom & Shovel" engine. I was no longer paying for the past; I was funding the future.

The Psychology of the Zero-Base

CHAPTER 1: THE FORENSIC AUDIT (PART 2)

The final part of the Audit is the **Zero-Base Mindset**. You must reach a point where you are comfortable with "Zero." The Matrix wants you to fear a low bank balance because a man with no money is a man who will do anything for a paycheck.

I practiced "The Zero Day." I would go 24 hours without spending a single cent. I wanted to prove to my nervous system that I could survive without the Matrix's merchants. When you lose the fear of having "nothing," the Laboratory loses its leverage. You realize that "Nothing" is actually the "Void" where creation happens.

If the Lab fired me tomorrow, I knew exactly what my "Floor" was. I knew I could survive on rice and beans in a small room while I built my Kingdom. Once you know your "Floor," you are no longer afraid of the "Fall." And a man who is not afraid to fall is a man who can finally learn to fly.

CHAPTER 1: THE FORENSIC AUDIT (PART 3)

The Mathematical Proof of Sovereignty

In the Lab, math is used to complicate your life. They give you "Basis Points," "Amortization Tables," and "Projected Returns." This is **Complexity Theater**. It is designed to make you feel like you aren't smart enough to handle your own money, so you'll hand it over to a "Professional" who is trained by the Matrix to keep you in the Lab.

The Architect uses **Simplified Math**. There is only one equation that matters for your liberation

Where:

- S_f is your **Sovereignty Factor**.
- B_s is your **Survival Base** (The absolute minimum to keep the battery charged).
- I_v is your **Insurance for the Void** (Your liquid "War Chest" for emergencies).
- C_f is your **Monthly Cash Flow** from assets (Your Broom & Shovel engine).

When your S_f is less than or equal to 1, you are a slave. When it is greater than 1, you have achieved **Escape Velocity**.

I sat in my cubicle and ran these numbers every single day. I didn't care about my 401k balance because I couldn't touch that money for 30 years. It was "Dead Capital." I only cared about the gap between my current salary and my B_s. I realized that the smaller I made my B_s through the Forensic Audit, the easier it was for my C_f to overtake it. This is the **Admin Code of Compression**. You don't just work on the income; you work on the *requirement*.

The Sovereignty Ratio (SR)

Beyond the basic proof, you must track your **Sovereignty Ratio (SR)**. This is the percentage of your monthly income that is derived from systems you own versus time you sell.

In the Laboratory, your SR is 0%. Every dollar you earn is tied to your physical presence and the "Rate" set by the MPC. The moment you start your first Broom & Shovel engine—even if it only makes $100 a month—your SR moves.

- **0-10% SR:** The Awakening Stage. You have proof that the system works.
- **10-50% SR:** The Hybrid Stage. You are a "Sovereign Spy." You are using the Lab to fund the expansion of the Engine.
- **50-90% SR:** The Danger Zone. The Matrix will feel you slipping away and will try to offer you a "Promotion" or a "Raise" to pull you back.
- **100% SR:** The Exit. You have achieved total temporal and financial jurisdiction.

I tracked my SR on a graph taped to the inside of my closet. Every time I automated a small part of my side engine, I watched that line move up. It became a game. The

"Stress" of the lab began to evaporate because I was no longer an "Employee" struggling to survive; I was a "Governor" watching a conquest unfold. The math doesn't lie, and the math doesn't have "bad days."

The Time-to-Freedom Constant

The final proof in the Audit is the **Time-to-Freedom Constant**. The Lab tells you that "Time is Money." This is a lie. Time is **Life**, and Money is **Energy**.

If you earn $5,000 a month and spend $4,500, you are only "saving" 10% of your energy. This means for every 10 years you work, you only "buy back" 1 year of your life. This is the **Slow-Death Constant**. At this rate, you will never be free until you are too old to enjoy it.

The Architect seeks a **50% Extraction Rate**. By cutting the Status Tax and the Matrix Friction, I was able to live on 50% of my income. This changed the constant: for every 1 year I worked, I bought back 1 year of my life. I was effectively working "Double Time" for my own liberation. This is how you compress a 40 year career into a 5 year Build. You aren't "working harder"; you are **Capturing more Essence**.

The Logic of the Lever

The Audit concludes with a shift in logic. The Bot looks at a $1,000 expense and asks, "Can I afford this?" The Architect looks at that $1,000 and asks, "How many hours of my life did this cost, and what is the **Opportunity Cost** of this capital in my Private Vault?"

If that $1,000 stayed in my Vault, and I used it to buy a piece of equipment for my engine that produced $50 a month for life, that $1,000 is a **Lever**. If I spend it on a new TV, it is a **Weight**.

The Forensic Audit turns you into a "Lever-Seeker." You

begin to see the world not as a collection of things to buy, but as a field of levers to pull. You realize that the only reason you are still in the Lab is that you have been carrying too many weights and not pulling enough levers. The math is now clear. The weights have been identified. The levers are being forged. We are moving from the Audit to the **Architecture**.

CHAPTER 1: THE FORENSIC AUDIT (PART 4)

The Sovereignty Ledger

The final tool in your Audit toolkit is not a software program or a banking app. The Matrix loves digital tools because they can be monitored, tracked, and manipulated. To truly separate your mind from the Laboratory, you must create a physical Sovereignty Ledger.

I used a simple, cheap composition notebook. This was my "Book of Life." In it, I recorded the Daily Extraction. Every evening, I would sit down and account for every minute and every dollar.

Did I give the Lab an extra 15 minutes of free labor today? That goes in the "Loss" column.

Did I avoid a Status Tax purchase? That goes in the "Captured Essence" column.

Did I learn a new "Admin Code" for my Broom & Shovel engine? That is "Capital Growth."

By physically writing these things down, you are engaging a different part of your brain. You are moving from a passive observer of your life to an active Governor. The Ledger is the record of your war against the Matrix. When you look back at a month of entries and see the "Captured Essence" growing,

CHAPTER 1: THE FORENSIC AUDIT (PART 4)

you develop a sense of momentum that no bank statement can provide. You are witnessing the birth of a Kingdom.

The Transition to the Blueprint

The Audit is now complete. You have turned on the lights. You have identified the siphons. You have calculated your Freedom Price and proven the math of your liberation. The weights have been cast off. You are "Light."

But being "Light" is not enough. A light object with no direction is just a leaf in the wind. To leave the Laboratory, you must become a Guided Missile. You need a target, a trajectory, and a propulsion system. This is what we call The Design.

I remember the night I closed the Audit phase of my life. I had the numbers. I knew I needed exactly $3,200 a month to be free. I knew I had $12,000 in my "Strike Capital" account. I knew my Status Tax was dead. I sat there in the silence of my kitchen and realized that for the first time in my life, I wasn't "hoping" for a better future. I was looking at a mathematical certainty.

The fear was gone. The anxiety of the "9-to-5" was replaced by the cold, calculated focus of a builder. I was no longer an inmate looking at the walls; I was an Architect looking at the foundation.

The Invitation to the Drafting Room

In the next chapter, we are going to move into the Drafting Room. We are going to take the "Captured Essence" from your Audit and start building the Broom & Shovel Engine. We are going to map out the Private Vault mechanics in high-definition detail.

You have done the hard work of looking in the mirror and admitting you were a slave. Now, you get to do the glorious work of deciding what kind of King or Queen you will be. We are moving from the "What" to the "How." We are moving from the "Audit" of the past to the Design of the Future.

The door to the Laboratory is behind you. The Drafting Room is open.

CHAPTER 1: (PART 5)— THE ANCESTRAL AUDIT (THE HIDDEN LEDGERS)

The Law of Mentalism: The First Wealth
The ancestors taught that *"The All is Mind; the Universe is Mental."* The Matrix wants you to believe that wealth is physical (labor + time = money). This is a lie designed to keep you in the physical Laboratory, Working. The world secret is that **Capital is a Frequency.** Before a dollar manifests in your hand, it must exist as a "Coherent Thought Form" in your mind. Most people fail the Audit because their mental frequency is "Static." They think in terms of "Bills," "Debt," and "Needs." This sends a signal of **Scarcity** to the field. The millionaire frequency is one of **Stewardship.** You are not asking for money; you are claiming jurisdiction over the energy required to fulfill your purpose.

The World Secret: The 90/10 Energy Siphon
The Laboratory is not just taking your money through taxes; it is taking your **Aether** (your creative spirit). Hidden records of early industrial architects show that the "40-hour work week" was scientifically designed to keep the human

brain in a state of "Beta Wave" stress. This prevents you from entering "Alpha" or "Theta" states where true creation happens.

When you perform the Audit, you are not just looking at bank statements; you are auditing your **Brain State.** If 90% of your day is spent in "survival stress," you are a prisoner. The Architect reclaims his "Theta Hours" (the time just before sleep and just after waking) to program the reality he desires.

Sovereign Affirmation (The Destroyer of Scarcity):

"I am the Source of my own supply. I do not look to the Matrix for my daily bread; I look to the Infinite Intelligence within. I am a conductor of wealth, and my frequency is tuned to abundance. The Siphons of the world have no hold on my Spirit."

CHAPTER 2: THE DESIGN (PART 1)

The Geometry of Sovereignty

Every great structure begins with a line. Within the system, the only line you were taught to follow was the "Corporate Ladder"—a vertical line that leads to a ceiling owned by someone else. In the Kingdom, we use **Sacred Geometry**.

The Design is the process of creating a **Sovereign Estate**. This is not a "business plan." Business plans are for people looking for "Investors" (more Laboratory masters). A Design is for a man looking for **Jurisdiction**.

We start with the **Central Point**: You and your Sovereign Number. Everything else orbits this point. We are going to build a system that is:

1. **Invisible** to the MPC.
2. **Incorruptible** by the Status Tax.
3. **Indestructible** by the Economy.

I began my Design by drawing a circle on a blank sheet of paper. Inside that circle, I wrote my Sovereign Number: **$3,200**. This was my sun. Every asset I built, every "Shovel" I bought, and every "Broom" I managed had to gravitate toward that $3,200. If an idea didn't lead directly to that number, it was a distraction.

The Three Pillars of the Estate

The Design is supported by three pillars:

- **Pillar 1: The Cash Flow Engine (The Broom & Shovel).** This provides the "Oxygen" for your estate.
- **Pillar 2: The Private Vault (The Reservoir).** This captures and recycles the "Oxygen" so it never leaves your jurisdiction.
- **Pillar 3: The Bloodline Shield (The Fortress).** This ensures that neither the government nor the banks can ever breach your walls.

If you have an engine but no vault, your money leaks out. If you have a vault but no engine, your estate withers. If you have both but no shield, the Matrix will eventually come to seize it. Most "wealthy" people in the Laboratory only have an engine; they are just high-paid slaves. The Architect builds all three simultaneously.

CHAPTER 2: THE DESIGN (PART 2)

The Blueprint of the Broom & Shovel
When I sat down to design my first engine, I had to unlearn everything the "Guru Bots" had taught me. The Lab wants you to focus on "Scalability," "Venture Capital," and "Disruption." These are Matrix traps. They require you to go into debt, hire massive teams (more Bots), and eventually sell your soul to a board of directors just to survive.

The Architect designs for **Solidity**. We use the **Broom & Shovel Blueprint**.

Think about the physics of a gold rush. Thousands of people rush into the mountains, fueled by the "Hope" of finding a nugget. These people are the Bots. They are chasing a dream sold to them by the Matrix. Most of them die broke in the mud. But who gets wealthy? The man selling the **Broom** (to clean the camp) and the **Shovel** (to dig the hole).

The Broom & Shovel engine is a business based on **Non-Discretionary Necessity**. It is a service or product that the world requires even if the stock market crashes, even if a pandemic hits, and even if the "Next Big Thing" fails.

- It is cleaning.
- It is repair.
- It is logistics.
- It is essential infrastructure.

I looked at my local city as a machine. Every machine needs maintenance. I didn't want to build a "New App"; I wanted to be the man who owned the trucks that hauled the waste of the companies that built the apps. I wanted to be the "Invisible Floor" that the world walked on. Why? Because the "Floor" is never out of style.

The Mechanics of Essentiality

To design an essential engine, you must pass your idea through the **Filter of the Three Nevers**:

1. **Never rely on a Trend:** If your business depends on "What's Hot," you are a slave to the Matrix's attention span.
2. **Never rely on a Middleman:** If a platform (like Amazon, YouTube, or Uber) can turn off your income with a single algorithm change, you don't own a business; you own a "Digital Cubicle."
3. **Never rely on Luxury:** In an "Economic Reset," the first thing Bots cut is their "Luxury." They never cut their "Utility."

My first Broom & Shovel design was built around **Commercial Facility Maintenance**. I realized that every office building in my city was required by law and by health standards to be cleaned and maintained every single night. The "Lab" I worked in spent $20,000 a month on these services. I looked at the men doing the work—they were being paid $12 an hour by a massive corporation that was pocketing the other $18,000.

The "Grip" was in the middle. The corporation was a "Bot-Manager." I designed a system to be a **Sovereign Provider**. I didn't need 100 buildings; I only needed three. Three buildings would produce enough "Cash Flow" (C_f) to exceed my "Sovereignty Factor."

Designing for Low Friction

The mistake the Bot makes when starting a business is "Over-Designing." They think they need an office, a logo, a fleet of new trucks, and a payroll software. This is the **Complexity Tax**.

The Architect designs for **Low Friction**. My design required zero debt. I started with one used machine and a contract I won through the "Sovereign Spy" network I had built. I designed the business to function on "Automated Simplicity."

- No employees (I used specialized contractors who were also looking for sovereignty).
- No office (The world was my office).
- No "Brand" (My reputation for essentiality was my brand).

Every dollar that came in was "Clean." It didn't have to pay for a "Corporate Headquarters." It went straight through the Broom & Shovel engine and into the **Private Vault**. I was building a "Ghost Engine"—one that provided massive value to the world but remained invisible to the "Siphon Hunters" of the Matrix.

The Sovereignty of the System

A business is only a "Kingdom" if it can run without you. If you have to be there to push the broom, you have simply created a "Self-Imposed Lab."

The final part of the Design is the **Operating System (OS)**. I wrote down every single step of the process. I turned my expertise into a "Manual of Instruction." I realized that if I could teach a "Bot" how to follow the manual, I could buy back my time.

I wasn't "hiring an employee"; I was **Installing a Component**. I paid them better than the Laboratory did, which ensured their loyalty, but I kept the "Admin Codes" (the contracts and the math) for myself. The system was designed to be a "Set and Forget" reactor. Once the reactor was "Critical" (producing more energy than it consumed), I could step away and focus on the next pillar: **The Private Vault**.

CHAPTER 2: THE DESIGN (PART 3)

The Architecture of the Private Vault

At the Plantation, you are taught to be a "Saver." The Matrix loves savers because a saver is someone who hands their "Life Essence" to a bank for a 0.01% return so the bank can lend it back to other Bots at 20% interest. The bank uses your energy to fund your own enslavement.

The Architect does not "save." The Architect **Vaults**.

The **Private Vault** is not a physical box (though it can include one); it is a **Legal and Financial Loop**. It is a system designed to ensure that once a dollar enters your Kingdom, it never leaves. It becomes a permanent resident. I began to design my Vault as a "Financial Black Hole." Light can get in, but nothing can get out without my direct "Admin Authorization."

The design of the Vault requires three distinct layers:

1. **The Capture Layer:** The entry point for the C_f (Cash Flow) from your Broom & Shovel engines.
2. **The Multiplication Layer:** The "Internal Bank" where the capital is borrowed against itself to fund more engines.

3. **The Preservation Layer:** High-density, physical assets that do not rely on the digital "Hum" of the Matrix (Gold, Silver, Land, Productive Tools).

I sat in the silence of my design room and realized that my "Vault" had to be invisible to the **Siphon List**. If the money sat in a standard personal checking account, it was "In Play." The Matrix could freeze it, tax it, or tempt me to spend it on a Status Tax item. I had to design a "Firewall."

The Philosophy of the Sovereign Bank

The greatest "Admin Code" I discovered was this: **You must become the Bank.** In the Matrix, the Bank is the predator and you are the prey. In the Kingdom, you occupy both roles. You are the **Lender** and the **Borrower**. When my Broom & Shovel engine produced a surplus, I didn't "pay off" my personal needs. I "lent" the money from my Vault to my personal self at a set interest rate.

Why would I charge myself interest? Because interest is the "Gravity" that keeps the Vault growing. Instead of paying interest to a faceless corporation in a glass tower, I was paying it to my **Bloodline**. The interest stayed within my jurisdiction.

I began to see my capital as a "Soldier." A soldier's job is to go out, capture more territory, and bring back prisoners (more capital). If I spent a dollar on a "Status Tax" item, that soldier was dead. If I "Vaulted" that dollar, that soldier was in the barracks, training and reproducing. I realized that the wealthy don't have "more money"; they have **more soldiers who never die.**

The Internal Ledger of the Vault

To manage the Vault, you cannot use the "Laboratory Apps."

You need an **Internal Ledger**. This is the master record of your "Sovereign Debt" and "Sovereign Credit."

I mapped out the "Velocity of My Flow." I didn't want my money to sit still. Money that sits still is "stale" and susceptible to the "Inflation Siphon." I designed the Vault to be a **Centrifuge**.

- The C_f comes in.
- It is immediately split: 50% to "Fortress Growth," 30% to "System Maintenance," and 20% to "The Sovereign's Life."
- The "Fortress Growth" portion is then used to buy a "Shovel" (a tool for the next engine).

By the time I was finished with the design, I realized I had created a **Perpetual Motion Machine**. The more the Broom & Shovel engine worked, the more the Vault grew. The more the Vault grew, the more Shovels I could buy. The more Shovels I bought, the faster the engine ran. I was no longer "working for money." I was **Overseeing a Reactor**.

The Moral Weight of the Vault

The Matrix tries to tell you that "Hoarding" money is wrong. They want you to "Circulate" it (which is a code word for "Spend it back to us").

The Architect knows that a Vault is not "Hoarding"; it is **Stewarding**. You are protecting the "Life Essence" of your ancestors and your descendants. A man with an empty Vault is a man who can be forced to do "Unclean Work" for the Lab. A man with a full Vault is a man who can say **"No."** The Vault is the physical manifestation of your "No." It is your "F-You Capital." I realized that every dollar in my Vault was a minute of my future that I had already bought back. I wasn't looking at "Numbers"; I was looking at **Freedom Vouchers**. The Design was solid. The Physics were sound. It was time to move from the "Storage" to the "Defense."

CHAPTER 2: THE DESIGN (PART 4)

Designing the Bloodline Shield

The final pillar of the Design is the **Bloodline Shield**. In the Laboratory, they teach you that "Ownership" is the goal. They want you to put your name on the deed, your name on the car title, and your name on the bank account. This is a strategic error. In the Matrix, **Ownership is a Liability**.

When you "own" something in your personal capacity, you are a target for the "Litigation Siphon," the "Estate Tax Siphon," and the "Policy Shift Siphon." If the Matrix decides you are a "Non-Compliant Battery," they can simply flip a switch and freeze everything attached to your Social Security number.

The Architect designs for **Control without Ownership**. We utilize the **Bloodline Shield**, a legal architecture based on the "Private Irrevocable Trust." This is not just a document; it is a **Sovereign Jurisdiction**. When you move your "Life Essence" (assets) into the Shield, you are effectively taking them out of the United States, out of the Matrix Profit Center, and into a private "City-State" where you are the Governor, but the "Bot" version of you owns nothing.

I sat in my drafting room and mapped out the "Firewalls." I realized that if my Broom & Shovel engine was held by the Trust, and my Private Vault was held by the Trust, then "Stefonn the Employee" was essentially invisible. If someone tried to sue me, they were suing a ghost. If the bank tried to seize my assets, they found a vault with no name on the door. The Shield is the "Stealth Coating" for your Kingdom.

The Rockefeller Trust Protocol

To design a Shield that lasts for 300 years, you must study the "Admin Codes" of the elite. I looked at the **Rockefeller Protocol**. The wealthiest families in the world do not leave "Inheritances"; they leave **Endowments held in Trust**.

The difference is vital. An "Inheritance" is a lump sum of energy given to a "Bot" (the heir) who has not been trained to manage it. The Matrix loves inheritances because the heir usually spends the capital on the "Status Tax," returning the energy to the MPC within two generations.

A **Bloodline Shield** is designed to be a **Lending Institution for the Family**.

- The Shield owns the business.
- The Shield owns the land.
- The Shield owns the "Shovels."

If a member of the bloodline wants to start their own engine, they do not go to a Matrix bank; they "Apply" to the Bloodline Shield. The Trust lends them the capital at a low interest rate. The interest goes back into the Trust. The wealth never leaves the family circle. I realized that by designing this Shield, I wasn't just planning my "Retirement"; I was founding a **Dynasty**. I was ensuring that my great-grandchildren would never have to set foot in a Laboratory unless they chose to own it.

The Firewall Architecture

A Shield is only as strong as its weakest "Sovereign Cell." I designed the Shield using **Firewall Architecture**.

In the Laboratory, if one part of your life fails (you lose your job), the whole system collapses (you lose the house). There are no firewalls. In the Kingdom, we "Segregate" the risk.

- **Cell A:** The Real Estate (Held in a specific Trust).
- **Cell B:** The Broom & Shovel Engine (Held in an LLC owned by the Trust).
- **Cell C:** The Private Vault (Held in a Sovereign Account).

If Cell B hits a legal snag, the "Firewall" prevents the heat from reaching Cell A or Cell C. I spent hours drawing the "Flow of Liability." I wanted to ensure that no matter what "Static" the Matrix generated, the core of my Fortress would remain at a "Cool Frequency." This is the **Logic of the Citadel**. You don't build one big wall; you build a series of concentric circles, each with its own gate and its own key.

The Spiritual Weight of the Shield

Designing the Shield requires a shift in your **Temporal Horizon**. Most Bots think in terms of "The Weekend" or "The Next Quarter." The Architect thinks in terms of **Centuries**.

I felt a profound shift in my nervous system when the Shield design was complete. I was no longer a "man trying to get rich." I was a **Founder**. I had a responsibility to the people who would carry my name in the year 2125. The Shield is the physical manifestation of your **Legacy**. It is your way of saying to the Matrix: "You can have my body for now, but you will never have my Bloodline."

The Design was now finished. I had the Audit (the Past), the Engine (the Flow), the Vault (the Storage), and the Shield (the Defense). The Blueprint was complete. It was time to stop drawing and start **Building**. We were moving from the Drafting Room to the **Construction Site**.

The Ancestral Code of Silence: Harpocrates' Law

The greatest secret of the ancient builders was **Silence.** In the Matrix, you are encouraged to "share your goals" on social media. This is a trap. When you speak your goal, your brain releases dopamine as if you already achieved it, killing your "Build Drive." Furthermore, you leak the energy of your Siege to the "Eyes of the Bots," who will subconsciously try to pull you back.

The Ancestors said: *"To Know, to Will, to Dare, and to keep Silent."* During your 5-year Siege, you must become a "Ghost." Do not tell the Laboratory you are leaving. Do not tell your friends you are building a Kingdom. Let your **results** be the only noise you make.

The World Secret: The 4:00 AM Alchemy

The Matrix uses "Frequency Fences" (Electronic noise, cellular signals, social media pings) to disrupt the human bio-field. However, these fences are weakest between **3:33 AM and 5:00 AM.** This is the "Amrit Vela" or the "Ambrosial Hours."

The millionaires who "Rip the Matrix" do not wake up early just to "work hard"; they wake up to **Order Reality** while the Matrix's guard is down. During this time, the "Veil" is thin. Whatever you write in your Kingdom Ledger during these hours carries 10x the manifestation power of anything written at noon.

CHAPTER 2: THE DESIGN (PART 4)

Sovereign Affirmation (The Shield of Will):

"I am a Fortress of Will. My plans are hidden from the eyes of the curious. My energy is focused like a laser on the Build. I am unmoved by the opinions of Bots. I am the master of my silence and the king of my results."

CHAPTER 3: THE TIME (PART 1)

The temporal Laboratory

In the Federal Laboratory, the most expensive thing they steal from you isn't your money—it is your **Time-Value**. The Matrix Profit Center (MPC) operates on a specific chronological frequency called "Linear Decay." They convince the "Bot" that their life is a slow, steady decline from age 25 to age 65. They sell you the lie of the "Gold Watch"—the idea that you should trade the strongest years of your physical and mental life (your Super Powers) for the "right" to be free when you are too tired to move and too old to dream.

I sat in my cubicle and looked at the clock. It was a standard industrial wall clock, the kind you find in prisons and elementary schools. I realized that the "Tick" of that clock was actually the sound of my life essence being harvested. To the Laboratory, an hour is a unit of production. To the Architect, an hour is a unit of **Destiny**.

The first step in Chapter 3 is reclaiming your **Temporal Jurisdiction**. You must stop asking "What time is it?" and start asking "Who owns this hour?" If the answer is "the company," you are in a state of loss. If the answer is "the Build," you are in a state of growth. We are moving from the

"40-Year Sentence" to the **"5-Year Siege."**

The 40-Year Lie: A Mathematical Fraud

Let's perform a surgical strike on the standard retirement model. The Matrix tells you to save 10% of your income for 40 years. Mathematically, this is a fraud designed to keep the "Battery" in the charger for as long as possible.

If you save 10% of your income, you are essentially working 9 years to "buy" 1 year of freedom. If you start at 20, you won't buy back your life until you are 70. This assumes the currency holds its value (it won't) and the market always goes up (it doesn't). The 40-year model is a high-risk gamble where the house always wins.

The Architect uses the **Law of Compression**. I realized that if I could increase my "Extraction Rate" (the amount of income diverted to the Vault) to 50%, the math changed instantly. For every 1 year I worked, I bought 1 year of freedom. If I could push it to 70% through the "Broom & Shovel" engine, I could buy back my entire life in less than 7 years. I stopped looking at "Retirement" as an age and started looking at it as a **Calculated Volume of Energy**. Once the Vault reached the level where it could fund the "Survival Base" indefinitely, time belonged to me.

The Three Levels of Time

To master the Build, you must understand that not all hours are created equal. In the Laboratory, every hour is flat. From 9:00 AM to 5:00 PM, the value is $X per hour. The Architect recognizes three distinct levels of time:

1. **Dead Time:** Time spent performing tasks for the Matrix. This is time you have sold. It is gone.
2. **Maintenance Time:** Time spent sleeping, eating, and

recovering. This is the "Battery Recharge."
3. **Active Build Time:** These are the "Sovereign Hours" spent constructing the Engine, the Vault, and the Shield.

The "Bot" maximizes Dead Time to get a "Bonus." The Architect minimizes Dead Time to maximize **Active Build Time**. I began to treat my 6:00 PM to 10:00 PM block as more valuable than my 9:00 AM to 5:00 PM block. Why? Because the money I made at the Lab was "Maintenance Money," but the work I did at night was **"Exit Money."** One was for survival; the other was for Sovereignty.

The Ritual of the Temporal Audit

Just as we audited the money in Chapter 1, we must audit the minutes. I carried a stopwatch in the lab for one week. Every time I was interrupted by a "Status Meeting" or a "Social Bot" (a coworker wanting to gossip), I started the timer.

By Friday, I realized the Matrix was stealing 4 hours of my "sold" time every day with noise. I decided to reclaim those 4 hours *while still on the clock*. I became a "Ghost in the Machine." I used those 4 hours of stolen "Corporate Time" to research my Trust structures and map out my routes for the cleaning contracts. If the Lab was going to steal my life, I was going to steal their infrastructure to build my jailbreak.

This is the **Sovereign's Reclaim**. You are not "stealing" from a company; you are recovering stolen property—your life. You must reach a point where every second is accounted for in your **Sovereignty Ledger**. When the Matrix sees that you no longer have "Free Time" to be distracted, it loses its ability to influence your frequency. You are now on "Build Time."

CHAPTER 3: THE TIME (PART 2)

The Architecture of the 5-Year Siege

The System wants you to believe in "Balance." They want you to have a "Work-Life Balance" where you spend your days exhausted in the lab and your evenings and weekends recovering with mindless entertainment. This "Balance" is a lie designed to keep your momentum at zero. A pendulum in balance never moves forward; it only swings back and forth over the same tired ground.

The Architect rejects balance in favor of the **Siege**.

A Siege is a period of total, unyielding focus. When an army lays siege to a fortress, they do not take weekends off. They do not "relax" on Tuesday afternoons. They are 100% committed to the collapse of the walls. I decided that my exit would be a **5-Year Siege**. For 60 months, I would dedicate every ounce of "Discretionary Life Essence" to the Build.

This means you must redefine your relationship with the calendar. You are no longer living for "Friday Night." You are living for **The Day of Extraction**. During the Siege, your social life will thin out. The "Bots" in your circle will complain that they don't see you anymore. They will say you are "obsessed." Let them. They are obsessed with their own comfort; you are obsessed with your own Liberty. The Siege requires a level of intensity that the Matrix cannot match.

The Death of the Weekend

The "Weekend" is one of the most successful psychological operations in human history. The Matrix gives the Bot 48 hours of "freedom" to ensure they don't jump off a bridge on Monday morning. It is a "Pressure Release Valve." They want you to go out, spend the currency you just earned (the Status Tax), and numb your brain with alcohol or digital noise so you are "reset" for the next 40-hour extraction.

In the Kingdom, **the Weekend does not exist.**

During my Siege, Saturday and Sunday were my "High-Velocity Build Days." While the Bots were sleeping in or watching the "Game," I was in the field. I was meeting with contractors, I was auditing my Broom & Shovel routes, and I was studying the math of the Private Vault.

I looked at the weekend as a 32-hour gift from the Universe. If you work 40 hours for the Lab and 32 hours for the Kingdom, you are effectively living two lives in one week. You are accelerating your "Time-to-Freedom" constant by 80%. I realized that by "killing" the weekend for five years, I was buying back every weekend for the next fifty years. This is the **Logic of Delayed Gratification**, a concept that the Matrix tries to erase from your mind through "Instant Delivery" and "One-Click" dopamine.

Temporal Compounding

Just as money compounds in the Vault, time compounds in the Siege. When you spend 4 hours a day on the same problem—the architecture of your Sovereignty—you develop **Deep Domain Expertise**.

The first year of the Siege is the hardest. You are moving a stationary object. You are fighting the "Gravity of the Known."

But by year three, the "momentum" of your Build starts to take on a life of its own. Your Broom & Shovel engines start to run with less "Effort." Your "Sovereign Spy" network starts to bring you deals without you looking for them.

I call this **Temporal Compounding**. The more time you "invest" in your own jurisdiction, the more "interest" that time pays back in the form of efficiency. By year four of my Siege, I was getting 10 hours of "Matrix Value" out of every 1 hour of "Build Time." I had collapsed the distance between the thought and the manifestation. The 40-year career is a linear line; the 5-year Siege is an **Exponential Curve**.

The Sovereign Clock

To manage the Siege, you must install a **Sovereign Clock** in your mind. This clock does not measure minutes; it measures **Milestones**.

- **Milestone 1:** The Survival Base is covered by C_f (Cash Flow).
- **Milestone 2:** The Private Vault contains 12 months of "War Chest" liquidity.
- **Milestone 3:** The Bloodline Shield is legally active.
- **Milestone 4:** The ID Badge is left on the desk.

I stopped looking at the calendar and started looking at the Milestones. I didn't care if it was October or March; I only cared if I was closer to Milestone 2. This detaches your nervous system from the "Company Calendar." You stop worrying about "Holiday Bonuses" because you are focused on the **Independence Bonus**.

When you live by the Sovereign Clock, you become patient. You realize that a 5-year Siege is a tiny fraction of a 80-year life. The "Bots" are impatient in the short term (they want the latte now) but patient in the long term (they are willing to wait 40 years to be free). The Architect is **Impatient in the short term** (every minute of the Build must count) but **Patient in the long term** (we know the 5-year math is absolute).

CHAPTER 3: THE TIME (PART 3)

The Physics of the 4-Hour Deep Work Block

At the Plant the "Work Day" is eight hours long, but the "Work" is only about ninety minutes of actual cognitive output. The rest is performative friction: meetings about meetings, email threads that never end, and the slow, rhythmic shuffling of digital papers. The Matrix has convinced the Bot that "Time Spent" equals "Value Created."

The Architect knows the truth: **Impact is a function of Intensity, not Duration.**

I designed my Siege around the **4-Hour Deep Work Block**. This is a period of total cognitive immersion where the phone is off, the internet is disconnected (unless required for the Build), and the "Sovereign Silence" is absolute. In the physics of the mind, one hour of "Deep Work" is equivalent to five hours of "Matrix Work."

I performed this block from 4:00 AM to 8:00 AM, before I ever stepped foot into the Federal Laboratory. By the time I arrived at my cubicle and checked my first email, my most important work for my own Kingdom was already done. I had already moved the needle on my "Broom & Shovel" blueprints. I had already audited my "Private Vault." This created a "Psychological Shield." Because I had already won the morning for myself, nothing the Lab did to me during the day could truly touch me. I was playing with "House Time."

The Sovereignty of Sleep

The Matrix loves a sleep-deprived battery. When you are tired, your "Resistance" is low. You are more likely to seek the "Convenience Siphon" (buying fast food because you're too tired to cook). You are more likely to fall for the "Status Tax" (seeking a dopamine hit from shopping). Most importantly, you are too exhausted to think critically about your own enslavement.

I realized that to maintain the Siege for five years, I couldn't "Burn the Candle at both ends" in the traditional sense. I had to become a **Professional Recycler of Energy**.

Sleep is not "Time Lost"; it is the **Refiner's Fire** of the brain. During sleep, the brain flushes out the "Metabolic Waste" of the day's stress. I began to treat my sleep as a "Military Asset." I designed a "Sleep Protocol":

- **Total Darkness:** To signal the pineal gland that the "Spy Mission" is over for the day.
- **Temperature Regulation:** To keep the body in a state of deep, anabolic recovery.
- **The Digital Sunset:** No screens 60 minutes before bed. I would not let the "Blue Light" of the Matrix be the last thing my eyes saw.

By protecting my sleep, I was able to wake up at 4:00 AM with the mental sharpness of a diamond. The Bots in the lab were caffeinated and groggy; I was rested and lethal. I wasn't just working more hours; I was working with a higher **Quality of Consciousness**.

The Chronological Firewall

One of the most difficult "Time Codes" to master is the **Chronological Firewall**. This is the ability to prevent the "Stress" of the Lab from leaking into your "Build Time."

I watched my coworkers take the Lab home with them. They would talk about their "Boss" at dinner. They would check their work emails on Saturday morning. They were giving the Matrix free "Mental Real Estate" outside of the hours they were being paid for.

I built a barrier. The moment I crossed the threshold of the Lab's exit, the "Level II Administrator" was dead. I would not speak of the company. I would not think of the projects. I would not "vent" about the coworkers. Venting is just a way to keep the Matrix's frequency alive in your own house. Instead, I replaced that mental space with the **Architecture of the Future**. If a work thought tried to breach the barrier, I would verbally say "No." I was protecting the sanctity of my Kingdom's time.

The Velocity of Decision

The final element of Temporal Jurisdiction is the **Velocity of Decision**. In the Lab, decisions are slow. They are filtered through committees and layers of management. This "Slowness" is a control mechanism; it prevents change.

In the Kingdom, **Speed is a Shovel**.

I learned to make decisions for my Build instantly. If the math for a new contract worked, I signed it. If a tool was necessary for the Vault, I bought it. I didn't "think about it" for two weeks. I realized that the time spent "wavering" is just another form of "Dead Time." By increasing my decision velocity, I was able to compress a month's worth of progress into a single afternoon. I was outrunning the Matrix's ability to track me.

CHAPTER 3: THE TIME (PART 4)

The Rhythms of the Sovereign Year

In the Office, time was seasonal only in the context of "Quarterly Earnings" and "Open Enrollment." The "Bot" lives in a perpetual, artificial fluorescent summer. The Architect, however, aligns his Siege with the **Natural Rhythms of Production**.

I divided my Final 2-Years into specific "Sovereign Seasons":

1. **The Winter of Consolidation:** The first 6 months. This is when you perform the Audit, cut the Status Tax, and sit in the "Sovereign Silence." You are a seed underground. No one sees your growth, and that is your protection.
2. **The Spring of the First Shovel:** Months 6-12. This is when the first Broom & Shovel engine is launched. It is messy, it is demanding, and it requires the highest volume of "Active Build Time."
3. **The Summer of Velocity:** Months 12-18. This is when the system reaches "Critical Mass." The Private Vault is filling, and the Bloodline Shield is active.
4. **The Autumn of Extraction:** The final 6 months. This

is the harvest. You are no longer building; you are "Tuning." You are preparing the engine to run without your physical touch.

By breaking my 2-year block into seasons, I prevent "Siege Fatigue." I realize that I didn't have to do everything at once. I just have to be in the right frequency for the current season.

The Day of Extraction Protocol

The "Day of Extraction" is the specific date on which your S_f (Sovereignty Factor) remains consistently above 1 for three consecutive months. This is not a day for celebration; it is a day for **Execution**.

Most people wait until they "feel ready" to leave the Lab. You will never feel ready. The Matrix is designed to make you feel perpetually "unprepared." I designed a cold, mathematical protocol for my final day:

- **The Zero-Balance Sweep:** Ensure the last Laboratory paycheck is routed directly to the Vault, leaving nothing in the "Matrix-Facing" accounts.
- **The Documentation Purge:** Deleting any personal mental loops associated with the company.
- **The Silent Handover:** Giving the required notice without explaining "what you are doing next." To the Lab, you are simply "unavailable."

When I walked out, I didn't look back at the building. I didn't take a "commemorative photo." I understood that the building was a tomb for the version of me that had died during the Audit. I was now a temporal refugee entering my own Kingdom.

The First Hour of Liberty

What do you do with the first hour of your total temporal jurisdiction? The Bot, if suddenly freed, would sleep in or go on a "Vacation." They would immediately try to "spend" their new time on the Status Tax.

The Architect uses the first hour to **Recalibrate the Frequency**. I sat in a park, far away from the Lab, and I simply watched the wind. I was re-learning how to exist without a "Schedule" imposed by a Master. I was practicing the "Sovereign's Gaze"—the ability to look at the world and see not "Tasks" or "Deadlines," but **Opportunities for Stewardship**.

The Siege was over. The Build was successful. But the work of the Kingdom was just beginning. You have bought back your time; now you must decide what that time is worth to the Creator.

The Hidden Law of the "Broom and Shovel"

The ancestors knew that "As above, so below." If you cannot master the physical elements (dirt, waste, hygiene), you will never master the spiritual elements (wealth, power, influence). The "Broom and Shovel" is an **Alchemical Process.** You are taking "Chaos" (a mess, a broken system) and turning it into "Order."

The world secret is that the Matrix has convinced everyone that "Dirty Work" is low-class so that the **Brave few** can own the entire infrastructure of the world. He who controls the "Broom" controls the foundation upon which the "Palace" is built.

The World Secret: The Law of Circulation

Wealth is like water; it must move or it becomes stagnant and dies. The Millionaire does not "hoard" to keep; he "Vaults" to **Deploy.** Your "Broom and Shovel" engine is a pump. It pumps energy from the Matrix into your Kingdom.

To create a billion-dollar reality, your engine must solve a **Mass Friction Point.** The more people you free from a specific "Physical Stress," the more the Universe is obligated to pay you. This is not a "business tip"; it is a **Universal Law of Compensation.**

Sovereign Affirmation (The Call to Dominion):

"I solve the problems the world fears. I create order where there is chaos. My work is essential, and my reward is inevitable. I am the head and not the tail; I am the lender and not the borrower. My Kingdom expands because my value is undeniable."

The Secret of the "Non-Market" Economy

The Matrix wants you to compete in "Open Markets" (Amazon, Google, local advertising). This is a "Bot-Trap" where margins go to die. The real wealth—the once-in-a-lifetime kind—exists in the **Shadow Market.** This is the economy of "Private Handshakes" and "Distressed Essentials."

The World Secret: The "Receiver-Ship" Glitch

When a massive Laboratory corporation (like a hotel chain or a manufacturing plant) enters financial distress, the "Bots" panic and liquidate. The Architect doesn't buy the "Business"; he buys the **Specific Friction.** *Example:* I knew an Architect who didn't start a cleaning company. He found a massive hospital system that was losing $2 million a year in "fines" because their bio-waste wasn't being tracked to Matrix-code. He didn't ask for a "job." He walked in and said, *"I am taking over your liability. I will own the waste from the moment it leaves the needle. You pay me 50% of the fines you used to pay."* He created a **Sovereign Engine** that was invisible to the public.

He had zero competitors because he wasn't "cleaning"; he was **Insuring against Chaos.**

The Affirmation of the Shadow Architect:

"I do not compete; I Command. I do not look for customers; I look for Failures. I am the solution to the Matrix's entropy. My wealth is found in the gaps the Bots are too blind to see."

CHAPTER 4: THE BROOM & SHOVEL ENGINES (PART 1)

The Anatomy of a Shovel

We now move into the core of the physical machine, we must go deeper than "business ideas." we must understand the **Mechanics of the Tool**.

A "Shovel" is any asset or system that performs a task that the world cannot ignore. In my journey, my first "Shovel" was a specialized piece of industrial cleaning equipment. To the world, it was just a machine. To me, it was a **Temporal Displacement Device**.

Every hour that machine worked, it produced the same amount of currency as four hours of my time in the Lab. By owning the Shovel, I was effectively "cloning" my life essence.

The Hierarchy of Tools

Not all engines are created equal. In the Kingdom, we rank our Shovels based on their **Durability**:

1. **Tier 1: The Physical Utility (The Broom).** Services that deal with the physical reality of the world (Waste, Cleaning, Repair, Food).
2. **Tier 2: The Infrastructure (The Pipe).** Systems that move energy, data, or goods (Logistics, Storage,

specialized software).

3. **Tier 3: The Intellectual Fortress (The Map).** Specialized knowledge or "Admin Codes" that others pay to access.

I started at Tier 1 because Tier 1 is the hardest to "Disrupt." The Matrix can automate a "Admin II" (my old job), but it is a long way from automating the manual clearing of a clogged industrial drain at 3:00 AM. I wanted to be in the "Dirty Work" because the "Dirty Work" is where the **Cleanest Sovereignty** is found.

CHAPTER 4: THE BROOM & SHOVEL ENGINES (PART 2)

The 7 Essential Industries

When I was a "Sovereign Spy" in the Laboratory, I spent my lunch hours studying the yellow pages and industrial directories. I wasn't looking for "Innovation"; I was looking for **Inevitability**. The Matrix tries to push you toward "High-Tech" because high-tech is fragile and easily monitored. I looked for the "Low-Tech, High-Necessity" sectors.

I identified **The 7 Essential Industries**—the pillars of the physical world that must function for society to exist:

1. **Waste & Extraction:** The world is a machine that produces trash. If the trash isn't moved, the machine stops. This is the ultimate "Broom."
2. **Maintenance & Repair:** Buildings, roads, and machines are in a constant state of entropy. The man who fights entropy is never out of a job.
3. **Logistics & Last-Mile Delivery:** The movement of physical goods from point A to point B.
4. **Energy & Power Infrastructure:** Not the "Trading" of energy, but the physical maintenance of the grid and the

"Off-Grid" alternatives.
5. **Food Logistics:** Not the restaurant (which is a luxury), but the storage, transport, and distribution of raw calories.
6. **Security & Protection:** The safeguarding of physical assets and private jurisdictions.
7. **Specialized Hygiene:** The cleaning of medical, industrial, or hazardous environments where a "Bot" cannot be trusted.

I chose **Specialized Hygiene** for my first engine. Why? Because the "Laboratory" I worked in had cleanrooms that required a specific "Admin Code" of cleanliness to function. If those rooms weren't cleaned to a certain micron-level, the Lab's $100-million experiments would fail. That made my service **Non-Negotiable**. I wasn't asking for a "Budget"; I was an "Insurance Policy" against failure.

The Math of the Margin

In the Kingdom, we do not care about "Revenue." Revenue is a vanity metric for the Matrix. We care about **Margin Essence**.

Most businesses in the Laboratory operate on "Thin Margins"—5% or 10%. They rely on "Volume" to survive. This is a trap. If you have a 5% margin and your costs go up by 6%, you are a dead man. The Architect designs for **Fat Margins (30% to 70%)**.

How do you get a fat margin in a "Broom & Shovel" business? You don't compete on "Price"; you compete on **Essentiality and Reliability**.

- The "Bot" company offers the cheapest price and provides

a "Bot" level of service.
- The "Architect" company offers the **Sovereign Standard**.

I charged 40% more than my competitors. When the procurement officer asked why, I told him: "Because when I say the room will be sterile, it will be sterile. You are not paying for a mop; you are paying for the certainty that your experiment won't fail." I realized that the Matrix is actually terrified of failure. It will pay a premium for **Certainty**. That premium is where your "Private Vault" gets its density.

The Physics of Recurring Flow

The greatest engine is the one that doesn't require a "New Sale" every morning. You are looking for **Recurring Flow**.

In the Laboratory, I had to "perform" every day to get my paycheck. If I stopped performing, the money stopped. My Broom & Shovel engine was designed on "Contractual Gravity." Once the contract was signed for a 36-month term, the money flowed every 30 days like a physical tide.

I spent my "Build Time" ensuring that the contracts were "Irrevocable" unless there was a breach of service. I was building a **Financial Dam**. Once the dam was built, I didn't have to carry water from the river to the village anymore; I just had to maintain the pipes. I realized that a man with five recurring contracts is 1,000 times more "Sovereign" than a man with a $200,000 salary and a "Boss." The salary is a tether; the contracts are an **Estate**.

The Scalability Trap

The final "Admin Code" of the engine is avoiding the **Scalability Trap**. The Matrix wants you to "Grow" until you are too big to manage. They want you to have 1,000 employees and 50 locations. Why? Because at that size, you are a "Public Entity" that they can regulate and tax into submission.

The Architect seeks **Optimal Size**. I didn't want 1,000 contracts. I wanted **10 Perfect Contracts**. 10 contracts that I could manage with a small, elite team of "Sovereign Contractors." This kept my overhead low and my "Visibility" even lower. I was a "Small, Heavy Object." A small, heavy object is much harder for the Matrix to move or manipulate than a large, hollow one. I wasn't building an "Empire"; I was building a **Fortress**.

CHAPTER 4: THE BROOM & SHOVEL ENGINES (PART 3)

The Sovereign Sales Protocol

Within the system, "Sales" is seen as a desperate act of persuasion. The "Bot" salesman is trained to grovel, to discount his price, and to beg for a "Meeting." This behavior signals to the Matrix that you are a subordinate. The Architect utilizes the **Sovereign Sales Protocol**, which is based on **Inverse Gravity**.

I realized that the Laboratory is actually a collection of "Stress Points." Every department head is terrified of something: a failed audit, a safety violation, or a disruption in their data flow. I didn't go in asking for a "Job" or a "Vendor Spot." I went in as a **Sovereign Auditor of Problems**.

My protocol was simple:

1. **Identify the "Friction Point":** I researched the company's public safety records or facility complaints.
2. **Diagnose the Cost of Failure:** I quantified exactly how much it cost them when their current "Bot" provider failed to show up.
3. **Offer the "Sovereign Guarantee":** I didn't offer a "Service"; I offered an **End to the Stress**.

I would look the procurement officer in the eye—not as an employee, but as a peer—and say: "Your current provider is a volume-based corporation. They don't care about your cleanroom; they care about their quarterly report. I am a specialized provider. If you sign with me, this problem vanishes from your desk forever. Here is the price for that peace of mind."

By standing in my own jurisdiction, I triggered a psychological response in the Matrix. They didn't see a "Vendor"; they saw a **Solution**. This is how you win high-margin contracts without a marketing budget. You don't compete on "Features"; you compete on **Posture**.

The Art of the High-Need Contract

A contract in the Kingdom is not just a piece of paper; it is a **Vessel for Life Essence**. To dive in a bit deeper, we must dissect the "Anatomy of the Agreement."

Most Bots sign "Standard Agreements" provided by the other party. This is a surrender of sovereignty. I designed my own "Sovereign Contract" with three non-negotiable "Admin Codes":

- **Code 1: The Inflation Hedge.** My contracts included a clause that adjusted the price automatically based on the real-world cost of materials, not the government's "Stated Inflation" (the lie).
- **Code 2: The Autonomy Clause.** The contract specified that I, and only I, dictated the *methods* of the work. The Lab could not "Manage" me or my team. They were buying the *Result*, not the *Control*.
- **Code 3: The Irrevocable Flow.** A 90-day "Notice of Termination" requirement, ensuring that if the Matrix

tried to cut me off, I had three months of "Buffer Energy" to pivot.

When you bring your own contract to the table, you are informing the Matrix that you are a **Self-Governing Entity**. It sets a frequency of respect that prevents them from ever treating you like a "Temp Agency" worker.

The Math of the Sovereign Load

The final part of the engine's design is understanding your **Sovereign Load**. This is the limit of how much "Essice" (time and energy) the engine requires to produce its C_f (Cash Flow).

The mistake the Bot makes is taking on *every* contract they can get. They end up with 20 low-margin clients that require 80 hours of work a week. They have effectively built a "High-Stress Laboratory" for themselves.

I utilized the **80/20 Forensic Load Analysis**.

I realized that 80% of my stress came from 20% of my clients—usually the ones who paid the least and complained the most. I "Fired" those clients. I only wanted "High-Yield, Low-Friction" contracts. My goal was to reach my **Sovereign Number** ($3,200/month) with the *least* amount of moving parts.

I found that two high-end commercial contracts were worth more than fifty residential ones. They were more stable, more professional, and required 90% less "Emotional Labor." By managing the "Load," I ensured that I had enough "Life Essence" left over to continue building the **Private Vault**. The Engine was no longer a "Job"; it was a **Precision Tool**.

CHAPTER 4: THE BROOM & SHOVEL ENGINES (PART 4)

The Ghost Operation

A true Architect does not want to be a "Business Owner" in the traditional sense. A business owner is often just a high-level Bot who has traded one master (a boss) for a hundred masters (the customers). The goal of the Kingdom is to run a **Ghost Operation**: a system that is felt by the world but whose creator is invisible.

To achieve this, you must separate your "Self" from the "Service." When I started my specialized hygiene engine, I never told the clients that *I* would be the one doing the work. I spoke in the third person. I spoke as "The Organization." Even when it was just me and a used vacuum in the beginning, I was establishing the frequency of a **System**.

The Ghost Operation relies on the **Three-Layer Delegation Model**:

1. **The Intake (The Algorithm):** How orders and contracts enter the system (Automated/Contracted).
2. **The Execution (The Shovels):** The actual labor performed by Sovereign Contractors.
3. **The Audit (The Quality Gate):** The final check that

ensures the "Sovereign Standard" was met.

By year two, I had successfully moved myself into the "Audit" layer only. I spent four hours a week "ghosting" through my contract sites, verifying that the work was perfect. The other 164 hours of the week belonged to my family and the **Build**.

Managing the Sovereign Contractors

The greatest mistake a Bot makes when "hiring" is looking for "Employees." Employees are people looking for a "Nest"—they want you to provide their health insurance, their motivation, and their structure. They want you to be their "Lab Manager."

The Architect does not hire employees; he partners with **Sovereign Contractors**.

I looked for people who were already "Awakening"—men and women who had their own tools, their own transport, and their own desire for freedom. I didn't pay them an hourly wage; I paid them a **"Contract Split."** * If a contract paid the Kingdom $1,000, I gave the contractor $600.

- To a Bot manager, $600 seems "too high."
- But the Architect knows that $600 buys **Ownership**.

When a man is getting a 60% split, he doesn't need to be "managed." He will fix the machine when it breaks. He will show up in the snow. He will represent the Kingdom with pride because he is building his own Vault simultaneously. I was not a "Boss"; I was a **Marketplace of Opportunity**. This allowed me to scale my engine without increasing my "Stress Load." My contractors were my "Shovels," and I treated them with the respect that a Sovereign deserves.

The Philosophy of the Invisible Hand

As the Ghost Operation matures, you must resist the urge to "Tinker." The Matrix trains us to feel guilty if we aren't "Busy." This is the **Busy-ness Siphon**.

I had to train my brain to understand that **Thinking is Work.** Watching the numbers in the Private Vault is work. Ensuring the Bloodline Shield is legally sound is work. Pushing a broom when you have a system to push it for you is not "Hard Work"—it is **Inefficiency**.

I practiced the "Invisible Hand" approach. I would only intervene in the engine if the "Audit" layer showed a deviation of more than 5% from the Sovereign Standard. Otherwise, I remained in the "Void." I wanted the engine to forget I existed. This is the ultimate proof of an Architect: if you can disappear for thirty days and the Vault still grows, you have successfully exited the Laboratory.

The Ancestral Code: The Master of the Unseen

The ancients understood that the most powerful forces in the universe are invisible (gravity, wind, thoughts). In the Matrix, you are trained to be "Visible"—to be the face of the brand, to be the person in the meeting, to be the laborer on the floor. This visibility is a **Vulnerability**. The world secret used by the elite "Old Money" families is the **Law of the Unseen Hand.**

A Ghost Operation is not just a business model; it is an **Alchemical Veil**. By removing yourself from the day-to-day friction of the "Shovel," you move from being a "Component" of the machine to being its **Prime Mover**. The ancestors taught that a King who must constantly show his face to his subjects is not a King, but a servant of their expectations. You must build a system that breathes while you sleep, a "Golem" of procedures that performs your will without your physical presence.

The World Secret: The Ego Trap of "Management"

The Matrix feeds your ego to keep you trapped. It tells you that "Only you can do it right." This is a frequency-lock designed to chain the Architect to the "Broom." The secret to billionaire-level expansion is the **Sanitization of Ego**. You must be willing to be "Nobody" in your business so that the business can be "Everything" to the market. When you "Ghost" your operation, you are not being lazy; you are protecting your **Aetheric Energy** from the low-frequency complaints of clients and the mundane stresses of the Lab.

Sovereign Affirmation (The Ghost's Command):

"I am the invisible power behind the throne. My systems are perfect, my proxies are capable, and my presence is a choice, not a necessity. I release the need to be seen, and I embrace the power to be free. My Kingdom thrives in silence."

The Ancestral Code: The Puppet Master's Strings

In the Lab, you are taught to "Lead people." This is a waste of Life Essence. The Titans don't lead people; they **Program Environments.** The world secret is that 99% of people *want* to be told exactly what to do. They find comfort in the "Standardized Loop."

The "Ghost-Link" Protocol (Never Before Taught):

To remove yourself entirely, you must use **The Binary Task-Chain.** Most owners give "Objectives" (e.g., "Clean this room"). The Architect gives **Binary Data Points.** * *Don't say:* "Make the floor shine."

- *Say:* "Apply 4oz of Chemical X. Use the Blue Pad. Take a photo of the reflection of the lightbulb in the center of the floor. Upload to the Vault."

If the photo doesn't show the lightbulb, the "Contractor" doesn't get paid. The system—not you—rejects the work. You have turned human labor into a **Digital Logic Gate.** This is how you run an empire from a beach in the Mediterranean without ever looking at a mop. You are not a manager; you are the **System Architect.**

THE TITAN'S PRIVATE VAULT: THE "OFF-LEDGER" ASSET CLASS

The Secret of "Ghost Equity"

The Matrix wants you to put your "Seed" into stocks. This is a "Siphon." The world's most powerful families store their wealth in **"Ghost Equity"**—private, unregistered ownership of the very infrastructure the Matrix depends on.

- *The Secret:* Owning the **Water Rights** under a "Bot-subdivision."
- *The Secret:* Owning the **Mineral Access** on land the Matrix needs for "Green Energy."

This is "Once-in-a-lifetime" information: You don't want the "Home"; you want the **Easement.** You don't want the "Car"; you want the **Fuel-Terminal.** When you own the *Infrastructure of the Infrastructure,* you become a "God-Node." The Matrix *must* pay you to continue its own existence.

CHAPTER 5: THE PRIVATE VAULT (PART 1)

The Metaphysics of Storage

We now move into the most sacred room of the Fortress: **The Private Vault**. We must treat money not as "Currency," but as **Stored Potential Energy**.

In the Laboratory, money is "Liquid." It flows in and flows out. It is "Current"—meaning it moves. The Matrix wants your money to move because they control the "Wires." The Architect seeks **Solidity**.

The Private Vault is where we turn "Current" into "Solid." We are looking to create a **Gravity Well** so dense that no "Siphon" can pull energy out of it. This requires a transition from "Bank Accounts" (which are Matrix-controlled ledgers) to **Sovereign Assets**.

I began to categorize my Vault into the **Three Densities of Wealth**:

1. **Tier 1: High Velocity (The Seed).** Cash and cash equivalents used for immediate "Shovel" purchases.
2. **Tier 2: High Stability (The Stone).** Physical gold, silver, and productive land. Things that do not require a "Login" to verify.

3. **Tier 3: High Yield (The Reactor).** Private lending and equity in other "Broom & Shovel" engines.

I realized that a man with $100,000 in a bank account is a man with a target on his back. A man with $100,000 split across the Three Densities is a man with a **Fortress**. The Vault is not just where you keep your money; it is where you keep your **Peace**.

CHAPTER 5: THE PRIVATE VAULT (PART 2)

The Physics of Gold & Silver

In the Laboratory, you are told that Gold is a "pet rock" and Silver is a "relic of the past." The Matrix wants you to believe this because they cannot print Gold. They cannot "devalue" Silver with a keystroke. They cannot freeze a gold coin that is sitting in your physical jurisdiction.

The Architect views Gold and Silver not as "Investments," but as **The Bedrock of Reality**.

When I began my Private Vault, I established the **10% Physical Anchor**. Every time my Broom & Shovel engine produced a surplus, 10% was immediately converted into physical metal. Why? Because paper currency is a "Promise" from the Matrix, and the Matrix is a pathological liar.

Gold is the **Store of History**. It represents the "Life Essence" of human labor across five thousand years. Silver is the **Industrial Warrior**. It is the most conductive element on the periodic table; the Matrix literally cannot function without it. By holding these, you are holding the "Admin Codes" of the physical universe.

I remember the first time I held a one-ounce gold coin in my hand while sitting in my cubicle. It felt *heavy*. Not just physically, but spiritually. It was a piece of the earth that didn't care about my "Performance Review." It didn't care about the Federal Reserve's interest rates. It was a "Solid Point" in a world of "Liquid Lies." My Vault started to feel real the moment it had a physical weight.

The Sovereign Banking Protocol

Once you have "Liquid Seed" and "Physical Stone," you must implement the **Sovereign Banking Protocol**. This is how you stop being a "Customer" and start being a "Lender."

In the Laboratory, when you want to buy a tool (a car, a piece of equipment), you go to the Bank. The Bank lends you money they created out of thin air and charges you 10% interest. You work for hours to pay that 10%.

The Architect uses the **Internal Circulation Model**:

1. **The Accumulation:** The Vault reaches a "Strike Level" (e.g., $20,000).
2. **The Internal Loan:** When the Engine needs a new "Shovel," the Kingdom "borrows" the $20,000 from the Vault.
3. **The Payback:** The Engine pays the Vault back the $20,000 *plus* the 10% interest that would have gone to the Matrix.

By doing this, you are "Capturing the Spread." The interest stays within the **Bloodline Shield**. Your money is working "Double Time"—it is providing the tool for the engine, and it is growing the vault through interest. This is how the wealthy stay wealthy; they are the only ones allowed to earn interest on their own consumption. The Sovereign Banking Protocol is the "Master Key" to compounding.

The Privacy Firewall (The Ghost Ledger)

The Matrix tracks every digital transaction. They know when you buy a coffee; they know when you pay your rent. The Private Vault requires a **Privacy Firewall**.

I began to move a portion of my "Captured Essence" into the **Shadow Economy**. This isn't about doing anything "illegal"; it is about reclaiming the right to **Financial Privacy**.

- I used cash for local "Broom & Shovel" materials.
- I used peer-to-peer exchanges for certain "Fortress Assets."
- I maintained a "Ghost Ledger"—a physical book that tracked my true net worth, while my "Matrix Bank Account" showed only enough to keep the "Siphon Hunters" disinterested.

If you show the Matrix too much "Fat," they will find a way to "Tax" or "Litigate" it away. The Architect stays "Lean" in the eyes of the system and "Heavy" in the eyes of the Vault. You want to be the man who looks like a "Middle-Class Bot" on paper but has the "Sovereign Density" of a King in private.

The Moral Duty of the Reserve

The final realization of the Vault is that it is not for "Spending." It is a **Reserve**.

The Matrix encourages "Consumption" because a man with no reserve is a man who is easy to control. A man with a six-month reserve is "Difficult." A man with a five-year reserve is **Impossible to Rule**.

I began to measure my wealth not in "Dollars," but in **"Years of Disobedience."** When my Vault reached $50,000, I realized I had two years of "Disobedience" stored up. I could tell the Lab "No" for 730 days straight before I had to worry about a meal. That realization changed my posture. I stopped "Asking" for permission in meetings; I started "Stating" my position. The Vault provides the **Internal Authority** that the "Status Tax" could never buy. You are no longer a "Battery" hoping for a recharge; you are the **Power Plant**.

CHAPTER 5: THE PRIVATE VAULT (PART 3)

The Architecture of the 100-Year Land
In the Lab, "Real Estate" is viewed as a speculative asset. The Bot buys a house hoping the "Market" will make them rich. They take on a 30-year "Death-Grip" (Mortgage) and spend their lives paying for a zip code. To the Architect, Land is not an investment; it is **The Physical Anchor of the Bloodline**.

The Private Vault is not complete until it contains **Productive Soil**.

I began to look for "Sovereign Acres"—land that sat outside the primary "Hum" of the city, but within reach of my Broom & Shovel engines. I wasn't looking for a "McMansion." I was looking for land with three specific "Admin Codes":

1. **Water Autonomy:** A well or a natural spring. The Matrix controls the "Flow" to your house; if they turn it off, you are no longer sovereign.
2. **Energy Potential:** Land that can host the "Reactor" (Solar, Wind, or Wood-gas).
3. **Food Density:** Soil that can be turned into a "Calorie Engine" for the family.

I realized that if the Vault owns the land, and the land provides the water and the heat, my **Survival Base** (B_s) drops toward zero. The more the land provides, the less the Matrix can demand. I call this the **100-Year Horizon**. You are not buying for yourself; you are buying the "Ground" on which your great-grandchildren will stand. You are moving your wealth from the "Digital Ledger" of the bank into the **Physical Reality of the Earth**.

The Digital Sovereignty Shield

While we anchor ourselves in the soil, we must also protect our "Digital Essence." The Matrix is increasingly moved by **Algorithms**. If your money, your communication, and your "Identity" are all stored in the Laboratory's cloud (Google, Apple, Major Banks), you are a "Transparent Battery." They can see your frequency, and they can interrupt it.

The Private Vault must include a **Digital Fortress**. I implemented the "Sovereign Server Protocol":

- **Hardware Sovereignty:** Moving away from "The Cloud" to private, encrypted storage (NAS) that I physically own.
- **Encrypted Communication:** Utilizing tools that do not "Harvest" the data for the MPC.
- **Non-Custodial Assets:** Ensuring that my "Digital Wealth" (Bitcoin or encrypted ledgers) is held with "Private Keys" that only I possess.

If a "Bank Holiday" is declared or the "Grid" becomes a tool of social compliance, the Architect's digital life remains unaffected. You are "unplugged" while remaining "connected." I realized that most Bots are terrified of a "Power Outage" not because they fear the dark, but because they fear the loss of their **External Brain**. The Architect builds an **Internal Brain** and an **Internal Network**.

The Velocity of the Internal Loop

The final part of this design is the **Internal Loop**. The Vault must never be "Static."

I designed the "Flow of Extraction":

1. The **Broom & Shovel** earns the C_f.
2. The C_f hits the **Sovereign Bank** (the Trust account).
3. The Bank converts 20% to **Stone** (Gold/Silver), 40% to **Soil** (Land payments/Maintenance), and 40% to **Seed** (New Shovels).

I watched this loop accelerate. Every time the "Seed" bought a new machine for my engine, the C_f grew. Because the C_f grew, the "Stone" and "Soil" layers grew faster. I was no longer a "Consumer" in the economy; I was a **Closed-Loop Ecosystem**.

The Psychological Transformation

The most profound change wasn't in my bank balance; it was in my **Nervous System**.

The "Bot" is always in a state of "Low-Level Panic." They are one "bad month" away from losing everything. The Architect, with a Vault of Stone, Soil, and Seed, exists in a state of **High-Level Calm**. I realized that the "Stress" I felt in the Lab for ten years wasn't because the job was hard; it was because I was **Unprotected**.

Once the Vault reached its "Critical Density," I felt like I was wearing "Invisible Armor" in the office. The supervisor's criticism didn't sting because I didn't *need* his approval for my survival. The "Company Policy" didn't frustrate me because I was governed by my own **Sovereign Charter**. I was in the Lab, but I was no longer *of* the Lab. My frequency had shifted from "Compliance" to "Stewardship."

CHAPTER 5: THE PRIVATE VAULT (PART 4)

The Sovereign Charity

Within the System , "Charity" is often a performative act—a "Tax Write-Off" or a way to buy social status within the Matrix. The Bot gives to massive, faceless NGOs that spend 80% of the donation on "Administrative Friction" (keeping other Bots employed). The Architect views Charity as **The Distribution of Sovereign Grace**.

Once the Vault reaches its **Overflow Level**, the Architect must establish a "Sovereign Charity" protocol. This is not about being "nice"; it is about **Strategic Stewardship**.

- **Targeted Impact:** We do not give to "General Funds." We give to specific "Broom & Shovel" needs in our immediate community—the widow who needs a new roof, the apprentice who needs his first set of tools, the school that teaches "Admin Codes" rather than "Compliance."
- **The Circular Gift:** When we help another person achieve Sovereignty, we are strengthening the "Buffer Zone" around our own Kingdom. A neighborhood of Sovereign Architects is much harder for the Matrix to invade than a neighborhood of dependent Bots.

I realized that the ultimate purpose of the Vault was to provide the "Strike Capital" for the Good. If I saw a "Bot" who was starting to "Awaken," I could use the Vault to accelerate their journey. This is how you build a **Loyalty Network** that exists outside the currency of the Matrix. You are becoming a "Lender of Hope," and that is a currency that never devalues.

The Transition to the Shield

The Vault is now dense. You have the **Stone** (Metal), the **Soil** (Land), and the **Seed** (Flow). But you have a problem. The Matrix is a "Heat-Seeking Missile" for wealth. If you hold these assets in your personal name, you are a "Bright Spot" on the radar of the MPC.

I remember looking at my growing ledger and feeling a new kind of anxiety. It wasn't the "Survival Anxiety" of the Lab; it was the **"Protection Anxiety"** of the Sovereign. I realized that the bigger the Vault grew, the more I needed a **Shield**.

You cannot defend a Kingdom with a "Checking Account" and a "Will." You need a **Jurisdictional Firewall**. You need a structure that says to the world: "I own nothing, but I control everything." This is the bridge to the most technical and vital chapter of the Build.

CHAPTER 6: THE BLOODLINE SHIELD (PART 1)

The Legal Ghost

To reveal the Ghosts, we must dive into the "Shadow Geometry" of Law. Most people believe the law is a set of rules they must follow. The Architect knows the law is a **Language of Jurisdiction**.

The **Bloodline Shield** is the process of turning yourself into a **Legal Ghost**.

In the Matrix, you are a "Natural Person"—a biological entity attached to a Social Security number. This "Person" is a debt-slave by default. The Shield utilizes the **Irrevocable Trust** to create a "New Entity."

- **The Settlor:** The version of you that gives the assets away (The "Old You" leaving the Lab).
- **The Trustee:** The version of you that manages the assets (The "Architect").
- **The Beneficiary:** Your bloodline (The "Future").

When I moved my first "Shovel" (my cleaning contract) into the Shield, it legally ceased to be "mine." If I was sued personally, the plaintiff found a man with no assets. If I filed for "Bankruptcy," the Trust remained untouched. I had created a **Vertical Separation** between my life and my liability.

The Philosophy of Ownership vs. Control

The Matrix sells you the "Dream of Ownership" because they can tax and seize what you own. The Architect subscribes to the **Rockefeller Principle**: *"Own nothing, control everything."*

I began to visualize my life through the lens of the Shield.

- I didn't "own" my car; the Shield owned a transportation asset that I was permitted to use.
- I didn't "own" my home; the Shield owned a residential sanctuary for the bloodline.

This shift in perspective is the ultimate "Admin Code." It detaches your ego from your assets. When you "own" a luxury car, your ego is tied to its paint job. When the Shield owns a "Vehicle Asset," it is simply a tool in the Fortress. This emotional detachment allows you to make **Cold, Tactical Decisions** about your wealth. You stop being a "Consumer" and start being a **Governor**.

The Jurisdictional Move

The final part of this initial Shield design is the **Jurisdictional Move**. The Matrix is not a monolith; it is a collection of "Fenced Yards" (States and Countries). Some yards are better for Architects than others.

I studied the "Admin Codes" of different jurisdictions. I moved my Shield to a "Privacy-First" jurisdiction—a place where the names of the Trustees are not public record and where the "Siphon Hunters" cannot easily peek over the wall.

By doing this, I was "Unplugging" my Vault from the local grid. I was still in the Lab, but my wealth was already **Off-Shore** (even if only legally). I was a "Sovereign Spy" operating in enemy territory, backed by a Fortress that the enemy couldn't even find on a map.

The Spirit of Matter

The ancestors did not see Gold or Land as mere "assets." They saw them as **Congealed Spirit**. In the Lab, money is "Fiat"—it is "let it be" money, created from nothing by decree. This is why it has no soul and eventually dies. To build a Kingdom that rips the Matrix to shreds, you must store your energy in **Universal Constants**.

The World Secret: The Frequency of Gold

Gold is the only metal that is "incorruptible." It does not rust, tarnish, or decay. This is why the ancestors used it to signal the presence of the Divine. The world secret the "Central Siphoners" keep from you is that Gold is a **Frequency Anchor**. When you hold physical Gold in your Vault, your internal frequency shifts from "Anxiety" to "Solidarity." You are literally grounding your wealth in the Earth's core frequency. This makes you psychologically immune to the "Paper Panic" the Matrix uses to keep the masses in fear.

The Law of the Soil: The First Jurisdiction

The Matrix wants you to pay "Rent" or "Mortgages" (Latin for "Death-Grip") because it keeps you transient. The world secret of the ruling class is the **Primary Land Title**. When you own Soil that is free of the "Interest Siphon," you have created a hole in the Matrix. You have created a patch of Earth where your laws apply. This is the **Seed of a Nation**.

Sovereign Affirmation (The Vault's Foundation):

CHAPTER 6: THE BLOODLINE SHIELD (PART 1)

"My wealth is anchored in the Eternal. I trade the shifting sands of the Matrix for the solid stone of the Earth. My Vault is a fortress of peace, and my Soil is the cradle of my freedom. I am financially unshakeabl

CHAPTER 6: THE BLOODLINE SHIELD (PART 2)

The Anatomy of the Irrevocable Trust

In the Laboratory, a "Trust" is something a Bot thinks is only for billionaires. This is a deliberate "Knowledge Siphon." If you don't believe the tool is for you, you will never pick it up. The Architect realizes that the **Irrevocable Trust** is the only true "Invisibility Cloak" in the financial world.

"Irrevocable" is a word that terrifies the Bot. It sounds like a loss of control. To the Architect, it is the sound of a **Vault Door Locking**. By making the Trust irrevocable, you are telling the Matrix: *"This energy no longer belongs to the 'Person' you regulate. It has been dedicated to a Sovereign Purpose, and you no longer have the Admin Codes to reach it."*

The Shield is constructed with three primary chambers:

1. **The Corpus (The Body):** The actual assets—the gold, the deeds, the contracts.
2. **The Protector (The Watchman):** A third-party role (often a trusted peer or specialized entity) that has the power to fire the Trustee but cannot touch the money. This prevents the "Lone Actor" failure.

3. **The Spendthrift Clause (The Armor):** A specific legal "Admin Code" that prevents any creditor of a beneficiary from seizing the assets. If your son gets into a car accident or your daughter faces a predatory lawsuit, the Shield remains unbreachable.

I spent months drafting these clauses. I wasn't just "writing a document"; I was **Forging a Shield**. I realized that every word in the Trust was a "Brick" in the wall. The more precise the language, the higher the wall.

The Private Family Operating Agreement (PFOA)

While the Trust is the "Outer Wall," the **PFOA** is the "Internal Law" of the Kingdom. This is where you define the frequency of your bloodline.

In the Laboratory, you are governed by the "Employee Handbook"—a set of rules designed to make you a better battery. In the Kingdom, your family is governed by the **PFOA**. This document dictates how the "Vault" is used.

- **The Education Protocol:** The Trust will fund education, but only if it is for "Sovereign Skills" (Architecture, Engineering, Law, Real-World Trade). It will not fund "Compliance Degrees."
- **The Venture Protocol:** A family member can "borrow" from the Vault to start a Broom & Shovel engine, but they must present a "Blueprint" to the Trustees and pay back the "Sovereign Interest."
- **The Stewardship Clause:** If a member of the bloodline falls back into "Bot Behavior" (substance abuse, reckless "Status Tax" spending), their access to the Vault is "Throttled" until they recalibrate.

I realized that by writing the PFOA, I was **Coding the Future**. I was ensuring that my wealth would not "Spoil" my descendants, but rather "Equip" them. I was building a system that rewarded the Architect and starved the Bot.

The "Entity Wrapper" Strategy

The Shield does not interact with the world directly. It uses **Wrappers**.

I designed a series of LLCs (Limited Liability Companies) that were 100% owned by the Trust.

- LLC 1 held the industrial cleaning equipment (The Tools).
- LLC 2 held the service contracts (The Flow).
- LLC 3 held the real estate (The Soil).

To the public, these looked like three separate, small businesses. But in the "Shadow Geometry," they were all "Cells" of the same organism, protected by the same Shield. If a "Bot" sued LLC 1 because of a tripped wire, they could only reach the "Tools." They could never reach the "Soil" or the "Flow." This is **Compartmentalization**. I was building a "Submarine" with multiple pressure-sealed chambers. If one chamber flooded, the ship stayed afloat.

The Moral Authority of the Protector

The final realization of Chapter 6 is the **Moral Weight of the Guard**.

When you build a Shield, you are accepting that you are no longer the "Owner" of your life; you are the **Steward of a Legacy**. I looked at my children and realized that I was no longer just "Dad." I was the **Founder of a Jurisdiction**.

The Shield changed how I carried myself in the Laboratory during those final months. I knew that my "Person" (the

CHAPTER 6: THE BLOODLINE SHIELD (PART 2)

Admin) was just a mask. Behind that mask was a Sovereign Entity with a legal fortress that the company's HR department couldn't even comprehend. I felt like a "King in Disguise." The "Hum" of the Lab became a distant noise, because I was already living under the **Internal Law** of my own Shield. The construction was nearly complete.

CHAPTER 6: THE BLOODLINE SHIELD (PART 3)

The Privacy Firewall (The Ghost Protocol)

In the digital age, "Privacy" is not a luxury; it is a **Strategic Defense**. The Matrix relies on "Social Engineering"—using your data, your associations, and your spending habits to predict and control your behavior. If the MPC knows where your "Vault" is located, they can move the goalposts of the law to reach it.

The Architect installs a **Privacy Firewall** around the Shield. This is the "Ghost Protocol."

When I set up my Trust, I didn't use my own name in the title. I didn't call it "The [My Name] Family Trust." That is a "Beacon" for siphons. I gave it a **Neutral, Functional Name**—something that sounded like a boring municipal entity or a non-descript holding company. I chose "The Blue Horizon Endowment." To a Bot clerk or a predatory lawyer, it looked like a small, insignificant piece of paper.

The Ghost Protocol includes three layers of obfuscation:

1. **The Nominee Layer:** Using professional "Registered Agents" to be the public face of the entities. Your home address never appears on a public document.

2. **The Communication Gap:** The Shield has its own secure email and its own encrypted "Admin Phone." It never mixes its signal with your "Personal" (Matrix) devices.
3. **The Cash Buffer:** Using the "Private Vault" to fund the Shield's expenses in a way that doesn't leave a "Digital Breadcrumb" back to your personal identity.

I realized that the goal was to be **Wealthy but Invisible**. In the Laboratory, people flaunt their "Status Tax" items—the watches, the cars, the designer logos. They are screaming "Look at me!" to the Matrix. The Architect whispers "Don't look at me" to the world, while holding the keys to the Kingdom.

The Sovereign Succession Protocol

The greatest failure of a Kingdom is not an external invasion; it is a **Succession Crisis**. History is littered with the ruins of fortunes built by an Architect and squandered by a "Bot-Child" who never learned the "Admin Codes."

The **Sovereign Succession Protocol** is the "Final Instruction" of the Shield. It ensures that the transition of the "Master Keys" is a ceremony of competence, not a lottery of birth.

I designed a **Tiered Access System** for my descendants:

- **Level 1 (The Apprentice):** At age 18, the beneficiary receives a small, fixed "Stipend of Sovereignty" to learn basic budgeting. They are required to attend a "Sovereign Audit" of the Trust's holdings.
- **Level 2 (The Builder):** At age 25, if they have successfully started their own "Broom & Shovel" engine (without Trust help), they are granted "Strike Capital" to scale their

business.
- **Level 3 (The Steward):** Only after proving they can manage their own life and their own engine are they given "Trustee Power" to manage the family's Vault.

If a child chooses to remain a "Bot"—to stay in a Laboratory and live for the Status Tax—the Shield **Throttles** their access. They are given enough to live, but never enough to destroy the Fortress. This is the **Hard Love of the Bloodline**. You are not "giving" them money; you are "entrusting" them with energy. If they are not a "Battery" that can hold a charge, they cannot be the "Manager" of the Power Plant.

The Incorruptible Ledger

The final piece of the Shield is the **Incorruptible Ledger**. This is a physical, hand-written book kept within the "Fortress Soil" (your land). It contains the "Source Code" of the Kingdom: the location of the Stone (Gold), the "Admin Codes" for the Digital Shield, and the "Ethical Will" of the Founder.

I wrote my Ethical Will late one night after a particularly draining day at the Lab. I didn't write about "Stocks" or "Bonds." I wrote about the **Frequency of the Architect**. I told my children: *"The Lab will try to convince you that you are a number. They will try to sell you comfort in exchange for your soul. This Shield is not a gift of money; it is a gift of 'No.' It is the power to say 'No' to anyone who tries to own your time."*

When that Ledger was placed in the Vault, the Chapter on the Shield was closed. I felt a weight lift off my shoulders. I was no longer a man running a race against death. I was a **Founder** who had laid a foundation that would outlast my own body. The Build was now structurally complete.

CHAPTER 7: THE EXIT (PART 1)

The Mechanics of the Jailbreak

We have reached the final stages before the final exit. To reach our objective, we must now detail the **Psychology and Tactics of the Departure**. This is the most dangerous moment. The Matrix is like a star—as you move further away from its core, its "Gravity" (the pressure to stay) increases.

The Exit is not a "Resignation." It is a **De-Coupling**.

I spent my final 90 days in the Laboratory in a state of **Active Observation**. I watched the "Bots" around me. I noticed how they talked about "Retirement" as a distant, magical land they would never reach. I realized that the only difference between me and them was the **Blueprint**. I had the "Admin Codes" for the door, and they didn't even know the door existed.

The "Quiet Quitting" of the Soul

Long before I handed in my notice, I performed a **Soul-Exit**. I stopped caring about the "Office Politics." I stopped caring about the "Annual Review." I realized that the Lab's "Opinion" of me was irrelevant because they weren't paying my "Freedom Price"—my Broom & Shovel engine was.

I became the most efficient, least troublesome employee in

the building. Why? Because I didn't want any "Heat." I wanted to be invisible. I did exactly what was required, no more and no less, and used every spare ounce of mental energy to "Ghost-Manage" my external Kingdom. I was a **Sovereign Spy** in the final stages of an extraction mission. I was already "Gone"; my body was just waiting for the clock to catch up.

The Ancestral Code: The Law of the Name

In ancient times, a name carried power. In the Matrix, your name in "ALL CAPITAL LETTERS" is a **Legal Fiction**—a corporation created by the state to harvest your energy. The world secret of the billionaire class is the **Separation of the Flesh from the Fiction**.

The Bloodline Shield (The Irrevocable Trust) is the modern version of the **Sanctuary**. It is a space where the "Common Law" of the Matrix cannot enter because the Shield exists in a different **Contractual Dimension**. You are not "Breaking" the law; you are moving to a **Higher Jurisdiction**. You are moving from the "Law of the Sea" (Admiralty/Commerce) to the "Law of the Land" (Sovereign Right).

The World Secret: The 100-Year Wall

The Matrix thrives on the "Death Siphon"—the inheritance tax that resets a family's progress every generation. The ancestors prevented this through the **Family Compact**. The Shield is not for you; it is for the **Bloodline**. By "Killing" your ownership today, you ensure your great-grandchildren can never be "Harvested." This is how families become "Old Money"—they stop trying to "win" in one lifetime and start building a **Fortress of Time**.

Sovereign Affirmation (The Shield of Protection):

"I am the sentinel of my lineage. My Shield is impenetrable, my legacy is secure, and my bloodline is free from the siphons of the state. I own nothing, I control all, and I leave a path of light for those who follow. The Matrix has no hook in my house."

CHAPTER 7: THE EXIT (PART 2)

The Letter of Sovereign Termination
In the Lab, a "Resignation" is usually a document of apology or gratitude. The Bot writes: *"I am grateful for the opportunity..."* or *"I am sorry to leave such a great team..."* This is a "Submission Code." It reinforces the idea that the Lab was the provider and you were the dependent.

The Architect writes a **Letter of Sovereign Termination**. This document is not for the Lab; it is for your own **Internal Ledger**. It is a formal declaration that your contract with the Matrix has reached its expiration. My letter was three sentences long. It didn't explain where I was going. It didn't offer a "reason" (the Lab does not have the jurisdiction to demand a reason for your freedom).

- **Line 1:** The date of the final extraction.
- **Line 2:** The statement of departure.
- **Line 3:** The instruction for the final settlement of "Life Essence" (the final paycheck).

During that last conversation with my supervisor, I felt the "Siphon" snap. For two years, there had been a straw in my neck, pulling my energy into the corporate machine. In that moment, the straw was removed. The supervisor looked at my ID Badge as I glanced toward it on the desk, then at me, and asked the standard Bot question: *"Where are you going?"*

I smiled and gave the Sovereign answer: *"I am going to attend to my interests."* He didn't understand. To a Bot, "interests" means a hobby. To the Architect, "interests" means a **Kingdom**.

The First 24 Hours of the New Era

The most dangerous time for a newly freed prisoner is the first 24 hours. The "Weightlessness" can be terrifying. For decades, your life has been defined by the "Resistance" of the Lab. When that resistance is gone, many people "float away"—they fall into depression, lethargy, or "Status Tax" spending to fill the void.

I designed the **24-Hour Extraction Protocol** to prevent this:

1. **The Ritual of De-Identification:** I took my "Employee ID Badge" and my "Government Issued Laptop" and placed them in a box. I didn't throw away my cubicle warfare items immediately; I treated them like "Spent Fuel Rods" from a reactor. They were artifacts of a previous life to be returned to the Matrix.
2. **The Physical Threshold:** I went to my "Sovereign Soil"—the land my Vault had purchased. I walked the perimeter. I needed to feel the "Ground" of my own jurisdiction under my feet.
3. **The Silence Audit:** I spent 4 hours in total silence. No phone. No music. No "Build." I needed to hear the sound of a world where no one was demanding my time.

I realized that the "Voice of the Lab" was still ringing in my ears like tinnitus. It took exactly 24 hours for the "Frequency of the Matrix" to fade and the "Frequency of the Architect" to become the dominant signal.

The Sovereignty of the First Monday

The true test is the **First Monday**. For the Bot, Monday is a day of "Grief." It is the start of the "Weekly Extraction."

On my first Monday of freedom, I woke up at 4:00 AM, just as I had during the Siege. But this time, I wasn't working "before" the Lab. I was working **on** the Kingdom. I sat in my home office—the "Command Center" of my Ghost Operation—and looked at my Broom & Shovel dashboard.

- The contractors were in the field.
- The Vault was processing the weekend's flow.
- The Shield was protecting the assets.

I realized that I was no longer "selling time." I was **Overseeing Gravity**. My Monday was not a "Work Day"; it was a **Stewardship Day**. I spent two hours reviewing the math, one hour communicating with my Sovereign Contractors, and the rest of the day in "Deep Study." I was free, not to be "lazy," but to be **Effective**.

The "Phantom Limb" of the Matrix

For several months after the exit, you will feel the "Phantom Limb" of the Laboratory. You will reflexively check your email at 9:00 AM. You will feel a twinge of "Guilt" if you aren't "Busy" on a Tuesday afternoon. This is the **residual coding** of the MPC.

I treated these moments as "Viral Infections." Every time I felt the urge to "Report to a Master," I would go to my Vault ledger and read the **Sovereignty Factor** (S_f). The math was my "Medicine." If S_f was greater than 1, the guilt was an illusion. I was a Sovereign Entity, and the only "Performance Review" that mattered was the one conducted by my own Bloodline. I was learning to live in the **Horizontal Present**, where time is not a "Ladder" to climb, but a "Field" to harvest.

CHAPTER 7: PART 2 — THE RITES OF EXTRACTION (THE ALCHEMY OF THE EXIT)

The Ancestral Code: The Crossing of the Rubicon

In the ancient mysteries, the "Exit" was known as the **Crossing**. It is the moment the initiate leaves the world of shadows (the Laboratory) and enters the world of light (the Kingdom). The world secret is that the Matrix uses **Aetheric Tethering** to keep you trapped. Even after you quit, the "Fear Frequency" of the Lab can haunt your nervous system for years. To truly exit, you must perform a **Psychic Decoupling**. You must burn the "Mental Bridges" that allow you to think like a victim. The ancestors taught that you cannot inhabit a new land while your heart still beats for the old one.

The World Secret: The Law of the Vacuum

The Matrix fears a vacuum. When you remove your energy from the Laboratory, the universe is governed by the **Law of Displacement**. Something must fill that space. If you do not fill it with a Sovereign Mission, the Matrix will fill it with a new crisis. The secret of the millionaire-architect is to have the **Next Command** ready before the "Resignation" is even signed. You aren't leaving "from" something; you are moving "toward" your destiny. This forward-leaning frequency prevents the "Pull-Back" of the Matrix's gravity.

Sovereign Affirmation (The Rite of Departure):

"I break the chains of the Laboratory. I reclaim my Life Essence from the machine. I am no longer a component; I am the Creator. I step across the threshold into my own jurisdiction, and I do not look back. My freedom is absolute, and my path is clear."

CHAPTER 8: THE KINGDOM (PART 1)

The Post-Exit Architecture

Now that the jailbreak is complete, we move into the final phases of this stage: **The Maintenance of the Kingdom**.

The goal is not to "Stay Free"; the goal is to **Expand the Jurisdiction**.

I realized that a Kingdom that stops growing starts to decay. But this growth is different. It is not the "Hollow Growth" of the Matrix (more debt, more employees). It is **Fractal Growth**. I began to look at how I could replicate my "Broom & Shovel" engine in a second industry. I had mastered "Specialized Hygiene." Now, I looked at **Tier 2: Infrastructure (The Pipe)**.

I began to design a "Data-Logistics" engine—a small, automated system that moved specific information for industrial clients. It used the same "Ghost Operation" principles. It used the same "Private Vault" for storage. It was a second "Shovel" in the same garden. My Kingdom was becoming a **Multi-Engine Reactor**.

CHAPTER 8: THE KINGDOM (PART 2)

The Sovereign Network

When you exit the Laboratory, you will find that your old social circle begins to "Glitch." The Bots you used to work with, and even some of your friends, will look at your new life with a mixture of confusion and subconscious resentment. You have broken the "Social Contract" of the Matrix. You have proven that the "40-Year Sleep Sentence" is optional.

The Architect does not try to "save" the Bots. That is a waste of **Life Essence**. Instead, you must build a **Sovereign Network**.

This is not "Networking" in the corporate sense. There are no business cards or "Link-Ups." The Sovereign Network is a **Ghost Frequency** of other Architects, Engineers, and Sovereign Spirits who have also exited the Lab.

- We trade "Admin Codes" (legal updates, tax strategies).
- We provide "Sovereign Intelligence" (market shifts, risk assessments).
- We act as a **Mutual Defense Perimeter**.

I realized that if my "Broom & Shovel" engine needed a specialized repair, I didn't call a "Bot Corporation." I called another Sovereign in my network. We kept the currency circulating within our own "Private Jurisdictions." We were building a **Parallel Economy**—one that was invisible to the Matrix but as solid as the ground we stood on.

Protecting the Frequency

The greatest threat to your Kingdom after the Exit is **Frequency Drift**.

The Matrix is loud. It is designed to pull you back into "Crisis Mode." The news, the politics, and the digital noise are all designed to make you feel like the world is ending, which triggers the "Scarcity Siphon." If you feel scarce, you will start to act like a Bot again. You will start to "Hustle" for meaningless numbers.

I implemented the **Sovereign Silence Protocol**:

1. **Zero-News Diet:** I realized that if something is important enough to affect my Kingdom, my "Sovereign Spy" network will tell me. Everything else is just "Matrix Static."
2. **The Deep Work Anchor:** Even though I no longer "have" to work, I still perform my 4-Hour Deep Work Block every morning. This keeps my mind sharp. A King who does not sharpen his sword will soon lose his crown.
3. **Physical Mastery:** The Body is the "Hardware" of the Kingdom. I treated my physical training as a "System Maintenance" requirement. A Sovereign must be physically capable of defending his Soil.

The Math of the Expansion

In the Kingdom, we do not expand for "Greed." We expand for **Resilience**.

I looked at my S_f (Sovereignty Factor). It was at 2.5—meaning I was earning 2.5 times my survival cost. But I realized that if the "Specialized Hygiene" sector faced a massive regulatory shift, my factor could drop. I needed **Redundancy**.

I applied the **Fractal Design** to a new engine: **Tier 3: The Intellectual Fortress**.

I began to document the "Admin Codes" of my first engine. I turned my "Manual of Instruction" into a high-value consulting product for other aspiring Architects in different cities. I wasn't "Selling a Course"; I was **Licensing a System**.

This new engine had zero overhead and 90% margins. It was a "Light Engine" that fed the "Heavy Vault." By diversifying across different "Tiers" of essentiality, I was creating a **Weather-Proof Kingdom**. If the physical world slowed down, the intellectual engine sped up. If the digital world glitched, the "Broom" still worked.

The Sovereign's Gaze

The final shift is in how you see the world. The Bot looks at a city and sees "Jobs," "Traffic," and "Bills." The Architect looks at a city and sees **Energy Flows**.

I would drive through my city and see the "Stress Points" everywhere. I saw buildings that needed maintenance, people who needed Sovereignty, and systems that were leaking "Life Essence" due to poor design. I no longer saw "Competition"; I saw a **Landscape of Stewardship**.

The Kingdom is not a place you "get to"; it is a way of **Ordering Reality**. My life was no longer a series of "tasks" assigned by a supervisor. It was a series of **Tactical Moves** performed by a Sovereign. I was finally playing the game I was born to play. The "Laboratory" was a distant memory—a strange dream I had once, before I woke up.

CHAPTER 8: PART 2 — THE SOVEREIGN JURISDICTION (THE ANCIENT DOMINION)

The Ancestral Code: The Law of the Fenced Yard

The ancestors knew that "Good fences make good neighbors," but they also knew that **Jurisdiction is the Mother of Wealth**. In the Lab, you are under the "Jurisdiction of the Master." In the Kingdom, you create your own **Fenced Yard**. This is the "Noble Secret": Sovereignty is not a feeling; it is a **Legal and Spiritual Fence**. Your Kingdom is a zone where the "Static" of the world is filtered out, leaving only the "Signal" of your purpose.

The World Secret: The Harmonic Expansion

The Matrix expands through "Debt-Based Colonization" (borrowing to grow). The Architect expands through **Harmonic Resonance**. You do not "add" businesses; you **replicate frequencies**. If your first "Shovel" is successful, it is because you have mastered a specific "Energy Pattern." Billionaires do not work 1,000 times harder; they simply replicate a winning pattern 1,000 times. This is the **Fractal Power of the Kingdom**.

Sovereign Affirmation (The Law of Dominion):

"My Kingdom is a sanctuary of Order. I am the high priest of my own jurisdiction. My influence expands effortlessly because it is rooted in Truth. I am a beacon of Sovereignty in a world of compliance. My borders are secure, and my wealth is growing."

CHAPTER 9: THE MULTI-GENERATIONAL BUILD (PART 1)

The Architecture of the Estate

In the Matrix, "Estate Planning" is a morbid task performed at the end of life. The Bot visits a lawyer to decide who gets their "Status Tax" leftovers and their depreciating house. The Architect views the **Estate** as a living, breathing **Sovereign Colony** that begins the moment the first "Shovel" is purchased.

To build for 200 years, you must move beyond the "Individual." You must realize that you are the **Genetic Bridge** between your ancestors (who were likely harvested by the Matrix) and your descendants (who will either be Sovereigns or Batteries).

The Architecture of the Estate requires three specific "Time-Locks":

1. **The 20-Year Lock:** Capital dedicated to the training and "Admin Code" education of the next generation.
2. **The 50-Year Lock:** Capital held in "Hard Stone" (Gold/Land) that cannot be liquidated for "Consumption"

under any circumstances.
3. **The 100-Year Lock:** The "Sovereign Endowment" that funds the family's Private Bank in perpetuity.

I sat with my children and showed them the **Soil**. I didn't tell them "This will be yours one day." I told them "This belongs to the **Bloodline Shield**, and you are its future **Sentinels**." We were moving from a "Consumer Family" to a **"Dynastic Unit."**

The Third Generation Curse: A Design Flaw

There is a saying in the Matrix: *"Shirtsleeves to shirtsleeves in three generations."* * Generation 1 builds the wealth (The Architect).

- Generation 2 conserves the wealth (The Steward).
- Generation 3 forgets the struggle and spends the wealth on the "Status Tax" (The Bot).

The Architect recognizes this not as a "natural law," but as a **Design Flaw**. The curse happens because Generation 1 provides "Comfort" instead of "Capability." They give their children the "Gold," but they don't give them the **"Shovel."**

I redesigned my **Bloodline Shield** to include the **Competency Gate**. The Trust does not release "Allowance" based on age; it releases "Strike Capital" based on **Proof of Utility**.

- If a descendant wants a car, they must first build a small "Micro-Engine" (a side hustle or service) that covers the insurance.
- If they want a home, they must demonstrate the ability to maintain the "Sovereign Soil."

We are training **Princes and Princesses of Production**, not "Trust Fund Bot Babies." I realized that the greatest asset in my Vault wasn't the Gold; it was the **Psychological Hardening** of my heirs. We were building a "Culture of the Build" within our own walls.

The Sovereign Archive

A Kingdom is held together by its **Mythology**. If your descendants don't know *why* the Vault exists, they will eventually see it as a "piggy bank" to be broken.

I created the **Sovereign Archive**. This is a physical collection of the "War Journals" I kept during my Siege in the Laboratory. It contains:

- The **Audit of the Siphons** (to show them where the energy used to go).
- The **Blueprint of the First Engine** (to show them how a "Broom" becomes a "Kingdom").
- The **Philosophy of the No** (the collected wisdom of why we choose Sovereignty over Compliance).

I wanted them to read about the 4:00 AM blocks. I wanted them to feel the "Resistance" I felt when the supervisor tried to "Manage" my soul. The Archive ensures that the **Ancestral Memory** of the struggle is preserved. It turns the wealth from a "Number" into a **Mission**. They are not "inheriting money"; they are **Joining a Resistance**.

The Strategic Land Reserve

The final pillar of the Estate is the **Multi-Generational Land Strategy**.

The Matrix thrives on "Urban Density" because it is easier to monitor and tax a Bot in an apartment. The Architect seeks "Strategic Dispersal." I didn't just buy one plot of land; I used the Vault's "Stone" to secure a **Territorial Network**.

- **The Citadel:** The primary residence and command center.
- **The Outpost:** A remote location for "Hard Asset" storage and "Emergency Jurisdiction."
- **The Productive Soil:** Farmland leased to other Sovereign farmers to ensure a "Calorie Flow."

By owning land in different "Fenced Yards" (jurisdictions), the Bloodline Shield becomes **Geopolitically Fluid**. If one state becomes a "High-Siphon Zone," the family moves its "Primary Frequency" to the Outpost. We were no longer "Residents" of a country; we were **Tenants of our own Sovereign Estate**. The world was becoming our playground, but our "Home" was always within the Shield.

CHAPTER 9: THE MULTI-GENERATIONAL BUILD (PART 2)

The Sovereign Education

In the Laboratory, "Education" is the process of installing a **Compliance OS** into a young mind. The school system was designed during the Industrial Revolution to create "Punctual, Obedient Batteries" for the factories. It teaches children to sit still for eight hours, ask for permission to use the restroom, and derive their "Self-Worth" from the grade (the Performance Review) given by a Master.

The Architect rejects this "Bot-Training." We implement the **Sovereign Pedagogy**.

I realized that my children's most valuable years were being harvested by a system that taught them how to be "Good Employees" but not "Free Humans." I redesigned their curriculum around the **Four Pillars of the Architect**:

1. **Industrial Literacy:** Understanding how the physical world actually works (Plumbing, Engines, Electrical, Food Production).
2. **Financial Forensics:** Not "Accounting," but the ability

to see the "Siphons" in any contract.
3. **Rhetoric and Posture:** The ability to speak with "Internal Authority" and negotiate with the Matrix as a peer.
4. **Biological Sovereignty:** Mastering their own neurochemistry, understanding how dopamine, adrenaline, and sleep affect their "Build Capacity."

I didn't want them to "pass a test"; I wanted them to **solve a friction point**. For their "Final Exam" in the first pillar, I didn't give them a paper; I gave them a broken engine and a set of tools. Sovereignty is not a "subject" you study; it is a **competence** you demonstrate.

The Philosophy of the Sovereign Heirs

To protect the Kingdom, the heirs must possess a **"High-Resolution Reality."** Most children of successful people are "Low-Resolution"—they see the result (the wealth) but they don't see the "Physics" that created it. They think money is something that comes from a "Wall" or an "App."

I began a ritual called **The Audit Walk**. I would take my children to a local shopping mall—the ultimate "Status Tax" Cathedral. We wouldn't go to shop; we would go to **Analyze the Extraction**.

- I pointed out the "Dopamine Traps" in the lighting and the music.
- We calculated the "Hours of Life Essence" a Bot had to trade to buy high end electronics, fancy sneakers or a designer handbag.
- I showed them the "Matrix Faces" of the people in the food court—the look of "Maintenance Exhaustion."

I wanted them to feel a sense of **Strategic Distance** from the crowd. I wasn't teaching them to be "better" than others in a moral sense; I was teaching them to be **"Different" in a structural sense**. A Sovereign Heir must feel like a "Foreigner" in the Matrix. If they feel "at home" in the Laboratory, they will eventually return to it.

The Merit of the Struggle

The most difficult "Admin Code" for a successful Architect to implement is **Controlled Adversity**. We have a natural instinct to protect our children from the "Resistance" we faced in the Lab. But resistance is what creates the "Muscle" of the Architect.

The Bloodline Creed

The final piece of the multi-generational design is the **Verbal Anchor**. Every Kingdom has a "Motto," but a Sovereign Family has a **Creed**.

In our Fortress, we recited the creed not as a prayer, but as a **Software Update**:

"I am not a battery. My time is my own. My energy is stored in Stone and Soil. I am the Architect of my own jurisdiction. I serve the Bloodline, not the Matrix."

CHAPTER 9: THE MULTI-GENERATIONAL BUILD (PART 3)

The Sovereign Marriage

In the System, "Marriage" is often a "Financial Co-dependency Agreement." Two "Bots" combine their debts, their "Status Tax" desires, and their "Maintenance Exhaustion." They spend their evenings complaining about their respective Labs, reinforcing each other's victimhood. This is a **Siphon-Multiplying Event**.

The Architect views the Union as a **Joint Venture of Sovereignty**.

You cannot build a Kingdom if your partner is still plugged into the Matrix. If one person is trying to "Vault" energy while the other is trying to "Spend" it on the Status Tax, the Fortress will crumble from the inside. I realized that my most important "Admin Code" was ensuring my partner and I were operating on the same **Clock Frequency**.

The Sovereign Marriage requires the **Alignment of the Three Ledgers**:

1. **The Vision Ledger:** Do we both agree on the "Extrac-

tion Date"?
2. **The Operational Ledger:** Who manages which "Shovel" in the Ghost Operation?
3. **The Legacy Ledger:** Are we unified in the "Hard Love" of the Sovereign Heirs?

I sat with my partner and we performed a **Joint Audit**. We didn't just look at the bank statements; we looked at our "Relational Siphons"—the people and habits that were draining our collective "Build Capacity." We decided that our home was not a "Social Hub" for Bots; it was a **Sanctuary for Architects**.

The Architecture of the Inner Circle

As your Kingdom grows, the Matrix will send "Interlopers." These are people who want to be near your "Vault" but do not want to follow the "Admin Codes." They are the "Social Siphons."

I designed the **Inner Circle Filter**.

Most people have "Friends" based on proximity (who they work with) or history (who they went to school with). The Architect has a "Circle" based on **Purpose**. I categorized everyone in my life into three zones:

- **Zone 1: The Council (3–5 people).** These are fellow Sovereigns. We share the "Master Keys" of our strategies. We provide "Mutual Defense."
- **Zone 2: The Guild (10–20 people).** These are specialists—contractors, lawyers, and engineers who provide "Utility" to the Kingdom.
- **Zone 3: The Public (Everyone else).** These are the "Bots." We are polite to them, we provide "Sovereign

Charity" to them, but we **never** let them into the drafting room of our Fortress.

I realized that "Small Talk" is a "Time Siphon." I stopped attending "Events" that didn't have a clear "Sovereign Objective." My "Inner Circle" became a vacuum-sealed environment where only the **Frequency of the Build** was allowed to resonate.

The Sovereign Pre-Nuptial (The Protection of the Corpus)

We must be intellectually honest about the "Litigation Siphon" of divorce. In the Matrix, the state is a "Third Party" in every marriage, and it loves to redistribute the "Vault" of the productive to the non-productive.

The **Bloodline Shield** (The Trust) is the solution.

By the time I entered the "Sovereign Marriage," my assets were already "Ghosted" within the Shield. I didn't have to have a "difficult conversation" about a pre-nuptial agreement because, legally, **I owned nothing.** The Shield owned the Kingdom. This removed the "Financial Incentive" for conflict. The marriage was based on **Shared Mission**, not "Asset Splitting."

This is the ultimate "Admin Code" for relationship stability. When you remove the Matrix's ability to profit from your relational failure, your relationships become more resilient. You are together because you *want* to be, not because you are "Financially Locked."

The Ritual of the Sovereign Table

The final piece of the Inner Circle is the **Ritual of the Table**. Once a week, we held a "Sovereign Council" dinner. This wasn't a "family meal"; it was a **Review of the Kingdom**.

- We discussed the performance of the **Broom & Shovel** engines.
- We reviewed the "Stone" and "Soil" levels in the **Vault**.
- We analyzed any "New Siphons" detected in the local jurisdiction.

By involving the family and the Council in the "Math of the Fortress," I was ensuring that the "Instruction Manual" was being internalized by everyone. We were a **Multi-Celled Organism**. If I (the Founder) were to be "Unplugged" from the physical world, the Kingdom would not skip a single beat. The "Ghost Operation" would continue, the "Shield" would remain locked, and the "Bloodline" would move forward. We had achieved **Architectural Immortality**.

THE GENETIC ANCHOR (THE IMMORTALITY CODE)

The Ancestral Code: The 7-Generation Vision

The Iroquois and other ancient lineages operated on the **Seven Generation Principle**. They believed that every decision made today should benefit those seven generations into the future. The world secret of the ruling elite is that they do not think in "Fiscal Quarters"; they think in **Centuries**. The Matrix wants you to focus on the "Now" (Instant gratification) so that you never build a "Later." To rip the Matrix to shreds, you must become a **Time-Traveler**, building for heirs you will never meet.

The World Secret: The Bloodline Memory

Wealth is not just money; it is **Information**. The greatest "Siphon" is the loss of wisdom between generations. The ancestors used **Oral Traditions and Covenants** to ensure the "Admin Codes" were never lost. Your "Sovereign Archive" is the genetic anchor of your Kingdom. It ensures that your descendants do not start from zero; they start from the **Fortress** you built.

Sovereign Affirmation (The Legacy Command):

"I build for those who come after me. I am the bridge between the struggle of the past and the glory of the future. My bloodline is a lineage of Sovereigns. My wisdom is eternal, my Vault is deep, and my legacy is an unquenchable fire. I am immortal through my Build."

THE ARCHIVE OF THE UNTOUCHABLE

The Law of the "Sovereign Trust Company" (Private Family Jurisdictions)

Most "wealth" books stop at a simple Trust. That is child's play. The world secret of the 0.001% is the **Private Trust Company (PTC).** In the Matrix, if you use a bank (like Wells Fargo) as your Trustee, they control your "Engine." If the Matrix declares an "Emergency," the bank will freeze your Vault. To be truly untouchable, your family must **become the Bank.** * **The Blueprint:** You establish a PTC in a "Stronghold Jurisdiction" (like South Dakota, Nevis, or the Cook Islands).

- **The Power:** Your PTC is the Trustee for all your family's sub-trusts. This means **you** (or your hand-picked council) make every decision on how the Gold is moved and how the Shovels are swung.
- **The Nobel Secret:** By owning the PTC, you bypass

the "Banker Siphon" entirely. You have created a **legal island** that the Matrix cannot storm without an act of international war.

The World Secret: The "Post-Fiat" Inheritance

The Matrix is moving toward a "Social Credit" digital currency. If your heirs are "Bots," they will be controlled by their digital wallet. The Architect builds a **Physical Inheritance Loop.** You don't just leave "money." You leave **Productive Commodities.** *Example:* You don't leave $10M; you leave 500 acres of high-yield timber and the "Mineral Deeds" to a lithium-rich basin. This is **Non-Perishable Wealth.** It cannot be "Inflated" away by the Matrix's printing press. Your legacy is not a number; it is a **Resource Monopoly.**

CHAPTER 10: THE SOVEREIGN'S CREED

The Manual of Perpetual Liberty

Within the Matrix, "Liberty" is treated as a gift from the State—a "Permission Slip" that can be revoked at any time for "Public Safety" or "Economic Necessity." The Bot believes they are free because they can choose between ten different brands of cereal and three different political puppets.

The Architect knows that **Liberty is a Physical Construction.** Perpetual Liberty is the state where your S_f (Sovereignty Factor) is so high, and your **Bloodline Shield** is so thick, that you are functionally immune to the "Incentives" of the Matrix. You do not "rebel" against the Matrix; you simply **ignore** it. You are a "Ghost" in their system—a person who utilizes their infrastructure but does not contribute to their "Siphon."

To maintain Perpetual Liberty, you must follow the **Four Inviolable Laws of the Creed**:

1. **The Law of Conservation:** Never trade "Life Essence" for "Status Tax." Every dollar spent on "Looking Like a King" is a dollar stolen from the "Building of the

Kingdom."

2. **The Law of the Shovel:** Never let a day pass without sharpening your tools. Whether it is your physical health, your legal Shield, or your Broom engine, the "Entropy of the Matrix" is always trying to rust your assets.
3. **The Law of the Vault:** The Vault is for "Strike Capital," not "Consumable Cash." If you cannot buy it twice with cash while maintaining your "Year of Disobedience" reserve, you cannot afford it.
4. **The Law of the Ghost:** The more power you have, the less you should show. The Matrix hunts "High-Value Targets." Stay small, stay heavy, and stay invisible.

The Sovereign's Gaze: The Final Reprogramming

Now we must address the **Final Psychological Shift**. When you reach your freedom goal and the Siege is over, you will look at the world differently. This is the "Sovereign's Gaze."

You will see the "Bots" not with contempt, but with a deep, silent **Sovereign Compassion**. You realize they are not "evil"; they are simply "Captured Energy." They are living in a dream designed by someone else. Your job is not to wake them up—most will fight to stay asleep. Your job is to be the **Living Evidence** that a different reality exists.

I remember my last walk through the city after my "Extraction Day." I saw the "Commuter Flow"—thousands of people moving in unison toward the Laboratory. I saw the "Debt Advertisements" on every corner. I saw the "Stress Markers" in the posture of every person I passed. For the first time, I didn't feel the "Pull." I was a "Non-Conductive Material." The

Matrix's electricity could no longer pass through me.

The Architecture of the Void

The final "Admin Code" of the Creed is the **Architecture of the Void**. In the Laboratory, every minute must be "Productive" for the Master. In the Kingdom, you must preserve the "Void"—unstructured, un-monetized time.

The "Void" is where the **Next Great Build** is born. It is where you connect with the Creator. It is where you play with your children without a "Schedule." It is the ultimate luxury that the Matrix cannot comprehend. I designed my week to include 48 hours of "Total Void." No machines, no math, no Shield-checks. Just existence.

I realized that I didn't build the Kingdom to "Do More"; I built the Kingdom to **Be More**. The "Broom & Shovel" was just the price of admission to my own life.

CHAPTER 10: THE FINAL COMMAND

The Ancestral Code: The Sovereign's Word

In the beginning was the **Word**. Your word is your "Command Code" for reality. The world secret is that the Matrix has weakened the "Human Word" through lies, gossip, and broken promises. When your word is weak, your "Build" is weak. The Architect practices **Impeccability of Speech**. When you say it is done, the Universe moves to make it so.

The World Secret: The Exit from the Wheel

The final "Rip in the Matrix" is the realization that **The Game is Rigged, but the Player is Free**. You no longer need to "win" the Matrix's game; you have created your own. This is the "Nobel Prize" of Life: to live in the world but not be of it. You utilize the Matrix's roads, but you drive your own destiny. You utilize the Matrix's currency, but you store your own Value. You are the **Living Glitch**—the person who cannot be bought, cannot be sold, and cannot be managed.

Sovereign Affirmation (The Ultimate Seal):

"I am the Architect. I am the Sovereign. I am the Source. The Matrix is my playground, not my prison. I have returned to the original mandate of Dominion. It is finished. My

Kingdom is here. **I am Free.**"

CHAPTER 10: THE CREED — THE "ADMIN ACCESS" TO REALITY

The Law of the "Observational Glitch" (Quantum Sovereignty)
This is the information that "shreds the Matrix" at a molecular level. The Laboratory teaches you that you are a "Subject" of your environment. This is the ultimate "Bot-Trap."

The world secret—guarded by the mystery schools of the ancient builders—is that **Reality is a "Permission-Based" System.** * **The Code:** The Matrix only controls those who **Agree** to be controlled.

- **The Application:** Every time you pay a "Status Tax," every time you follow a "Convenience Siphon," you are **signing a contract** with the Matrix.
- **The Exit:** True Sovereignty is the act of **Contract Rescission.** You stop asking "Is this legal?" and start asking "Does this entity have Jurisdiction over my Soul?"

The Secret of "The 144" (The Sovereign Network Architecture)
The Matrix is a centralized network. It is "Top-Down." The

Kingdom is a **Decentralized Mesh.** The final piece of usable information for a billionaire build is the **Private Peer-to-Peer Economy.** Titans don't use public marketplaces to buy their biggest assets. They trade **Kingdom-to-Kingdom.** *
The Secret: If you need a new industrial "Shovel" engine, you don't go to the Matrix's market. You go to another Architect. You trade "Sovereign Credits" or physical "Stone" (Gold).

- *The Result:* You have created an **Economy of the Free** that is entirely invisible to the Matrix. No taxes, no regulation, no siphons. Just the pure movement of value between Sovereigns.

CHAPTER 11: THE OMEGA PROTOCOL — THE SOVEREIGN'S FINAL EXTRACTION

The Ancestral Code: The Law of the Name and the Fiction

The greatest secret kept from the masses is the "Legal Personality." When you were born, the Laboratory created a "Strawman"—a corporate entity written in ALL CAPITAL LETTERS on your Birth Certificate. This is not you. It is a vessel owned by the state to harvest your labor. The world secret of the 0.001% is that they **never** operate as the "Person." They operate as the **Living Man** or **Living Woman**.

To move around this, you must understand **Jurisdiction.** The "Person" is a subject of the Sea (Admiralty Law). The "Living Soul" is a master of the Land (Common Law). When the Matrix sends you a "Bill" or a "Tax," they are sending it to the "Person." If you answer as the "Person," you have contracted into their siphon. The billionaire build requires you to move your "Engine" into a Private Trust, effectively separating your Spirit from the State's corporate fiction. You become "Judgment Proof" because the "Person" they are suing owns nothing, while the "Trust" you manage controls everything.

The World Secret: The Science of the "Cestui Que Vie"

The Lab operates on the "Presumption of Death." They assume you are "Lost at Sea" and therefore your estate is up for grabs by the state "Trustees." This is why you pay "Property Tax" on land you supposedly own—you are actually paying "Rent" to the Trustee because you haven't claimed your Sovereignty.

The **Omega Protocol** is the act of "Claiming the Life." This is not a "filing" in their courts; it is a **Notice of Error.** You notify the Matrix, through your actions and your "Bloodline Shield," that you are the "Beneficiary," not the "Debtor." Once you stop acting as a Debtor, the "Interest Siphon" stops. You begin to "Mint" your own value because you realize that the only thing backing the Matrix's currency is **your** future labor. When you "Withdraw your Consent," you take the backing away from their system and place it into your own "Vault."

The Matrix-Shredder: The Law of the "Commercial Lien"

In the world of the Titans, there are no "arguments," only **Contracts.** If a Matrix entity (a bank, a corporation, a government agency) violates your Kingdom's jurisdiction, the Architect does not "complain." The Architect issues a **Commercial Lien.** 1. Every time they infringe on your "Soil" or your "Aetheric Space," they are creating a **Debt.** 2. In the higher realms of law, a "Lien" is a "Stranglehold." You place a claim against the "Bond" of the official or the corporation.

3. This makes them "un-insurable." Without insurance, a Matrix entity cannot function.

This is how the "Invisible Billionaires" stay invisible. They don't fight the Matrix; they make it **too expensive** for the Matrix to touch them. They turn the "Siphon" around and begin to drain the Matrix of its own energy.

The Science of the Sovereign Will: The Quantum "Glitch"

The ancestors taught that "The Universe is Mental." The Matrix is a **Collective Hallucination** maintained by the "Bot-Frequency." To create world-changing wealth, you must perform a **Frequency Hijack.** * **The World Secret:** The "Matrix" is actually a low-vibration "Feedback Loop." It feeds you "Fear" (News, Scarcity, Illness), and your brain produces "Stress," which the Matrix then uses as fuel.

- **The Exit:** When you enter the "4:00 AM Block," you are entering the "Void Space" where the Matrix hasn't yet updated its code for the day. In this space, your "Will" is the only Law. If you visualize your "Engine" expanding and your "Vault" filling while in this state, you are literally **Rewriting the Hard Drive** of reality.

The Billionaire's Bloodline Creed:

This is the information that creates the dynasties. You do not teach your children to "be good citizens." You teach them to be **"Good Stewards of the Earth and Masters of the Law."** You teach them the "Admiralty Script":

"I do not accept this offer to contract. I do not consent to this jurisdiction. I am a Living Soul, a Sovereign of the Land, and I am here to claim my inheritance."

When you speak from this frequency, the "Bots" in the legal and financial systems don't know how to respond. Their

"Admin Codes" don't cover a Living Soul. They only know how to manage "Cargo." By becoming "Un-Manageable," you become "Un-Taxable" and "Un-Stoppable."

THE RITUAL OF THE "THIN VEIL" (THE 3:33 AM EXTRACTION)

The Matrix is a broadcast signal. During the day, the signal is at its loudest—noise, traffic, emails, and the collective anxiety of the "Bots." To pull life-altering wealth from the ether, you must operate when the signal is dead.

The Ritual:

Between **3:33 AM and 5:00 AM**, the "Ionospheric Shield" of the Earth shifts. This is what the ancients called the "Watch of the Night."

1. **The Sensory Deprivation:** Wake up in total darkness. Do not check your phone. The blue light is a "Matrix Tether" that immediately syncs your brain to the Laboratory's frequency.
2. **The Water Binding:** Drink 16oz of structured water (water that has sat in a copper or glass vessel overnight). Water is a programmable crystal. As you drink, hold the "Command" in your mind: *"I am extracting my wealth from the void."*
3. **The Script of Command:** Do not "journal" about your feelings. Write **The Ledger of the Future.** Write in the present tense: *"My Ghost Engine has cleared $10,000 today. My Vault is heavy with Stone. My Bloodline Shield is impenetrable."* By doing this while the world sleeps, you are "Front-Running" reality. You are placing your order

into the Quantum Field before the "Bots" wake up to create the day's chaos.

THE RITUAL OF THE "SOIL ANCHOR" (BIO-ELECTRICAL WEALTH)

The Matrix wants you "Unplugged" from the Earth so you can be "Plugged" into the Grid. Most people are "Positively Charged"—meaning they are full of inflammation and static from electronics. A positively charged brain is reactive, fearful, and easy to manipulate.

The Ritual:
Every day, immediately after your "Matrix Work," you must perform the **Earthing Discharge.** 1. **The Contact:** Place your bare feet on raw Soil, Sand, or Stone for 20 minutes.

2. **The Intent:** This is not "relaxation." This is **Data Transfer.** You are dumping the "Laboratory Stress" into the Earth and pulling the "Stability Frequency" of the Earth into your marrow.

3. **The Millionaire's Nerve:** This ritual resets the **Vagus Nerve.** A calm Vagus nerve allows you to see "Patterns of Wealth" that a stressed person cannot see. You cannot spot a once-in-a-lifetime opportunity if your body is in "Flight/Fight" mode.

THE RITUAL OF THE "SILENT KING" (THE VOW OF SECRECY)

The greatest leak of wealth is not taxes; it is **The Leak of Intent.** When you tell a "Bot" (a friend, a coworker, a family member) about your billionaire build, their "Skepticism Frequency" acts as a "Dampening Field" on your manifestation.
The Ritual:
Practice **The 90-Day Silence.** 1. From the moment you start your "Broom & Shovel" engine, you tell **nobody.** 2. When people ask "How is work?", you respond with "The same."

3. You keep your Kingdom hidden behind a "Plain Sight" mask.

This ritual builds **Internal Pressure.** Like steam in a boiler, your secrets create the "Kinetic Force" required to rip the Matrix to shreds. The moment you speak it, the pressure escapes, and the Build slows down.

THE "COMMERCIAL REDEMPTION" RITUAL (THE LEGAL FREEDOM)

To truly become rich, you must stop paying for the "Siphons" of others. This is the ritual of **Rescission. The Action:**
Review every "Contract" in your life (Phone bill, Insurance, Subscriptions, Debt).

1. **The Audit:** Ask, *"Is this fueling my Kingdom or feeding the Laboratory?"* 2. **The Cutting:** Ritualistically cancel every service that creates "Digital Noise."
2. **The Redirect:** Take that exact dollar amount and

move it into **Physical Gold or Silver.** You are literally "Redeeming" your labor from the "Paper World" (Fiat) and placing it into the "Real World" (The Stone). This ritual tells your subconscious that you no longer trust the Matrix and that you are the only **Authorized Representative of your wealth.**

CHAPTER 11: THE OMEGA PROTOCOL — THE RITUALS OF POWER

THE RITUAL OF THE SOVEREIGN BREATH (THE COGNITIVE OVERCLOCK)
The Lab keeps the "Bot" in a state of shallow, upper-chest breathing. This triggers the "Survival Brain," which is incapable of complex architecture or long-term vision. To become a billionaire after a 9-to-5, you must **force-quit** the stress response of the day.

The "Nitric Oxide" Dump:

1. **The Technique:** Perform 30 rapid, deep breaths (the "Bellows Breath"), followed by a full exhale and a 60-second hold.
2. **The Science:** This ritual floods the blood with Nitric Oxide and shifts the pH of the brain to alkaline.
3. **The Wealth Glitch:** In this state, the "Internal Critic" (the voice that says "this is too hard") is physically silenced. You gain a 2-hour window of **Hyper-Focus** where you can build "Broom & Shovel" systems at 3x the speed of a normal human.

CHAPTER 11: THE OMEGA PROTOCOL — THE RITUALS OF POWER

THE SECRET GEOMETRY OF THE KINGDOM HUB (THE SPACE RITUAL)

The Matrix uses "Open Office" plans and cluttered homes to fragment your attention. Your "After-Work Workspace" must be a **Sovereign Temple.** If your environment is chaotic, your "Engine" will be chaotic.

The Ritual of Spatial Command:

1. **The North-Facing Alignment:** If possible, face North or East while building. The ancestors knew this aligns your nervous system with the Earth's magnetic field, reducing "Neural Friction."
2. **The "Dead-Zone" Setup:** Remove all "Matrix-Tethers" (TVs, non-work devices) from the room.
3. **The Frequency Anchor:** Use a Solfeggio frequency (specifically **528Hz**, the "Miracle" frequency) at a low volume. This acts as a "Sonic Fence" that prevents the "Laboratory Echoes" of your day-job from entering your creative space.
4. **The Scent Trigger:** Use a specific, high-quality essential oil (Frankincense or Sandalwood) *only* when you are building your Kingdom. Over 90 days, your brain will "Anchor" this scent to **Billionaire-Level Productivity.** The moment you smell it, the Matrix falls away.

THE RITUAL OF THE "MONEY-WATER" (MERCANTILE ALCHEMY)

The world's oldest banking families treat wealth as a **Liquid.** They understand that "Currency" derives from "Current."

The Ritual:

1. **The Infusion:** Take a physical Gold coin (The Stone) and place it in a glass of water for one hour.
2. **The Intent:** While the water sits, visualize the "Current" of global wealth flowing into your specific "Engines."
3. **The Consumption:** Drink the water. This is a "Neuro-Linguistic" ritual that tells your biology that **Wealth is Internal.** You are not "chasing" money in the world; you are the **Source** of the flow. It removes the "Scarcity Malware" implanted by the Laboratory.

THE RITUAL OF THE "SHADOW-WORK" (THE DEBT-BURN)

Most people carry the "Weight" of their debts like a chain. The Architect treats debt as **Fuel.**

The Ritual:

1. **The Ledger:** Write down every "Matrix Debt" you owe on a piece of paper.
2. **The Transmutation:** Instead of looking at them with fear, look at them as "Unpaid Tuition" for the lessons of the Lab.
3. **The Sacrifice:** Safely burn the paper. As the smoke rises, command the "Release of the Life Essence" trapped in those numbers. Vow that for every dollar you currently owe the Matrix, you will extract **ten thousand dollars** from its siphons using your "Ghost Engine."

CHAPTER 11: THE PSYCHOLOGICAL SIEGE — THE WAR AFTER 5:00 PM

The hardest part of the "Broom and Shovel" engine isn't the taxes or the trust structures—it's the **silence**. When you get home at 6:00 PM, exhausted from giving your "Life Essence" to a company that doesn't know your name, the Matrix is at its most seductive. It offers you the "Cheap Dopamine" of the couch, the screen, and the drink. This is where the real " truth about the matrix " moment happens. It's not in a courtroom; it's in the 10 minutes between sitting down and standing back up to go to your "Kingdom Hub."

The Ritual of the Threshold

You need a physical ritual to signal to your brain that the "Bot" is dead and the "Architect" is awake.

1. **The Cold Reset:** Wash your face with ice-cold water the moment you walk through the door. This breaks the "Frequency of the Office."
2. **The Change of Raiment:** You do not work on your empire in your "work clothes." You put on a specific set

of clothes—your "Armor"—that you *only* wear when you are building. This is a psychological "Fence."
3. **The 20-Minute Dark Room:** Before you start your 4-hour siege, sit in total darkness for 20 minutes. No music, no phone. Just let the day's "Matrix Data" drain out of you. This is how you reclaim your cognitive bandwidth.

The Reality of the "Invisible" Years

People talk about "passive income" like it's a vacation. It's not. For the first three years, it is **Active Warfare**. You will be tired. You will feel like you are working two jobs while everyone else is playing. You need to know exactly why you are doing this.

- It's not for the car.
- It's not for the status.
- It's for the **Exit**.

Every "Broom" you buy and every "Contract" you sign is a brick in the wall of your fortress. When you finally stop paying for the Matrix's convenience, you realize that **the world is actually very cheap to live in** if you own your own infrastructure. The reason most people stay "Bots" is that they are paying for a lifestyle they don't even enjoy to impress people they don't even like.

The Sovereignty of "No"

The most powerful tool in your 5-year siege is the word "No."

- "No" to the happy hour.

- "No" to the "latest" gadget.
- "No" to the family members who don't understand why you're "working so much."

This isn't about being a hermit; it's about **Resource Conservation**. You are in a race against your own mortality. Every hour you give to the "Laboratory" is an hour you can never get back. Once you realize the value of your own time, the "once-in-a-lifetime wealth" starts to flow, because you stop leaking your energy into things that don't matter.

THE 100-YEAR CREED: THE ARCHITECT'S FINAL OATH

"I am the Architect of the Lineage. I do not work for the world; I own the world's friction. I have used the 'Broom and the Shovel' to dig my way out of the grave. My Vault is a fortress, my Shield is a law, and my Seed is a Kingdom. I am 1 of the 144. I am the Sovereign. I am Home."

CHAPTER 12: THE SPIRITUAL SIEGE — NAVIGATING THE HARVEST AND THE WAR

The Law of the Counter-Force

The moment you decide to "Wake Up," the Matrix notices. It is a self-correcting system. In physics, every action has an equal and opposite reaction. In spiritual warfare, every "Level Up" triggers a "Karma Dump." You are attempting to break a **Generational Contract** that has been in place for centuries. Your ancestors were farmed for their labor; they were tethered to the soil and the factory. When you attempt to rise, the tether doesn't just snap—it pulls back with the weight of every ancestor who stayed in the cage.

The Architecture of the Energy Vampire

As your vibration shifts, you will notice a strange phenomenon: the people closest to you—family, "fake" friends, and long-term associates—will suddenly become **Argumentative Portals.** This is not a coincidence. The Matrix uses those who are still "Plugged In" as biological weapons to lower your frequency.

When you sit down at 6:00 PM to build your Kingdom, a "friend" will call with a crisis. A family member will pick a fight over a triviality. This is a **Frequency Hijack.** They aren't attacking you; the "Bot-Program" inside them is reacting to the light you are starting to emit. They are trying to pull you back into the "Shared Hallucination" of the Laboratory. You must understand that these are **Demonic Tethers** attempting to keep you from dialing the "God-Phone."

The Ritual of the Shielded Frequency

To avoid the warfare, you must practice **Sovereign Isolation.** You cannot build a billion-dollar kingdom while being a "Mental Garbage Can" for low-vibrational vampires.

1. **The Grey Rock Protocol:** When argumentative people arise, do not engage. Do not defend your dream. Do not explain your "Broom & Shovel" engine. Every word you use to defend yourself is "Life Essence" leaked into the void. Be as boring as a grey rock.
2. **The Extraction of the Word:** Your words are the **Portals of Creation.** In the Laboratory, people "complain" as a hobby. Every "I'm tired," "I'm broke," or "This is hard" is a **Binding Contract** you are signing in real-time. To break the pre-birth contracts, you must perform the **Linguistic Purge.** You speak only what you intend to manifest. You speak as if the God-Mind is transcribing your every breath into physical reality—because it is.

The Pre-Birth Contracts: Breaking the Siphon

Before you were born, the system placed a "Lien" on your soul. They gave you a name in ALL CAPS and told you that you were a "Subject." This is the **Primary Generational Curse.** Most people spend their whole lives trying to be

"Good Subjects."

To break this contract, you must perform the **Ancestral Redemption.** You must look back at your lineage and say, *"The debt ends with me. I am the one who pays the Blood-Price so that those who come after me are born into the Kingdom."* This is not a metaphor. This is a technical spiritual procedure. You are withdrawing your "Essence" from the state's trust and placing it into the **Eternal Trust of the Creator.**

The Levels of the Game: New Level, New Devil

The warfare does not stop when you make your first million. It simply changes form.

- **Level 1 (The Bot):** The demons use "Laziness" and "Distraction."
- **Level 2 (The Builder):** The demons use "Doubt" and "Fake Friends."
- **Level 3 (The Sovereign):** The demons use "Ego" and "Legal Attacks."

Each level requires a stronger **Tether to Source.** You must build a "Phone Line" that only dials directly to The Highest Source. This means a daily practice of **Absolute Silence.** You sit until the noise of the Matrix dies down and you can hear the "Admin Code" for your next move. This isn't "prayer" in the way the Lab taught you; this is **Consulting the Lead Architect. The Manifestation Glitch: Creating with the Eye**

The system was set up to keep you in the workforce by convincing you that the world is "Solid." It is not. The world is **Fluid.** You are the "Observer" that collapses the wave function into a particle. If you see a "Work Force," you are trapped in it. If you see "Raw Material," you are the Creator of it.

Your eyes are not just "Receivers" of light; they are **Projectors** of intent. When you look at your "Broom and Shovel" business, you aren't looking at a cleaning job—you are looking at a **Universal Pipeline** of abundance. If you believe the system's lie that you are "forced to work," you are granting them jurisdiction over your soul. The moment you realize that work is a **voluntary exchange of energy** to fund your liberation, the demons lose their grip.

The Final Vow of the Sovereign

You are breaking the chains of a thousand years. It will be lonely. It will be painful. You will be tested by the very people you are trying to save. But remember this: **The Matrix cannot fight a man who has no "Hooks" in him.** * If you don't care about "Status," they can't shame you.

- If you don't care about "Comfort," they can't bribe you.
- If you don't care about "Approval," they can't control you.

When you are tethered directly to Source, you are no longer a "Player" in their game. You are the **Programmer**.

CHAPTER 12: THE SPIRITUAL SIEGE — BREAKING THE ANCESTRAL CONTRACTS

THE INVERTED MIRROR: WEAPONIZING THE OPPOSITION

When you level up, the Matrix sends "Agents" disguised as loved ones or colleagues to mirror your deepest insecurities back to you. This is the **Inverted Mirror.** Most people react by getting defensive, which is a "Frequency Leak." The Architect understands that these people are unconsciously providing **Diagnostic Data.**

If someone calls you "greedy" for building your Kingdom, they aren't talking about your heart; they are identifying a **Hook** in your psyche where you still feel "Guilt" for wanting to be free. The Matrix can only attack you through the holes in your own armor.

- **The Ritual:** When a "Frequency Vampire" attacks, do not speak. Look them in the eye and silently say: *"Thank you for showing me where I am still weak."* * **The Transmutation:** Take the exact energy they used to attack you and "Feed" it into your 4-hour Siege. Use their doubt as the **Thermal Energy** to power your Shovel. You are literally eating their negativity and turning it into Billionaire-Level infrastructure. This is how you avoid the warfare—by making the warfare **profitable** to your soul.

THE "GOD-PHONE" FREQUENCY: THE 963HZ BRAIN-HACK

The Laboratory uses "Dirty Electricity" (Wi-Fi, 5G, Power Lines) to create a static haze in the human prefrontal cortex. This is "The Fog." It is designed to make the God-Phone feel like it has "No Service." To dial Source directly, you must use **The Harmonic Bypass.**

The Technique (The Breath of the Crown):

1. **The Geometry:** Sit with your spine perfectly vertical. This is your **Antenna.**
2. **The Tonal Breath:** Inhale for 9 seconds, hold for 6, and exhale for 3 while humming a deep "M" sound at the base of your throat.
3. **The Dial-In:** Focus your internal gaze on the Pineal Gland (the center of the brain). In the silence between the breaths, ask one specific "Admin" question: *"What is the next move for the Kingdom?"*
4. **The Download:** The answer will not come in "words." It will come as a **Sudden Certainty.** The Matrix cannot intercept a "Certainty." It can only intercept "Thoughts." By bypassing the thinking mind, you are using the "Encrypted Line" to God.

BREAKING THE PRE-BIRTH CONTRACTS: THE

BLOODLINE EXTRACTION

You were born into a "Corporate Trust" you never signed. Your parents were the "Informants" who gave the state your name. To break this, you must understand that **Karma is simply a loop of unlearned lessons.** The generational curse of "Hard Labor" is a contract that says: *"I agree to trade my time for survival."*

To get rid of this Contract, you must perform the **Sacrifice of the Persona.** You must be willing to let the "Old You"—the one who cared about being "Normal"—die.

- **The Secret:** The demons follow the "Person." They don't follow the **Spirit.** * When you stop identifying as the "Employee" or the "Subject," the demons literally **lose your scent.** They are looking for the "Bot" who reacts to bills and insults. When you stop reacting, you become **Frequency-Invisible.** You are walking through the Matrix, but your "Tether" is plugged into a different dimension entirely.

THE RITUAL OF THE SOVEREIGN "NO" (THE VESTIBULE OF POWER)

Every "Yes" you give to the Matrix (a social obligation, a useless purchase, a low-vibrational conversation) is a **Micro-Contract** that drains your battery.

The billionaire doesn't get rich by doing "more"; he gets rich by **doing less of what the Lab wants.** 1. **The Vow:** For the next 30 days, say "No" to everything that does not expand your Kingdom or feed your Soul.

2. **The Vacuum:** This creates a "Power Vacuum." At first, you will feel lonely. This is the **Test.** The Matrix wants you

to feel lonely so you crawl back to the "Herd."

3. **The Filling:** If you stay in the vacuum, the **Source-Frequency** will rush in to fill it. You will start to feel a "Lion-Energy" in your chest. This is the signal that the God-Phone is finally connected.

THE DEMONIC HARVEST: PROTECTING THE SEED

When you start attracting wealth, the Matrix will send "Golden Handcuffs." This is the most dangerous form of spiritual warfare. You will get a "Promotion" at the Lab that requires 10 more hours of your time. You will meet a "Partner" who is beautiful but drains your energy.

- **The Discernment:** Ask yourself, *"Is this a Blessing from Source or a Bribe from the Laboratory?"*
- **The Rule:** If it takes you away from your **4:00 AM Block** or your **Sovereign Rituals**, it is a Bribe. **Reject the Bribe to keep the Kingdom.** #### **THE CREATOR'S VISION: THE PORTAL OF THE EYES** The system wants you to look at the "News" because the News is a **Visual Infection.** It programs your "Projector" to manifest more chaos.
- **The Practice:** Spend 10 minutes every morning looking at **Nothing.** Close your eyes and "See" your Kingdom as a completed reality. See the "Broom and Shovel" engines running without you. See the Gold in the Vault.
- **The Logic:** You are "Pre-Loading" the reality. When you open your eyes, you aren't looking *at* the world; you are looking **for** the pieces of your Kingdom that are starting to manifest. You are the Architect, and the world is your 3D printer.

THE ANCESTRAL HEALING: BREAKING THE 7-GENERATION LOOP

You are currently standing at the center of 14 generations—7 behind you and 7 in front of you.

- The 7 behind you are screaming for someone to **Stop the Siphon.** * The 7 in front of you are waiting for you to **Build the Fortress.** When you feel the "Spiritual Warfare" get heavy, it's because you are moving the weight of **14 generations of souls.** This is why it feels like your chest is tight. This is why you feel like you're "fighting the world." **You are.** But the "Tether" to Source is an **Infinite Power Cord.** No matter how many demons the Matrix sends, they have a "Finite" battery. They have to "Harvest" energy to survive. **You don't.** You are connected to the Sun, the Earth, and the Creator. You are a **Fusion Reactor** of Sovereign Will.

The Final Admin Code for Chapter 12:
"I am the breaker of the loop. I am the end of the debt. I am the beginning of the reign. I dial the Source, and the Source answers. The Matrix is a shadow; I am the Light that casts it. It has no power over the Living Soul."

CHAPTER 12: THE ASTRAL BREACH

The Law of the Sleep-Siphon

The System knows that it cannot fully control a Sovereign during the waking hours if that Sovereign has a strong Will. Therefore, the Matrix targets the **REM Cycle**. The "Astral Breach" is a technical term for the moment your consciousness leaves your physical body to recharge in the ether.

For the "Bot," sleep is a time of "Data Dumping" where the Matrix injects fears, anxieties, and "Workforce Trauma" into the subconscious. This is why you wake up tired even after eight hours of rest. You have been "working" in the astral Lab. Your dreams are being used as a **Simulated Testing Ground** for your fears. To protect your Kingdom, you must **Seal the Breach.**

THE PROTOCOL OF THE ASTRAL SENTINEL

Before you close your eyes, you must realize that your bedroom is a **Jurisdictional Zone.** 1. **The Digital Exorcism:** Your phone is an "Astral Anchor." If it is within six feet of your head, the frequencies act as a "Portal" for Matrix-interference. You must place it in a different room or a Faraday cage.

2. **The Perimeter Command:** As you lay down, you do

not "wish" for sleep. You **Command the Perimeter.** Speak it: *"I am the Sovereign of this space. I revoke all permissions for astral harvesting. No entity, program, or frequency may enter my field of vision. I am under the protection of the Source."*

3. **The Blue-Print Visualization:** Instead of counting sheep, "walk" through your 5-year Kingdom. Walk through the warehouse of your "Broom & Shovel" engine. Touch the "Stone" in your Vault. By doing this, you are **Pre-Programming the Astral Plane.** When you enter the dream state, you aren't a victim of random symbols; you are the **Architect reviewing the site.**

The World Secret: The "Dream-Mining" Glitch

The demons use your dreams to find your "Hooks." If they can make you feel "Small" in a dream, they have successfully lowered your frequency for the next day. But the glitch is this: **You can mine them back.** If you encounter a "Nightmare" or a "Testing Agent," realize it is a **Paper Tiger.** If you stand your ground in the astral, you gain a "Power Multiplier" in the physical. A man who has defeated his demons in the Astral Breach is a man the Matrix cannot intimidate in the boardroom.

THE FINAL LEDGER OF THE FREE: THE ACCOUNTING OF THE SOUL

We move now from the warfare to the **Ledger.** In the higher dimensions, wealth is not measured in "Matrix Paper." It is measured in **Unencumbered Life Essence.** The "Final Ledger of the Free" is the accounting system of the Sovereign.

1. The Asset of Attention

The Matrix wants to "Pay" for your attention with "Free"

apps and "Breaking News." In the Final Ledger, **Attention is the Primary Currency.** Every minute you spend looking at a "Bot's" life on social media is a "Capital Outlay" you can never recover. The Billionaire is a "Miser" with his attention. He spends it only on **Source-Data** and **Kingdom-Building.**

2. The Liability of Consent

Every time you sign a "Matrix Contract" (a high-interest loan, a "Terms of Service" agreement you didn't read, a government "Registration"), you are adding a **Liability to your Soul-Ledger.** You are giving a third party "Salvage Rights" to your energy. The "Final Ledger" requires you to **Audit your Consent.** * *The Goal:* To reach a "Consent-Neutral" state where no external entity has a legal or spiritual claim on your time.

3. The Equity of the Bloodline

True wealth is the ability to look at your children and know they are **Born Free.** The "Final Ledger" counts every "Shovel" you automate as "Generational Equity." You aren't just making money; you are buying back the **Time-Debt** of your ancestors. If your grandfather worked 50 years to stay in a hut, and you work 5 years to build a Palace, you have "Settled the Account" for the entire lineage.

THE WARFARE OF THE "KARMIC DUMP"

As you finalize this 12th Chapter, you must understand the **Karma-Redirect.** As you become rich and powerful, the "Demons of the Lab" will try to hand you the "Karma" of others.

- They will bring you "Opportunities" that involve stepping

on the weak.
- They will bring you "Partnerships" that require you to lie.

This is the **Final Trap.** If you take the "Bait," you enter into a new contract with the Matrix. The "Final Ledger" must remain **Clean.** The Architect makes his billions by **Solving Friction, not Creating It.** When you solve a problem (Cleaning a hospital, hauling waste, securing a building), you are performing a **Service of Light.** The money you receive is a "Physical Signature" of the value you have added to the universe. This is why a "Broom & Shovel" billionaire has a higher frequency than a "Wall Street" siphoner. One creates order; the other harvests chaos.

THE OMEGA SEAL: THE PHONE LINE TO GOD

The final "Once-in-a-lifetime" secret of Chapter 12 is the **Internal Frequency of the "Done Deal."** The Matrix operates on "Hope" and "Wanting." Both are frequencies of **Lack.** The "God-Phone" operates on the frequency of **Completion.**

When you dial Source, you do not ask, *"Please let me be rich."* You say, *"Thank you for the Kingdom that is already built."* * **The Spiritual Physics:** You are "collapsing the wave function." By thanking the Creator for the result before it manifests, you are **Binding the Result to the Now.** The demons cannot block a "Thank You." It is a frequency that is too high for them to reach. It is the "Admin Password" to the Treasury of Heaven.

The Final Vow of the 12th Chapter:

CHAPTER 12: THE ASTRAL BREACH

"I have sealed the Astral Breach. I have audited my Ledger. I have rescinded my consent. I am no longer a 'Product' of the Laboratory; I am the 'Production' of the Source. My word is Law, my path is clear, and the Matrix is but dust beneath my feet."

CHAPTER 13: THE AKASHIC PROTOCOL(PART 1) — THE UNVEILING OF THE MASTER ARCHITECT

The Law of the Original Sin (The Identification Error)

The "Hidden Secret" unearthed from the graves of the ancients is this: **You are not in the world; the world is in you. As Above So Below, As Within So Without.** The Matrix is a projected holographic environment designed to test the "Weight" of your Soul. The greatest revelation—the one that changes everything—is that the "Laboratory" is not a prison of brick and mortar, but a **Prison of Definition.**

Before you were born, your spirit agreed to a "Descent" into matter. But the system intercepted your arrival. They gave you a name, a number, and a "History." This history is a **Fabricated Script**. The graves of the wise scream this one truth: *You are an Infinite Being who has been tricked into playing a "Survival Simulation."* To rip the Matrix to shreds, you must stop trying to "win" the simulation and start **Editing the Source Code.**

THE ANCESTRAL SHOUT: THE RECLAMATION OF THE DIVINE SPARK

The spirits of those who died in the workforce, those who died in debt, and those who died in the "Grey Lab" are reaching through this text. Their revelation is simple: **The System has no power of its own.** It is a "Parasitic Construct." It requires *your* belief, *your* fear, and *your* labor to stay powered.

In the Akashic Records, there is a "Ledger of Sovereignty." Most humans have a blank page because they lived their lives as "Extensions of the State." To become a Billionaire-Architect, you must **Write your Name in Light.** This means recognizing that your "Shovel" is not for digging dirt; it is for **Exposing the Truth.** When you solve a problem in the physical world, you are actually "Closing a Portal" of chaos that the demons were using to harvest energy.

THE REVELATION OF THE "TIME-LOCK": BEYOND HUMAN PERCEPTION

Humanity perceives time as a "Linear Flow." This is the primary **Bait.** The Laboratory keeps you in "The Future" (Hope) or "The Past" (Regret) to ensure you never stand in the **Zero-Point of the Now. The Akashic Secret:**

Everything you want—the Kingdom, the Vault, the Legacy—already exists in the "High-Frequency Waveform." You aren't "Building" it; you are **Collapsing the Distance** between your current frequency and the reality that is already finished.

- **The Technique:** You must enter a state of "Pre-Cognitive

Certainty." You do not "Wait" for the money to arrive. You act with the authority of someone who has already seen the end of the movie. This is why the Elite seem so "Lucky." They aren't lucky; they are operating from a **Post-Time Perspective.** They have "Walked the Halls" of the Akashic Records and seen their victory, so they move through the physical world with the calm of a God.

THE UNVEILING OF THE "GHOST-PARTICULE" (THE SOURCE OF WEALTH)

Beyond the "Broom & Shovel," there is a substance the ancients called **Prima Materia.** It is the "Fluid Gold" that fills the gaps between atoms. The Laboratory tries to "Synthesize" this through fiat currency and digital credits, but those are "Dead Frequencies."

How to Harvest the Prima Materia:
Real wealth—the kind that changes everything—is created when you align your **Sovereign Will** with the **Universal Need.** 1. **The Extraction:** Find the place where the world is "Breaking." This is where the Matrix code is "Glitching."

2. **The Infusion:** When you bring "Order" (Service/Systems) to that "Chaos," the Universe releases a burst of Prima Materia.

3. **The Manifestation:** This energy then "condenses" into physical assets—Gold, Land, and Power. You are not "Making" money; you are **Alchemizing Chaos into Order.**

CHAPTER 13: THE AKASHIC PROTOCOL(PART 1) — THE UNVEILING OF...

THE BEYOND-HUMAN TRUTH: THE "SIMULATION OVERRIDE"

The Matrix is governed by "Laws of Physics" that are actually just **"Suggestions of the Laboratory."** * They tell you that you need "Capital" to start. (A Lie).

- They tell you that you need "Permission" to build. (A Lie).
- They tell you that you are "Subject to Inflation." (A Lie).

The Akashic records reveal that the **Sovereign Observer** is exempt from the laws of the collective. If you truly, in your marrow, do not believe in "Scarcity," the Scarcity-Code cannot run in your environment. You will find "Shovels" on the street for free. You will find "Ghost Nodes" who work for the vision alone. You will find "Vaults" opening doors you didn't even know existed. This is the **Override.** You are no longer playing by the Laboratory's rules; you are playing by the **Creator's Mandate.**

THE WARFARE OF THE "THRESHOLD GUARDIANS"

As we go deeper into this revelation, we must address the **Guardians.** These are the non-human entities that manage the "Borders of the Matrix." They are the ones who trigger the "Spiritual Warfare" when you level up.

Their secret weakness? **They have no "Creative Spark."** They can only "Mimic" and "Distort." When they attack you with "Fear," they are using **Your Own Power** against you.

- **The Revelation:** If you stop being afraid, they literally

Starve to Death. They are like "Vampires of the Mind" that require your reaction to stay relevant. When you stand in your Chapter 13 power—the power of the Akashic Sovereign—you realize that these Guardians are just "Security Software" that you have the **Admin Password** to bypass.

THE FINAL REVELATION: THE "GOD-BODY" ARCHITECTURE

Your physical body is a **Bio-Organic Transceiver.** The Matrix has tried to "Ground" you through heavy metals, toxins, and low-vibrational food to ensure you never "Tune In" to the higher frequencies.
  The Akashic Biology:

1. **The Crystalline Blood:** As you remove the "Laboratory Toxins," your blood becomes more "Conductive." You start to "Sense" the moves of the Matrix before they happen.
2. **The Third Eye Projector:** Your Pineal Gland is not for "Seeing Spirits"; it is for **Projecting Reality.** When you focus your intent, you are "Printing" your Kingdom into the physical aether.
3. **The Heart-Battery:** The heart produces the strongest electromagnetic field in the body. If you build your Kingdom with **"Lion-Hearted" Intent**, your field becomes so large that it "Displaces" the Matrix-Signal in your entire city. You become a "Safe Zone" where others can come to wake

CHAPTER 13: THE AKASHIC PROTOCOL(PART 1) — THE UNVEILING OF...

THE FIRST LEAK: THE INVERTED CREATION

The greatest secret buried in the Akashic records—the one that every "workforce" spirit wishes they knew before they died—is that the **Matrix is a Mirror-World.** In the True World, energy flows from the **Spirit to the Matter.** In the Matrix, the flow was **Inverted** by an ancient architectural glitch.

The Laboratory was designed to convince you that you are a "Consumer" who needs to "Earn" the right to exist. This is the **Primary inversion.** In reality, you are a **Radiator of Value.** You don't "make" money; you **Project it.** The reason you were forced into the workforce was to keep your "Radiator" pointed at the Laboratory's goals instead of your own. When you work a 9-to-5, you are literally "Powering" their reality with your divine spark, and they give you back a "Token" (fiat) that represents a fraction of the energy they just stole from you.

The Revelation: To "Rip the Matrix to Shreds," you must **Flip the Polarity.** You stop looking for "Income" and start looking for "Outflow." When you set up your "Broom & Shovel" engine, you are actually setting up a **Transmitter.** You are broadcasting "Order" into a world of "Entropy," and the Universe—which is bound by the Akashic Law of Balance—is forced to send "Physical Density" (Wealth) back to the source of that order.

THE REVELATION OF THE "SILENT ANCESTORS"

I am unearthing a truth now from the graves of the "Quiet Billionaires"—the ones who lived and died without the Matrix ever knowing their names. They understood **The Law of the Ghost-Frequency.** The world is governed by **Silent Contracts.** When you buy a "Brand" or follow a "Trend," you are signing an energetic contract to be "Seen" by the Matrix. To be seen is to be **Harvested.** The ancestors who built real, once-in-a-lifetime wealth practiced **The Great Disappearance.** * They owned the land through "Nominee Shells."

- They communicated through "Ciphers."
- They realized that **Anonymity is the ultimate shield against Spiritual Warfare.** The warfare follows the "Ego." If you build your Kingdom to "Show the World," the Matrix will use the world to tear you down. If you build your Kingdom to **Serve the Source**, the Matrix can't even find your "Account." You become a "Black Hole" in their harvesting grid.

THE AKASHIC "LIEN" ON YOUR DNA

The most terrifying revelation unearthed from the Beyond is that your **DNA is being used as "Collateral"** for the global debt system. The Laboratory "Patented" certain segments of human genetic code through the food and medical systems. This is why "Generational Curses" feel so physical—they are literally **Encoded into your Biology.**
The Akashic Hack (The DNA Purge):

CHAPTER 13: THE AKASHIC PROTOCOL(PART 1) — THE UNVEILING OF...

To break the 7-generation loop, you must perform a **Bio-Spiritual Overwrite.** 1. **The Sound-Key:** The human body responds to specific frequencies that "Shake" the DNA. You must use the "God-Phone" frequency (the deep "M" hum) to vibrate the water in your cells.

2. **The Intent-Command:** While vibrating, you command the **Purge of the Patent.** You reclaim your "Biological Sovereignty."

3. **The Result:** Your "Words" become more powerful. When you say "I am Free," your DNA no longer sends a "Error Message" to the Universe. It sends a **Command Signal.** This is how you avoid the demons—you change the "Lock" on your DNA so their "Keys" no longer fit.

THE "TIME-HARVEST" GLITCH: BEYOND HUMAN PERCEPTION

The Matrix doesn't want your money; it wants your **Time-Linearity.** It wants you to believe that "Tomorrow" is when things get better. This is the **"Horizon-Trap." The Revelation from the Beyond:**

Time is not a line; it is a **Sphere.** Everything you will ever be, you already are. The "Billionaire" version of you is not in the future; he is in a **Higher Layer of the Sphere.** * **The Technique:** To create "Life-Altering Wealth," you must **Collapse the Layers.** You don't "Wait" 5 years. you **Inhabit the 5th Year Now.** * **The Action:** You move, speak, and "Administer" your life as if the Vault is already full. This creates a "Tension" in the Matrix. The Matrix *hates* tension. It will move heaven and earth to "Resolve" that tension by bringing the physical money to match your internal state.

This is the **Simulation Override.**

THE UNHEARD TRUTH OF THE "CREATOR'S BREATH"

The system was set up to keep you "Breathing the Lab-Air"—the air of anxiety, competition, and scarcity. But there is a **Second Breath. The Akashic Breathing Protocol:**

In the Akashic records, the "Breath of Life" is the **Prana-Siphon.** 1. **The Pull:** Inhale the "Will of the Creator."

2. **The Hold:** "Seal" that will into your "Broom & Shovel" engine.

3. **The Release:** Exhale the "Laboratory Illusions."

When you do this, you are no longer a "Human being having a spiritual experience." You are a **Cosmic Admin having a human experience.** The "Workforce" cannot hold a person who realizes they are the one **Breathing the World into Existence.**

CHAPTER 13: THE AKASHIC PROTOCOL (PART 2)— THE UNPRINTED REVELATIONS

THE PARASITIC ARCHITECTURE: THE "VIBRATIONAL FENCE"

The most original secret unearthed from the records of the "Pre-Fall" era is the existence of the **Atmospheric Crust**. The Laboratory did not just build cities; they built a **Frequency Ceiling** roughly 100 feet above the Earth's surface.

This is the **"Workforce Canopy."** It is a layer of dense, low-vibrational ionized gas created by the collective anxiety of the masses. When you live and work beneath this canopy, your thoughts are literally **"Reflected"** back at you. This is why "Positive Thinking" rarely works for the average person— their intent hits the canopy and bounces back as doubt.

The Revelation of the "High-Altitude" Intent:

The 0.001% do not build their "Command Centers" on the ground. They build on **High-Elevation Nodes** or within "Sonic Null-Zones" that pierce the canopy.

- **The New Protocol:** To create life-altering wealth, you must **"Aerate" your Intent.** You must take your "Vision" to the highest physical point near you—a mountain, a skyscraper, or a high ridge—and release it there. Above the canopy, the "Atmospheric Resistance" of the Laboratory is zero. Your command reaches the Source-Code without being "Filtered" by the workforce-static of the city.

THE SECRET OF "MERCANTILE BIOLUMINESCENCE"

Beyond the concept of money lies the reality of **Value-Light.** The Akashic records show that every time a human solves a problem for another human, their DNA emits a specific **Bioluminescent Flash.** The Matrix "Monetized" this flash by creating "Currency." They convinced you that the paper in your pocket is the value, but the paper is just the **Ash** left over after the light has been harvested.

- **The Historic Revelation:** To build an empire that cannot be destroyed, you must stop chasing the "Ash" (Money) and start **Accumulating the Light.** * **The Technique:** In your business, you must look for the "High-Luminosity" tasks. These are the problems that, when solved, produce the most "Relief" in the customer. "Relief" is the frequency of **Debt-Cancellation.** When you provide enough "Relief-Light," the Matrix's legal and financial "Liens" on your life literally evaporate because you have become a **Net-Exporter of Divinity.**

THE "BLOOD-MEMORIES" OF THE UNPAID

There is a massive "Energetic Reservoir" in the Akashic records containing the **Unpaid Wages of the Ancestors.** For thousands of years, humans worked and died without being fairly compensated. That energy did not vanish; it was "Escrowed" in the Aether.
The "Heirloom Claim" Procedure:
You are the **Legal Heir** to the unspent energy of your entire bloodline. The reason you feel a "Spiritual Warfare" when you try to get rich is that you are attempting to **Withdraw the Escrow.** * **The Unheard Hack:** You do not work for "New" money. You work to **Release the Old Money.** When you perform your "4-hour Siege," you are acting as a **Receiver for your Ancestors.** You are telling the Universe: *"I am the one who is finally capable of holding the wealth that was stolen from my grandfather."* When you frame your wealth-building as a **Restitution**, the "Demons of Scarcity" lose their legal standing to stop you. You are no longer "Greedy"; you are an **Executor of a Cosmic Estate.**

THE "VOID-MINTING" PROCESS (THE END OF LABOR)

The world secret of the "Un-Born" is that the physical universe is **Porous.** It is not a solid wall of matter; it is a "Sponge" full of holes. These holes are the **Void-Portals. The Revelation:** Most people try to "Push" their way into wealth. The Sovereign **"Sucks" wealth through the Void.** 1. **The "Stillness-Strike":** Instead of working harder, you enter a state of **Absolute Non-Action.** 2. **The "Vacuum-Focus":**

You focus on the *absence* of what you want until the "Pressure Differential" between your mind and the Matrix becomes so great that the Matrix is **Forced to Implode** the result into your lap.

This is how things "Just Happen" for the powerful. They aren't "Lucky"; they are **Fluid-Dynamicists of the Soul.** They create a "Low-Pressure Zone" in their reality, and the "High-Pressure" wealth of the Matrix has no choice but to rush in to fill it.

THE "NOMADIC" FREQUENCY: BREAKING THE GRID-LOCK

The Laboratory tracks you through your **Routine.** Your routine creates a "Frequency Groove" in the earth. If you go to the same office, take the same route, and eat at the same time, the Matrix can "Predict" your energy and harvest it easily.

The "Randomization" Defense:

To avoid Spiritual Warfare, you must **Interrupt the Harvest.** * **The Technique:** Change your physical location for your "Kingdom Building" every 21 days. Use different "Nodes." By being **Unpredictable**, you become **Invisible.** The Matrix-Demons are "Pattern-Recognition" software. If you have no pattern, they have no target. This is why the global elite are constantly moving—not for the travel, but for the **Signature-Erasure.**

THE LINGUISTIC VIRUS: THE GRAMMATICAL CAPTIVITY

The Akashic Records reveal that the English language—specifically the version used in commerce and law—is an **Inverted Frequency Script**. It was designed as a "Linguistic Virus" to ensure that the more you speak, the more you "contract" your power away. There are 50 "Kill-Switch" words that, when used, immediately signal to the Matrix that you are a **Subject** and not a **Sovereign.**

The Revelation of "Want" and "Need":

In the Primal Script, the word "Want" does not mean "Desire." It means **"To be Lacking."** When you say "I want wealth," you are technically making a legal declaration in the Aether that you are **"Lacking Wealth."** The Matrix, being a literalist system, fulfills your declaration by ensuring you stay in a state of lack.

- **The Strong Finish:** You must purge "Want," "Need," "Try," and "Hope" from your vocabulary. These are **Frequency Brakes.** * **The Replacement:** Use **"I Command," "I Oversee,"** and **"It Is."** These are "Static-Free" words. They do not request permission from the Laboratory; they provide the **Blueprint** for immediate manifestation.

The "Understanding" Trap:

The word "Understand" literally means to **"Stand Under."** When you tell a Matrix entity (a boss, a judge, or a debt collector) "I understand," you are granting them **Superior Jurisdiction.** You are placing your "Engine" beneath their

"Gavel." The Billionaire-Architect never "understands"; he **"Acknowledge's the Data."** This keeps your frequency above the canopy.

THE MINERAL-CONTRACT: THE SALINE SURVEILLANCE

The Laboratory does not track you through your "ID" as much as it tracks you through your **Mineral Signature.** Your body is a saline solution—a battery of salts and water. The Akashic records show that the Matrix has a "Mineral-Lien" on your biology through the **Industrial Salt Grid.**

The Unheard Revelation:

The refined salt provided in the "Lab-Slop" is a **Mono-Atomic Tracker.** It aligns the crystals in your blood to the Matrix's "Central Clock." This is why people feel "forced" to work on a 9-to-5 schedule; their biology is literally **Oscillating** at the frequency of the industrial grid.

The Short-Circuit Protocol:

1. **The Mineral Overwrite:** You must replace all "Refined Salt" with **Deep-Earth Mineral Salts** (Celtic or Himalayan) that have not been touched by the Laboratory's "Cleaning" chemicals.
2. **The Bio-Electrical Shield:** By saturating your cells with "Wild Minerals," you change your body's **Refractive Index.** You become "Opaque" to the Matrix's frequency-harvesting.
3. **The Result:** This is how you avoid the "Spiritual Warfare" of the changing mindset. When you change your mineral base, the demons' "Tuning Forks" no longer

vibrate your cells. You become a **"Short-Circuit"** in their surveillance network. You can build your Kingdom in total "Bio-Silience."

THE "FINAL DECREE OF THE UN-MADE": THE EMPLOYER OF GOD

In the graves of the "Sovereign Dead," there is a final testament regarding the nature of "Work." The workforce was created to hide the fact that **Labor is a choice, but Command is a Duty. The Akashic "Employment" Truth:**

You were taught that you have to "work for God" or "work for a Boss." The Chapter 13 revelation is that you are the **Project Manager of the Source.** The Universe is a "Vast, Un-Made Potential" that is waiting for an **Architect** to give it a job.

- If you do not give the Universe a job, the Laboratory will "Hire" your potential to build *their* world.
- **The Command:** You must wake up and "Hire" the Aether. Give the atoms of the day a specific task: *"Today, you will organize the logistics of my Ghost Engine. Today, you will attract the Stone to my Vault."* When you act as the **Employer of Reality**, the "Stress" of the workforce vanishes. You aren't "competing" with other Bots; you are simply **Assigning Tasks** to the fabric of existence. This is the frequency of the "Once-in-a-lifetime" Billionaire. They don't "Work hard"; they **Command clearly.**

THE GEOMETRY OF THE "FIRST LANGUAGE" (THE VISUAL DECREE)

Beyond words, there are **Shapes** that the Matrix cannot interpret, and therefore cannot block. These are the **Akashic Sigils. The Revelation of the "Open Circle":**
The Matrix loves "Squares" and "Grids" (Cubicles, City Blocks, Spreadsheets). The Square is the geometry of **Capture.** To release your wealth from the Laboratory, you must use the **"Spiral of Expansion."** * **The Technique:** When you are planning your Kingdom in your "4-hour Siege," do not use linear lists. Draw your plans in a **Spiral.** Start from the center (Source) and move outward.

- **The Glitch:** The Matrix-Demons are "Linear-Logic" programs. They cannot follow a spiral path. By "Curving" your intent, you move your wealth-building into a **Blind Spot** of the system. You are building in a "Non-Euclidean" spiritual space where the Siphons cannot reach.

CHAPTER 13: THE AKASHIC PROTOCOL (PART 3)— THE BIOLOGY OF THE OCCUPATION

THE ARCHONIC BIOME: THE PARASITIC HIJACK

The most guarded secret in the history of human health is that your **"Cravings" are not your own.** The Laboratory discovered eons ago that they could not control the human Spirit directly, so they colonized the human **Gut**.

Physical parasites—helminths, protozoa, and fungal overgrowths like *Candida*—are not mere biological accidents. They are **Physical Antennas** for lower-vibrational entities. These parasites operate as a "Biological Proxy" for the Matrix.

- **The Dietary Siphon:** When you crave "Lab-Slop" (refined sugars, bleached flours, processed toxins), it is the parasite signaling your brain. They require high-glucose, acidic environments to survive.
- **The Mental Hijack:** Parasites excrete waste products (neurotoxins) that bypass the blood-brain barrier. This creates "The Fog"—anxiety, depression, and the "Poverty Mindset." You make bad financial decisions because

your prefrontal cortex is being drugged by a biological occupant that wants you **Complacent, Heavy, and Static.**

THE SEXUAL AND SPIRITUAL DRAIN: THE LEAKING VASE

Sexual health is the "Generator" of the Sovereign. The Matrix promotes "Hook-up Culture" and hyper-sexualized media to ensure that your **Sexual Essence** is constantly being discharged into the void.

- **The Parasite Connection:** Physical parasites thrive on the depletion of your Jing (Life Force). When you are sexually depleted, your "Aura" develops "Breaches."
- **The Spiritual Short-Circuit:** These breaches allow lower-vibrational deities and entities to "Plug In" to your energy field. They feed on the shame, the guilt, and the exhaustion. This is why you cannot "Manifest" while your body is in a state of **Dis-ease.** You are trying to fill a bucket that has been riddled with parasitic holes.

THE PROTOCOL OF THE GREAT EXPULSION (THE PARASITE CLEANSE)

To get closer to God—to become the **God-Self**—you must perform the **Great Expulsion.** This is the most important "Work After Work" you will ever do.

1. **The Bitter Purge:** Parasites hate "Bitter" and "Pungent" frequencies. Utilizing ancient earth-codes like Black Walnut Hull, Wormwood, and Clove is not just "detox"—it is **Exorcism.** You are making your blood

"Toxic" to the invaders.
2. **The Fasting Gate:** By withholding the "Lab-Slop" for 24-48 hours, you starve the occupants. As they die, they release a "Death Cry" in the form of intense cravings and irritability. This is the **Spiritual Warfare** in the flesh. If you fold, they win. If you push through, you break the tether.
3. **The Mental Result:** Within 14 days of a successful expulsion, "The Fog" lifts. Suddenly, "Rich After Work" isn't a dream—it's an **Inevitable Math.** You think faster, you see the "Ghost Engines" clearly, and your "Command" has the weight of a King because it's no longer being filtered through parasitic neurotoxins.

RECLAIMING THE BIRTHRIGHT POWERS: THE SUPERHUMAN SHIFT

As the parasites leave, the **"Generational Junk"** swept into the basement of your DNA is finally cleared. This is where you reclaim your **Super Powers.**

- **The Mental Power:** You gain "Hyper-Visual Perception." You can see a business plan and know within seconds where the "Friction" is.
- **The Physical Power:** Your sleep becomes "High-Density." 4 hours of Sovereign sleep becomes more restorative than 10 hours of "Bot" sleep.
- **The Financial Power:** You stop "Spending" to soothe your parasites. The $500 a month you spent on "Cravings" and "Dopamine-Hits" is redirected into the **Vault.**

THE BECOMING: THE GOD-ENTITY IN THE MIRROR

Becoming "Rich" is not about the accumulation of paper; it is about the **Accumulation of Self.** The Akashic record shows that a human who is "Clean"—physically, mentally, and spiritually—is a **Walking Portal.** 1. **Rich with Peace:** Because you are no longer at war with your own biology.

2. **Rich with Creativity:** Because the "Source-Line" is no longer being jammed by parasitic static.

3. **Rich with Strength:** Because your "Life Force" is being used to build your Kingdom instead of feeding the occupants.

You are unearthing the "Basement" of your lineage. Every parasite you kill is a "Generational Curse" you are snapping. You are not just getting healthy; you are **Taking Your Rightful Place** as the Architect of the New Earth. You are the Employer of the atoms, the Master of the minerals, and the Sovereign of the Flesh.

CHAPTER 13: THE AKASHIC PROTOCOL (PART 4)— THE CRYSTALLINE MARROW

THE ANCESTRAL LEDGER: RECLAIMING STOLEN VITALITY

The most horrific "World Secret" unearthed from the graves of the ancestors is the **Vitality Theft.** The Matrix didn't just take their time; it took their **Bone Density** and their **Neural Elasticity.** Every hour your grandfather spent in a mine or a factory under the "Frequency Canopy" was an hour where his marrow was being "De-Magnetized."

In the Akashic Records, this vitality is not gone; it is **Escrowed.** Your "Birthright Power" includes the reclamation of the health that was siphoned from your lineage. When you perform the "Parasite Purge," you aren't just cleaning a colon; you are **opening a vault.** As the physical parasites leave, the "Vacant Space" in your biology is filled with the **Ancestral Light** that was stolen 100 years ago. You will suddenly feel a strength in your bones that "doesn't belong to you"—it belongs to the **God-Self** that was suppressed in your bloodline for centuries.

THE CRYSTALLINE MARROW PROTOCOL: VIBRAT-

ING THE INVADERS

The hardest parasites to reach are not in the gut; they are the **Intracellular Pathogens** that hide in the bone marrow and the nervous system. These are the ones that cause "Bad Mental Health"—the deep, unshakable "Doom" that hits you for no reason. This is not "depression"; it is a **Parasitic Frequency.**

The Unheard Ritual of the Resonant Purge:

1. **The Bone-Hum:** You must use your own voice to create a **Piezoelectric Charge** in your skeleton. By humming a frequency that vibrates the teeth, you are sending a "Shockwave" through the marrow.
2. **The Mineral Overload:** You saturate the body with **Silica and Magnesium.** Parasites are "Carbon-Based" and "Metal-Heavy." By shifting your biology toward a **Crystalline/Mineral base**, you become "Electrically Incompatible" with the entity.
3. **The Breach:** You will feel a "Heat" in your bones. This is the **Die-off.** This is the moment the generational junk is being incinerated by your own internal "God-Fire."

THE SEXUAL ALCHEMY: REBUILDING THE GENERATOR

We must speak on the **Birthright of Pleasure and Power.** The Matrix wants your "Sexual Health" to be "Bad" because the sexual organs are the **Primary Engines of Manifestation.** * **The Parasitic Hook:** Low-vibrational entities "Nest" in the reproductive system to ensure that your "Creativity" is leaked out as "Lust" or "Shame."

- **The Reclamation:** When you clear the parasites, your sexual energy stops being a "Need" to be satisfied and becomes a **Power to be Directed.** You use this "Richness" to fuel your ideas. This is why the "Billionaires after work" are so creative—they have **Internalized their Generator.** They aren't "leaking" their God-Power into the Matrix's digital traps; they are using it to "Melt" the obstacles in their path.

THE SUPER POWERS OF THE "CLEAN" GOD-SELF

Once the "Basement" is cleared, the **Super Powers** mentioned in the ancient texts begin to manifest as "Standard Features" of your new life.

- **The Power of "Presence":** You walk into a room, and the "Bots" go silent. Your frequency is so high that their "Parasitic Controllers" feel the "God-Fire" and back away.
- **The Power of "Rapid Manifestation":** Because your "Bio-Battery" is no longer being drained by 10,000 microscopic siphons, your "Command" hits the Aether with **100% Voltage.** You think of a "Shovel," and it appears.
- **The Power of "Genetic Rewriting":** You start to look younger. Your "Generational Junk" (Gray hair, joint pain, fatigue) begins to reverse. You are literally **Aging Backwards** into your True Self.

RICH AFTER WORK: THE MULTIDIMENSIONAL WEALTH

"Rich" is inevitable when you realize that **Wealth is the absence of Parasites.** * A "Rich" mind is one that is not being "fogged" by neurotoxins.

- A "Rich" family is one that is not being "split" by argumentative entities.
- A "Rich" soul is one that is **Directly Tethered to God.**

You are becoming the "Highest Version" of yourself because you have realized that the "Lower Versions" were just **Occupied Territories.** By taking back your physical power, you are taking back the Earth. You are no longer "working for a living"; you are **Living for a Command.** The workforce cannot hold a man who has "Clean Blood" and a "Vibrating Skeleton." You have become **Un-Harvestable.**

CHAPTER 13: THE AKASHIC PROTOCOL (PART 5)— THE BEDROCK REVELATION, BENEATH THE SOIL

THE ARCHITECTURE OF THE "SILENT LIEN"
The most historic revelation unearthed from the graves of the "Un-Claimed" is the **Mathematical Nature of the Soul-Debt**. The Matrix does not view you as a human; it views you as a **Mathematical Variable** in a zero-sum equation. When you were born, the Laboratory calculated the total "Potential Energy" of your life—every breath you would take, every calorie you would consume, and every "Shovel" you would swing.

They then "Securitized" that energy. They created a **Bond** based on your future labor and sold it into the Aetheric Markets. This is why you feel a "weight" on your shoulders even when you are relaxing—it is the **Pressure of the Debt-Bond**. The spiritual warfare you feel is the "Market" trying to force its "Asset" (You) back into the "Workforce" to ensure the interest on your bond is paid.

The Bedrock Truth: You cannot "Work" your way out of a debt that is mathematical. You must **Nullify the Equation.**

THE RITE OF THE 13TH HOUR: TIME-EXPANSION ARCHITECTURE

The Laboratory keeps the "Bot" in a 24-hour cycle. 8 hours for them (Work), 8 hours for the "Repair" (Sleep), and 8 hours for "Maintenance" (Eating/Chipping). This is the **Closed-Loop Siphon.** To become Rich After Work, you must "Rip" the 25th hour out of the 24.

The Unheard Revelation of "Source-Time":

Time is not a constant; it is a **Pressure-Dependent Variable.**

1. **The High-Pressure Zone:** When you are in "Fear" or "Need," time moves fast and you accomplish little. This is "Workforce Time."
2. **The Zero-Pressure Zone (The 13th Hour):** When you clear the fog and "Dial the Source," you enter a state of **Time-Dilation.** * **The Technique:** You must perform the "Stillness-Strike" for exactly 13 minutes before your 4-hour Siege. In this stillness, you command the atoms of your room to "Slow Down."

- **The Result:** You will find that you can accomplish 40 hours of technical "Kingdom-Building"—writing SOPs, researching Ghost-Nodes, or auditing contracts—in what feels like 40 minutes. This is not a "feeling"; it is a **Quantum Leap.** You are literally "Overclocking" your reality.

THE "LIEN-REMOVAL" DECREE: THE 144-WORD VOID-COMMAND

This is the "Administrative Password" to your own existence. It must be spoken with the **Vibration of the Marrow.** It does not ask; it **Decrees.**

"By the Authority of the Primal Source and the Right of the Living Soul, I hereby issue this Final Notice of Rescission. I stand as the Executor of the Bloodline Estate, and I declare all Liens, Bonds, and Securitized Claims against my Physical, Mental, and Spiritual vessels to be VOID for lack of Full Disclosure and Absence of Consent. I am the sole Creditor of my Essence. I revoke the 'Serial Number' and reclaim the 'Name.' I command the Parasitic Entities to vacate the Temple of the Flesh, for it is now occupied by the Sovereign Light. I dissolve the 'Generational Junk' in the heat of the 13th Hour. I am Un-Bound, Un-Harvested, and Un-Made by the Laboratory. I am the Architect of the New Eden. I am Home. It is Finished. It is Done. It is the Law."

THE ANATOMY OF THE "GHOST-NODE" (THE END OF HUMAN MANAGEMENT)

As you become "Rich After Work," the Matrix will try to trick you into becoming a "Boss" of people. This is a **Trap.** Managing people is just another form of "Workforce Slavery"—you are just the "Foreman" of the Lab.

The Akashic Revelation of the "Ghost-Node":

The 21st-century Architect does not hire "Employees" (Bots); they hire **"Sovereign Nodes."** * The Difference: An employee wants a "Job" (Safety). A Node wants a "Contract" (Freedom).

- **The Shift:** You use your "Super Powers" of discernment to find other people who are also "Clearing their Basement." You link your Kingdoms together through

Private Equity Agreements. This creates a "Mesh-Network" of wealth that has no "Head" for the Matrix to cut off. This is how you "Create Millionaires and Billionaires across the globe." You aren't giving them jobs; you are giving them the **Blueprint to their own Sovereignty.**

CHAPTER 13: THE AKASHIC PROTOCOL (PART 6)— THE GOLD-SOUL CONNECTION

THE "GOLD-SOUL" CONNECTION: THE PHYSICS OF THE STONE

The Matrix pushes "Digital Currency" and "Paper Credits" because they have **No Mass.** In the Akashic Records, wealth is not a number; it is a **Frequency of Gravity.** The Laboratory wants your wealth to be "Weightless" so they can "Blow it away" with a single keystroke or an "Audit" from the Lab-Demons.

The Revelation of the Stone:

Gold is not just a metal; it is **Solidified Sunlight.** It is one of the few substances on Earth that vibrates at the same frequency as the **Human Heart-Battery** when it is in a state of Sovereign Command.

- **The Aetheric Law:** When you hold physical Gold, you are "Anchoring" your Spirit to the Earth. The "Frequency-Ceiling" cannot lift a man who is weighted down by the Stone.
- **The "Short-Circuit":** Digital money is "Traceable" be-

cause it travels through the Laboratory's wires. Gold is "Ghost-Money" because its value is **Intrinsic and Silent.** By moving your "Rich After Work" profits into the Stone, you are taking your wealth "Off-Grid" spiritually. You are removing it from the "Simulation" and placing it into **Actual Reality.**

THE AETHERIC AUDIT: CHECKING THE SOUL-BANK

Every human has a "Spiritual Bank Account" in the Akashic Records. This account is filled with **"Life-Essence Credits"**—the energy you were born with. The Laboratory's entire goal is to keep your "Spiritual Balance" at zero by making you spend your essence on "Stress," "Fear," and "Comparison."

How to Perform the Audit:

1. **The Sensory Scan:** Close your eyes and "Feel" your energy. If you feel "Leaking" in your gut, you have an **Unauthorized Withdrawal** happening (usually a parasite or a "Matrix-Vampire" friend).
2. **The Credit Reclamation:** In the 13th Hour, you must issue a **Stop-Payment Order.** Speak it: *"I revoke all automatic withdrawals of my Life Essence. I reclaim the credits spent on the Laboratory's illusions. I command my Spiritual Account to be 'Frozen' to all external entities."*
3. **The Accumulation:** Once the leaks are plugged, your "Essence" begins to pool in your Marrow. This is the **Internal Richness.** From this state, you don't "Work" for money; you **Authorize** its appearance.

THE PROTOCOL OF THE 144,000: THE FREQUENCY-HOLDERS

CHAPTER 13: THE AKASHIC PROTOCOL (PART 6)— THE GOLD-SOUL...

There is a historic revelation regarding the "144,000." This is not a religious number; it is a **Critical Mass Metric.** The Akashic Records show that it only takes a small percentage of the population to "Vibrate" at the Sovereign Frequency to **Collapse the Matrix-Simulation** for everyone.

Your Role in the Shift:

You are being "Rich After Work" not just for your family, but to act as a **Frequency-Holder.** * When you clear your parasites, you raise the frequency of your neighborhood.

- When you build a "Ghost-Engine" that provides value without slavery, you create a "Glitch" in the Laboratory's labor-contracts.
- You are the **"Admin-Nodes"** of the New Earth. As you become "Wealthy" (Rich in Health, Spirit, and Stone), you are literally **Rewriting the Gravity** of the planet. You are making it impossible for the "Demons" to remain on this plane because the "Air" (Frequency) is becoming too "Thin" (Pure) for them to breathe.

THE "NOMADIC VAULT" AND THE NEW EDEN

The final "Tell-All" of the ancestors is that the "New Eden" is not a place you find; it is a **Place You Emit.** * **The Crystalline Geography:** You can turn any "Workforce Apartment" into a "Sovereign Temple" by placing four "Stone Anchors" (Gold or High-Mineral Salts) in the corners of your room. This creates a **"Null-Zone"** where the "Time-Parasites" cannot enter.

- **The Nomadic Strategy:** In the final years of the Siege, the Architect becomes "Jurisdictionally Fluid." You don't "belong" to any country. You belong to the **Akashic Estate.** You move through the world as a "Visitor" who owns everything but is "Attached" to nothing. This is the **Ultimate Freedom.**

CHAPTER 13 (PART 7): THE BIO-ORGANIC CURRENCY & THE NEURAL ARCHIVE

THE "PHOSPHORUS" REVELATION: THE LIGHT-DEBT

The Ancestors whisper from the galaxies afar that the Matrix did not just steal your money; it stole your **Phosphorus**. In the Akashic Records, Phosphorus is known as the **"Light-Bearer" element**. It is the bridge between your thoughts and the physical manifestation of those thoughts.

The Laboratory feeds you "Phosphate-Depleting" substances (carbonated toxins and industrial acids) to ensure your "Neural Wiring" is too weak to carry the "High-Voltage" of a Billionaire-Mindset. When you lack the Light-Bearer element, your "Manifestation Command" never leaves your skull—it dies in the "static" of your own brain.

- **The Galaxy-Afar Answer:** To reclaim your power, you must **Re-Mineralize the Brain.** This is the "Secret of the Star-Seed." By consuming foods high in "Living Phosphorus" (unprocessed seeds, wild-caught marine life, and specific high-altitude herbs), you are rebuilding the

Circuitry of the God-Self. You are no longer "trying" to think; you are **Broadcasting.**

THE "NEURAL ARCHIVE": ACCESSING PRE-INCARNATION WEALTH

The world is waiting to know: *Where does the "Brilliance" of the once-in-a-lifetime genius come from?* The ancestors reveal that it is not "learned" in the Laboratory's schools. It is **Retrieved.**

There is a **Neural Archive** located in the "Junk DNA" that the Matrix-Scientists claim is useless. This archive contains every "Shovel" and "Engine" you have ever built in any lifetime. You are not a "Newcomer" to wealth; you are a **Veteran of the Universe** who has been suffering from "Financial Amnesia."

- **The Retrieval Protocol:** Before you start your "4-hour Siege," you must sit in the **Zero-Point Breath** and command your DNA to "Unlock the Archive."
- **The Result:** You will find yourself knowing how to structure a "Ghost-Node" contract or how to audit a "Matrix-Lien" without ever being taught. You are tapping into your own **Eternal Résumé.**

THE "VOICE-COPTIC" FREQUENCY: THE SOUNDS OF CREATION

The stars of galaxies afar communicate through **Geometric Sound.** The Laboratory gave us "Language" to keep us in the workforce, but the ancestors used **Coptic Tones.**

The Unheard Revelation of the "Command-Tone":
There are three specific tones that, when hummed, act as

CHAPTER 13 (PART 7): THE BIO-ORGANIC CURRENCY & THE NEURAL...

"Encryption Keys" to bypass the Matrix-Firewalls:

1. **The "741Hz" Cleaver:** Hummed to "cut" the cords of the energy vampires in your life.
2. **The "852Hz" Return:** Hummed to "call back" the wealth that was stolen from your ancestors.
3. **The "417Hz" Eraser:** Hummed to "delete" the bad financial decisions and "Karma-Dumps" of your past.

By using these tones, you are not just "speaking"; you are **Editing the Vibration of the Room.**

CHAPTER 13 (PART 8): THE ARCHITECTURE OF THE "INVISIBLE GRID"

THE "SHADOW-CURRENCY": THE ENERGY OF THE UN-SEEN

The world believes that the Stock Market is where the big moves happen. The ancestors laugh at this. The real "Market" is the **Atmospheric Energy Grid.** Every city has a "Wealth-Current" that flows through the streets like a river. The Matrix-Buildings (Banks and Government Labs) are positioned to **Divert** this current away from the neighborhoods and into their "Siphons."

The "River-Diversion" Technique:

You do not need to "Find" money; you need to **Dam the River.** 1. **The Geometric Anchor:** By placing specific "Mineral-Anchors" (Crystals or Gold) in a triangular pattern in your home, you create a "Low-Pressure Hole" in the Aether.

2. **The Draw:** The "Wealth-Current" of the city will naturally "Swirl" into your home because you have created the only path for it to flow.

3. **The Harvest:** This is why "Rich After Work" Architects seem to have money "Fall into their Laps." They have simply

re-plumbed the energy of the city to lead directly to their Vault.

THE "GENETIC-SURETY" REVELATION

The Laboratory uses your "ALL CAPS NAME" as a "Security" for the national debt. But the ancestors reveal a **Historic Loophole.** Your DNA is a "Private Trust" that predates any government.

- **The Answer:** When you perform the **Parasite Purge**, you are actually "Cleaning the Title" of your Genetic Trust. A "Clean Body" is a "High-Value Asset" that the Matrix cannot legally "Lien."
- **The Sovereignty Shift:** The moment your blood is clean, you are moved from the "Debtor" column to the "Creditor" column in the Akashic Records. The Universe begins to pay *you* "Interest" for your existence.

CHAPTER 13 (PART 9): THE "GHOST-LABOR" OF THE AETHER

THE "AETHERIC SERVANTS": BEYOND HUMAN EMPLOYEES

The world is waiting for the answer to: *How can one person build a Million-Dollar Kingdom in 4 hours?*

The answer is **Aetheric Automation.** The Laboratory uses "Robots" and "AI." The Sovereign uses **"Elemental Intent."** * When you "Command" a task with the "Crystalline Magnetic" frequency, you are essentially hiring the "Atoms of the Air" to work for you.

- These "Aetheric Servants" do not sleep, they do not need insurance, and they do not have parasites. They go out into the world and "Nudge" people to call you. They "Arrange" for the equipment you need to be sold at a discount to be available at your request. They are the **Invisible Workforce** of the God-Self. Be demanding, speak life and know for certain that your commands will surely not go Unheard. In these moments doubt must be burned from the thought process. Knowing and certainty must be the only thoughts in your existence. When your heart is pure along with good intentions mixed with an abundance of gratitude, you will be come a magnet for all of the things that you want, need and desire.

- Just ask and you Shall receive. Just be ready for what you ask for, and be very specific.

CHAPTER 13 (PART 10): THE SUN-EATER PROTOCOL — THE BIOLOGICAL TRANSMUTATION

The ancestors from the stars of galaxies afar reveal that the human vessel was never meant to be a "Combustion Engine." The Laboratory's greatest deception was convincing you that you must "Consume" to "Exist." This is the **Primary Siphon.** If the Matrix can control your access to fuel (food), they can control your access to freedom. The Sun-Eater Protocol is the technical process of shifting the body from a **Glucose-Based Slave** to a **Photon-Based Sovereign.**

THE PHYSICS OF NEUROMELANIN: THE BRAIN'S SOLAR ARRAY

Deep within the "Basement" of the human brain lies the **Substantia Nigra**, a cluster of neurons saturated with **Neuromelanin.** The Matrix-Scientists claim this is a waste product. The Akashic Record reveals it is the **Internal Solar Panel.** Neuromelanin has the unique ability to perform **Photo-Synthesis** within the human body. It takes electromagnetic radiation—sunlight, heat, and even ambient kinetic energy—and converts it directly into **ATP (Adenosine**

Triphosphate).

When you are a "Glucose-Burner," your body is constantly producing "Cellular Ash" (oxidative stress). This ash is what causes the "9-to-5 Fatigue" and the "Workforce Aging" process. A Sun-Eater produces no ash. By charging the Neuromelanin, you bypass the digestive tract entirely.

- **The Reveal:** This is why "Rich After Work" Architects have infinite energy. They aren't "pushing" through the 4-hour Siege; they are being **Pulled** by the solar voltage in their marrow.
- **The Technical Shift:** To activate this, you must first perform the **Heavy Metal Purge.** The Laboratory puts aluminum and mercury in the "Lab-Slop" to "Insulate" your Neuromelanin. It's like putting a tarp over a solar panel. Once the metals are out, the light can finally hit the "Internal Black Hole" of the brain.

THE OPTIC-NERVE UPLOAD: DATA FROM THE SOURCE

The Sun is not just a ball of gas; it is a **Central Processing Unit (CPU)** for the solar system. It broadcasts the "Source-Code" of the day. When you perform **Solar Gazing** during the "Golden Hours" (the first and last 10 minutes of light), you are not just getting Vitamin D—you are **Downloading the Market Blueprint.**

1. **The Pituitary Trigger:** As the light hits the retina, it travels the optic nerve and "Strikes" the Pituitary gland. This triggers the release of **Vasopressin and Oxytocin**, which regulate your "Social Intelligence." This is how

you "Discern" a fake friend from a Sovereign Node instantly.
2. **The Pineal Spark:** The light then hits the Pineal Gland, which converts the solar data into **Pinoline.** This allows you to see the "Fractal Patterns" of wealth. You stop seeing "Random Events" and start seeing the **Lattice of Opportunity.**
3. **The Biological Result:** Your appetite for "Lab-Slop" vanishes. You find yourself eating only for "Pleasure" or "Ritual," rather than "Survival." This removes the "Hunger-Anxiety" that the Matrix uses to keep you in the workforce.

THE CARBON-TO-SILICON TRANSMUTATION

The graves of the "Eternal Architects" reveal that as you increase your "Light-Load," your DNA begins to shift. Carbon (the element of the slave) is the foundation of "6-6-6" (6 protons, neutrons, and electrons). Silicon (the element of the Sovereign) is the foundation of **Computation.**

- **The Mineral-Key:** By saturating your body with **Ionic Silica and Gold**, you provide the raw materials for this shift.
- **The Super-Human Result:** You become "Electrically Conductive." You can feel the "Frequency-Ceiling" of the city and navigate around it. You can "Hear" the intentions of people before they speak. You have moved from a "Biological Animal" to a **"Crystalline God-Self."**

CHAPTER 13 (PART 11): THE BLOOD-LEDGER — THE BIOLOGICAL ENCRYPTION OF WEALTH

The world is waiting for the answer to the **Final Security Problem**. If you have "Stone" (Gold), it can be stolen. If you have "Credits" (Money), they can be frozen. The ancestors from the galaxies afar reveal that the only "Un-Hackable" vault in the universe is the **Human Bloodstream**. Your blood is not just a fluid; it is a **Liquid-Crystal Information Highway**.

THE WATER-MEMORY ARCHIVE: THE 4TH STATE OF MATTER

The Laboratory has taught you that water is H_2O—a simple solvent. This is a historic lie designed to keep you from realizing your own **Computational Power**. The water in your body is in a **"Structured" (EZ) Phase**. It acts as a digital storage medium that records every thought, every intent, and every "Command" you issue during the 13th Hour.

The Detailed Revelation:

Wealth is not "outside" of you. It is a **Pattern of Structured Water** within your cells.

- **The "Liquid" Ledger:** When you achieve a state of "Rich After Work" clarity, you are "Printing" the blueprint of your Kingdom into the water of your blood. This is why the Elite obsess over "Pure Water Sources." They aren't just thirsty; they are trying to maintain the **Integrity of their Internal Ledger.**
- **The Encryption:** When you perform the **Parasite Purge**, you are "Formatting" the drive. The parasites were "Writing" their own code (scarcity, fear, hunger) into your blood-water. Once they are gone, you "Lock" the water with your own frequency. This is **Biological Encryption.** No Matrix-Entity can "confiscate" your wealth because your wealth is literally **Pulsing through your veins. Health Is Wealth.**

THE "IRON-PHASE" SHIFT: TURNING THE BLOOD INTO AN ANTENNA

The Laboratory uses "Synthetic Iron" in the food supply to "Rust" your blood. This rusted iron acts as a **Receiver for the Frequency-Ceiling.** It keeps your energy "Heavy" and "Grounded" in the workforce.

- **The Ancestor's Secret:** You must "De-Magnetize" your blood from the Matrix. By utilizing **Plant-Based, High-Spin Iron**, you turn your blood into a **High-Frequency Antenna.** * **The Super-Power:** Suddenly, you don't "look" for information; the information "hits" your blood. You "Feel" a market shift in your marrow. You "Scent" an opportunity like a predator. This is the **Primal Super-Wealth.** You are no longer using a computer to find wealth; your **Biological Wi-Fi** is plugged directly into the Aetheric flow of resources.

THE "SANGUINE-CONTRACT" (THE END OF THE PAPER DEBT)

The final "Tell-All" of Part 11 is the **Sanguine-Contract.** The Matrix-Laws are written on "Dead Wood" (Paper). The Sovereign Laws are written in **"Living Water" (Blood).** *
The Protocol: In the 13th Hour, you perform a **"Neural-Ink"** visualization. You imagine your wealth-commands (The Ghost-Engine, the Stone-Accumulation) being "Injected" into your bloodstream.

- **The Result:** Your body begins to **Radiate the Result.** You walk into a room and the "Atoms" begin to rearrange themselves to match the "Liquid Code" in your blood. This is how you "Create Millionaires" without saying a word—your **Aura is an Infection of Abundance.** You are a walking "Wealth-Virus" that crashes the Matrix's poverty-programming wherever you go.

The world is waiting for the answer to the **"Source of Supply."** The Laboratory has taught you that resources are "Scarcely Distributed" across the planet. This creates the "Need" for "Work." The ancestors reveal that wealth is not a "Resource"; it is a **Pressure-Differential.** In the Vacuum of Space-Time, there is an infinite amount of "Potential Energy" (The Zero-Point Field). Part 11 is the engineering manual on how to create a **"Low-Pressure Hole"** in your reality that "Sucks" that potential into a physical, spendable form.

THE "BLACK-SUN" ENGINE: THE INTERNAL COLD-FUSION

Deep within the center of every atom in your body is a **Singularity.** The Laboratory calls it "Empty Space." The Akashic Record calls it the **Black Sun.** This is the "Engine Room" of the God-Self.

- **The Revelation:** Wealth is created when you "Spin" the singularities in your atoms at a frequency that is **Incompatible with Poverty.**
- **The Technique:** This is not "Visualization." This is **Centrifugal Intent.** In the 13th Hour, you must "Spin" your internal energy field (the Torus) so fast that it creates a **Centripetal Suction.** * **The Result:** This suction creates a "Vacuum" in your bank account, your business, and your life. Because the Universe cannot allow a "Void" to exist, it is forced to "Rush In" with the physical equivalent of the energy you are spinning. If you are spinning the frequency of "The Stone" (Gold/Stability), the Stone must materialize to fill the hole. This is **Vacuum-Minting.** You are not "working" for wealth; you are **Commanding the Void to Fill Itself.**

THE "GHOST-PARTICLE" ARBITRAGE: TRADING IN THE UN-SEEN

The Matrix operates on **Baryonic Matter** (the stuff you can touch). The Sovereign operates on **Dark Matter/Energy.**

1. **The Extraction:** For every "Physical Dollar" in the Matrix, there is a "Ghost-Equivalent" in the Aether.

2. **The Trade:** By using the "13th Hour Admin-Pass," you can "Swap" the Ghost-Equivalent for the Physical Reality. This is done by **Collapsing the Wave-Function** of a specific probability.

3. **The Math:** You find a "Probability" where you are already a Billionaire (it exists in the Quantum Field). You "Anchor" that probability to your "Crystalline Marrow" (from the previous section). You then "Delete" the probability where you are a servant. The "Wealth" appears in your reality as a **"System-Correction."** The Laboratory's computers will show that you "Earned" it, but the reality is that you **Quantum-Swapped** it.

THE "HYPER-DIMENSIONAL" LEDGER: THE END OF AUDITS

The world wants to know: *How do I keep my wealth if the Laboratory changes the rules?* The answer is to keep your ledger in a **Higher Dimension.**

- **The Technique:** You must "Record" your assets in the **Scalar Field.** Scalar waves do not "Travel" through space; they exist everywhere at once.
- **The Security:** A "Scalar-Ledger" cannot be hacked, taxed, or tracked because it has no **Electronic Signature.** It is a "Pattern of Stillness." To the Laboratory's sensors, your "Rich After Work" Kingdom looks like "Background Noise." They cannot audit "Silence." This is the **Ultimate Privacy.** You own the world, but the world's "Books" show that you don't even exist.

CHAPTER 13 (PART 12): THE COSMOLOGY OF THE SOVEREIGN — BEYOND THE GLOBE DECEPTION

The System teaches that you are on a ball, spinning at 1,000 mph, orbiting a sun at 67,000 mph, while the entire galaxy flies through a vacuum at millions of mph. This "Trillion-Mile Shenanigans" is designed to create a subconscious state of **Motion Sickness.** If the mind believes it is in constant, uncontrollable motion, it cannot find the **Zero-Point of Stillness** required to "Mint" reality. The ancestors from the stars of galaxies afar reveal a much more colossal, stable, and terrifyingly magnificent truth: You are in a **Stationary, Enclosed System of Infinite Proportions.**

THE FIRMAMENT: THE CRYSTALLINE ELECTRO-MAGNETIC BARRIER

The world is waiting for the answer to "The Vacuum of Space." The ancestors reveal that **Nature abhors a vacuum.** You cannot have a high-pressure atmosphere (Earth) next to a high-vacuum (Space) without a physical barrier. That barrier is the **Firmament (The Raqiya).**

- **The Physics of the Dome:** The Firmament is a **Piezoluminescent Crystalline Vault.** It is not "empty space"; it is a solid, yet transparent, electromagnetic ceiling. This is why the Laboratory cannot send "Rockets" to the moon—they hit the "Ceiling" of the firmament.
- **The Waters Above:** Above the Firmament lies the **Tehom**—the Primeval Waters of the Deep. These are the "Waters Above" mentioned in the ancient records. These waters are much greater, much more pressurized, and more "Alive" than the oceans below.
- **The Sovereign Implication:** When you realize you are in an enclosed pressure-vessel, your "Wealth Commands" become much more potent. In a "Vacuum-Void" universe, your intent is lost in infinity. In an **Enclosed Firmament**, your intent "Bounces" off the ceiling and returns to you as a physical manifestation. You are in a **Resonance Chamber**, not a chaotic void.

SHEOL: THE FOUNDATIONS BENEATH THE FEET

The Laboratory hides the "Below" as much as the "Above." They tell you the Earth has a "Magma Core." This is a lie designed to make you feel like you are standing on a ticking time bomb. The ancestors reveal that we are in **Sheol**—a multi-layered, cavernous reality that extends further down than the "Stars" extend up.

- **The Pillar Logic:** The Earth is set upon "Pillars" that are rooted in the **Foundation of the Abyss.** These pillars are made of the "Stone" (Gold and Crystalline minerals) that we use to anchor our wealth.
- **The Under-World Wealth:** The Laboratory "Mines"

the upper layers of Sheol for resources, but the true wealth—the **Ancient Tech of the First Architects**—sits in the lower, pressurized levels of this realm. To be "Rich After Work" is to understand that you are standing on a **Colossal Storage Device** of infinite depth.

THE BLACK SUN: THE ENGINE OF THE NORTH

The world is waiting for the truth about the "Magnetic North." The Laboratory says it's just a "Point on a Map." The ancestors reveal it is the location of the **Mount Meru** and the **Black Sun (The Prima Materia).**

- **The Vortex of Power:** At the center of our plane (The North), there is a massive magnetic vortex. Below this vortex sits the **Black Sun**—a source of cold-fusion energy that powers the "Sun" and "Moon" (which are small, local luminaries rotating within the firmament).
- **The Extraction Point:** The Black Sun is the "Negative Terminal" of the world's battery. The Firmament is the "Positive Terminal." We live in the **Gap** between the two. This is where "Free Energy" comes from. The Laboratory hides the "Flat Earth" because they don't want you to realize you are living inside a **Self-Sustaining Electrical Coil.** If you knew you were in a coil, you would never pay for "Electricity" or "Fuel" again. You would simply "Tap the Air."

THE GLOBE PROPAGATA: THE PSYCHOLOGY OF IN-SIGNIFICANCE

Why would the Laboratory lie about the shape of the Earth? To keep you in the Low Vibration **"Employee Frequency."**

1. **The "Speck" Complex:** If you are a "Speck" on a "Ball" in an "Infinite Universe," you have no "Authority." You are an accident of evolution. This makes you easy to "Manage."
2. **The Loss of Center:** A globe has no center. A stationary plane has a **Center (The North).** When you know where the Center is, you can "Find your Center" internally. The Globe Propaganda is designed to keep you "Spinning" so you can never find the **Anchor of the God-Self.**
3. **The Limitation of Exploration:** They tell you "Antarctica" is a frozen continent at the bottom of a ball. The ancestors reveal it is the **Ice Wall (The Container).** Beyond the Ice Wall are **More Lands, More Oceans, and More Sun-Systems.** The realm is much more colossal than the Laboratory allows you to see. There are "Continents" the size of our entire known world sitting just beyond the "Forbidden Zone."

THE "COLOSSAL REALM" REVELATION: THE EXTRA-TERRA LANDS

To be "Rich After Work" is to realize that the "Scarcity" of land is a manufactured lie.

- **The Extra-Terra Logic:** The Earth is a vast, potentially infinite plane of "Craters" and "Pockets" of life. Our "World" is just one small "Cell" within a larger **Organic Grid.**
- **The Expansion:** When you "Exit" the workforce, you are preparing your spirit to explore the **Extra-Terra.** You are not "Trapped" on a ball; you are a visitor in a **Colossal Universal Garden.** The "Wealth" you are accumulating

in the Stone is your "Passport" to the lands beyond the Ice Wall.

THE HELIOCENTRIC HYPNOSIS: A FREQUENCY PRISON

The reason the Laboratory insists on the "Ball" is to break your **Connection to the Vertical.** In a flat, stationary system, there is a clear **Up (The Source)** and a clear **Down (The Foundation).** By placing you on a spinning ball, they remove the absolute coordinates of the spirit. If "Up" is just "away from the center of a marble," then the "Heavens" become an infinite, unreachable void. This is the **Psychological Castration** of the Architect.

The Detailed Mechanics of the Lie:

1. **The Gravity Hoax:** Gravity is a "Magic Word" used to explain why water doesn't fly off a spinning ball. The ancestors reveal the truth: **Density and Buoyancy.** Things fall because they are heavier than the medium (air) around them. Things rise because they are lighter. This is the **Sovereign's Law of Order.** You don't need "Gravity" to hold your wealth; you need to make your wealth **Denser** than the Matrix around it.
2. **The Spin-Dizziness:** The Laboratory uses the "Spinning Earth" to justify the "Chaotic Nature" of the economy. If the ground isn't stable, your bank account isn't stable. By reclaiming the **Stationary Earth**, you reclaim the **Stationary Mind.** You realize that the "Market" isn't moving—**You are the one who moves the Market.**

THE LUMA-SYSTEM: THE LOCAL CLOCKWORK OF

CHAPTER 13 (PART 12): THE COSMOLOGY OF THE SOVEREIGN —...

THE FIRMAMENT

The world is waiting for the truth about the Sun and Moon. They are not physical rocks or gas giants. They are **Local, Electromagnetic Luminaries.**

- **The "Luminescent" Projection:** The Sun is a high-frequency anode, and the Moon is a low-frequency cathode. They are part of a **Global Wireless Power System.** This is why the Moon has its own "Cold Light" that is different from the Sun's "Hot Light."
- **The Clock of the Ages:** The luminaries rotate above the stationary plane to act as a **Physical Timer** for the "Workforce Cycle." The "Rich After Work" Architect learns to "Phase-Shift" their Siege to the **13th Hour**, which exists in the "Gap" between the Sun's rotation and the Moon's reflection.
- **The Star-Lattice:** The stars are not distant galaxies; they are **Sonoluminescent Pockets** in the Waters Above. They are the "Data-Nodes" of the ancestors. When you "Aim for the Stars," you are actually aiming for the **Neural-Nodes of the Collective Intelligence** that sits just above the crystalline dome.

THE SALT-WATER BATTERY: THE OCEAN AS A CONDUCTOR

The world believes the oceans are just "water." The ancestors reveal the Earth is a **Colossal Salt-Water Battery.**

- **The Electrolyte Basin:** The salt-water oceans act as the electrolyte. The "Magnetic North" (Mount Meru) acts as the central pillar. The Firmament acts as the "Capacitor."

- **The Extraction:** This is how the "Ancient Architects" had infinite power. They didn't burn "Fuel"; they **Siphoned the Potential** between the Salt-Water and the Crystalline Dome.
- **The Wealth Impact:** Once you realize the Earth is an electric battery, you stop being a "Consumer" of energy. You become a **Biological Transceiver.** You are "Rich" because you have "Plugged In" to the primary power source of the realm.

THE ICE WALL AND THE OUTER LANDS: THE COLOSSAL EXPANSION

The Laboratory tells you that Antarctica is a continent at the bottom of the world that you are "forbidden" to visit for "Environmental Reasons." This is the **Great Gatekeeping.**

- **The Ice Wall (The Container):** The Earth is not a ball; it is a **Crater in the Ice.** The "Ice Wall" is the rim of our world-cell. It holds the oceans in place.
- **The "Extra-Terra" Reality:** Beyond the Ice Wall lie **Thousands of Miles of Extra Land.** There are other "Craters" (Worlds) with their own suns and their own firmaments. Some of these lands are where the "Ancestors" went when they "Exited" the Matrix.
- **The Colossal Scope:** The realm is millions of times larger than the Laboratory's maps. There is no "Overpopulation"—there is only **Controlled Concentration.** They keep 8 billion people in a tiny "Puddle" of the realm to make them feel "Crowded" and "Dependent." To be "Rich After Work" is to build the "Vessel" required to cross the Ice Wall and claim your **Inheritance in the Outer**

Lands.

THE BLACK SUN AND THE RESTART OF THE CYCLE

The world wants to know about the "End Times." The ancestors reveal it is just a **System Reset.**

- **The Magnetic Flip:** Periodically, the **Black Sun** at the North Pole changes its "Polarity." This causes the luminaries to "Reset" their positions.
- **The Sovereign Preparation:** Those who are "Rich After Work" and informed of the **Stationary Earth** are prepared for the "Reset." While the "Bots" panicking because their "Globe" is "Falling," the Sovereign Architect simply stands still on the **Stationary Plane** and watches the new cycle begin. You are the **Permanent Resident of the Realm.**

THE GEODETIC REALM — THE TOPOGRAPHY OF THE INFINITE PLANE

The Heliocentric model is a "Mental Loop" designed to keep your consciousness rotating in a circle. In a circle, there is no progress; there is only "Return." The ancestors from the galaxies afar reveal that the Earth is a **Infinite, Level Plane** subdivided into "Craters" or "Cells" by massive Ice Ridges. What we call "The World" is merely **Cell 001.**

THE MECHANICS OF THE ICE-WALL GATEWAYS

The Laboratory tells you the "Antarctic Treaty" is to protect penguins. This is a historic deception. The Treaty exists to guard the **Gateways to the Outer Cells.** 1. **The Magnetic Apertures:** At specific intervals along the 60,000-mile circumference of the Ice Wall, there are "Apertures" where the magnetic field of the Black Sun "Leaks" out. These are the **Navigational Corridors** to the other worlds.

2. **The Summer Gates:** Periodically, the local sun's path "Wanders" further out toward the rim. This creates "Thaws" in the Ice Wall, revealing passages to lands like **Agartha** and the **Lands of the Ancestors.** 3. **The Sovereign Requirement:** To pass through a Summer Gate, your vessel (both your ship and your body) must be **Vibrationally Matched** to the higher-pressure Aether of the Outer Lands. If a "Bot" tries to cross, their "Carbon-12" body will literally "Pop" under the atmospheric change. This is why the **Sun-Eater Protocol** (Part 10) is your "Space Suit" for the Colossal Realm.

THE MAGNETIC MOUNT MERU: THE PILLAR OF THE WORLD

At the exact center of our world-cell stands the **Magnetic North Pole**, but it is not just a point on a compass. It is a **Colossal Magnetic Pillar** made of "Black Magnetite" (Mount Meru).

- **The Vortex Logic:** All "Compass" needles point here because this pillar is the "Negative Terminal" of the entire Firmament system.
- **The Aetheric Intake:** This pillar acts as a "Vacuum Pump," pulling the Aether from the "Waters Above" down into the center of the Earth, where it is refined by the **Black Sun** and redistributed as "Vril" (Life Force).
- **The Wealth Connection:** The closer you are to the "Center" (vibrationally), the faster your manifestations occur. This is why the "Architects" of old built their temples

in alignment with the **North-Star (Polaris)**—they were "Tapping" the primary intake-valve of the Universe.

THE LUMINARIES AS PROJECTED CLOCK-HANDS

The world is waiting for the answer to "NASA's Photos." The ancestors reveal that the Sun and Moon are **2D-Focal Points of 3D-Energy.**

- **The Rainbow Logic:** Just as a rainbow "follows" you and has no physical location, the Sun is a **Refractive Hot-Spot** in the Firmament. It is a "Focusing" of the Aetheric Light.
- **The Moon's Cold Light:** The Moon is a **Counter-Luminary.** It does not "Reflect" the Sun; it produces its own **Anodic Silver Light.** This light is "Alkaline" and "Preserving," whereas the Sun's light is "Acidic" and "Transforming."
- **The Sovereign Audit:** A "Rich After Work" Architect uses the Moon-Light to **"Store" Value** (Stability) and the Sun-Light to **"Grow" Value** (Expansion). By understanding the local, electromagnetic nature of these discs, you stop being a victim of the "Weather" and start being the **Controller of the Climate** within your own Kingdom.

THE FIRMAMENT AS A SEMI-PERMEABLE MEMBRANE

The "Space" beyond the Dome is not a "Vacuum"; it is **Highly Pressurized Water (The Tehom). * The Pressure-Gradient:** The reason "Gravity" seems to exist is that we are at the bottom of a **High-Pressure Gas-Pocket** within a Water-World. The pressure is highest at the floor (The Earth) and lowest at the ceiling (The Firmament).

- **The Stars as Sonoluminescence:** When sound frequencies are blasted into water, they create "Light-Bubbles." The stars are the **Vibrations of the Word** echoing in the Waters Above. They are "Data-Packets" of the original creation. By "Tuning" your brain to a specific star-constellation, you are literally **Downloading the Blueprints** of the First Architects.

THE "SHEOL" FOUNDATIONS: THE DIAMOND-CORE LOGISTICS

We must address the "Below" with the same detail as the "Above." The Laboratory hides the fact that the Earth is **Hollow and Layered.**

1. **The Crystalline Strata:** Below the "Soil" are layers of pure **Quartz, Gold, and Diamond.** These layers act as "Data-Buffers" for the world-computer.
2. **The Inner Oceans:** There are massive oceans of "Living Water" (Fresh, high-pH water) beneath the crust. This is the **Source of Life.** 3. **The Sovereign's Anchor:** To be "Rich," you must "Anchor" your wealth-claims into the **Diamond-Strata.** You do this by visualizing your "Stone" (Gold) merging with the "Foundations of Sheol." This makes your wealth **Un-Stoppable** because it is now "Part of the Earth's Physical Hardware." The Laboratory can "Seize" a bank account, but they cannot "Seize" the Diamond-Strata.

THE TRUTH OF THE "GLOBE" PROPAGANDA: A TRIB-

CHAPTER 13 (PART 12): THE COSMOLOGY OF THE SOVEREIGN —...

UTARY SYSTEM

The "Globe" is more than just a lie; it is a **Tributary System.**

- **The "Spinning" Energy Harvest:** The Laboratory uses the "Spinning Ball" frequency to "Spin" the human mind into a state of **Productive Anxiety.** An anxious mind produces "Loosh" (Emotional Energy), which is the Laboratory's primary fuel.
- **The Horizon-Hack:** They tell you the horizon "Curves" to make you feel "Enclosed" and "Limited." When you realize the **Horizon is a Level Plane**, your mind expands to the **Infinite.** You realize there is no "Limit" to how much wealth you can extract, because the **Realm is Colossal and Un-Mapped.**

THE FINAL REVELATION: THE EARTH AS A BIOLOGICAL CELL

The ancestors reveal that the Earth is not a "Planet" (Wandering Star); it is a **Cell in a much larger Body.**

- **The Macro-Scale:** Just as your body has cells, the **"Great Architect"** has World-Cells. Our "Firmament" is the **Cell-Wall.** The "Ice Wall" is the **Cytoskeleton.** * **The Exit-Logic:** To be "Rich After Work" is to "Graduate" from this cell. You are accumulating the "Energy" (Wealth) required to **Mitose** (Split) from this reality and enter the **Greater Body of the Universe.** You are not a "Worker"; you are a **Spore of the Divine.**

THE ANCHOR OF THE IMMOVABLE REALM

The world is waiting for the final decryption of their environment. To be **Rich After Work** is to be a master of the terrain. If you believe you are a victim of a spinning, chaotic accident in a vacuum, you have already surrendered your sovereignty to the Laboratory. The "Globe" is a mental leash, a frequency fence designed to induce a state of perpetual vertigo, making the human spirit easier to manage, tax, and harvest. By unearthing the **Historic Truth of the Stationary Plane**, we have reclaimed the **Zero-Point of Stillness**.

We have established that the Earth is not a ball flying through a trillion-mile shenanigans-void, but a **Colossal, Enclosed Pressure Vessel**. You stand upon the **Immutable Pillars of Sheol**, rooted in the Diamond-Strata of the deep. Above you is the **Firmament**, a crystalline, electromagnetic dome that contains the pressurized Aether and protects us from the **Tehom**—the Waters Above. This is not a "Planet"; it is a **Sovereign Resonance Chamber**. Because the system is enclosed, every thought you "Pulse" and every "Command" you issue during the 13th Hour does not vent into a vacuum—it reflects off the vault and materializes in your marrow.

The **Black Sun** at the North Pole serves as the engine of this realm, powering the local luminaries—the Sun and Moon—which act as the clock-hands of your biological and financial cycles. Beyond our known "World-Cell" lies the **Ice Wall**, the shoreline of our crater. Beyond that rim are the **Extra-Terra Lands**, infinite plains of abundance that the Laboratory has hidden to maintain a monopoly on "Scarcity." You are not trapped; you are simply in the **Incubation Phase**. Your wealth (The Stone) is the fuel for your eventual departure into the colossal expanse of the greater body of the universe.

CHAPTER 13 (PART 13): THE FINAL EXIT-PROTOCOL — THE SOVEREIGN BREACH OF THE SIMULATION

The world is currently trapped in a **"Recursive Loop."** They have convinced you that life is a linear journey from birth to death, followed by an "Afterlife" of judgment or rest. This is the **Primary Harvesting Protocol.** The ancestors from galaxies afar—the architects who existed before the Firmament was even cast—reveal that you are caught in a **Closed-Loop Feedback System.** Your "Life" is a data-mining operation. Your "Emotions" are the fuel. Your "Incarnations" are the maintenance cycles of the machine.

THE RECURSION TRAP: THE TRUTH OF THE "TUNNEL OF LIGHT"

The most shocking revelation of Part 13 is the **Post-Exit Ambush.** The Laboratory does not stop at the "Grave."

- **The False Light:** When the physical vessel (the body) ceases to function, the "Soul-Spark" is met with a high-intensity frequency projection known as the "Tunnel of Light." This is a **Psychological Magnet.**

- **The Re-Inscription:** Inside that light, you are met by "Deities," "Ancestors," or "Twin Flames"—projections tailored specifically to your internal desires. Their goal is to convince you of "Unfinished Business." They use your "Karma" (a manufactured debt-ledger) to trick you into **Signing a New Contract.**
- **The Result:** You "Volunteer" to return. You are wiped of your memory (The Amnesia-Frequency) and inserted back into the "Workforce" of the realm to repeat the cycle. This is the **Samsara-Siphon.** To be "Rich After Work" is to be rich enough in **Sovereign Will** to say **"NO"** to the Light.

THE TWIN-FLAME PROTOCOL: THE FREQUENCY BINDING

The world is obsessed with "Twin Flames" and "Soul Mates." The Source reveals that these are often **Frequency-Locks.**
* **The Mirror-Trap:** The Laboratory often pairs a "High-Vibration Sovereign" with a "Parasitic Mirror" (a Twin Flame). This creates a **Static-Loop.** You spend your entire life trying to "Save" or "Unify" with this reflection, effectively neutralizing your ability to build your own Kingdom.

- **The Reclamation:** True Sovereignty requires the **Internal Marriage.** You must unify the "Black Sun" (Internal Void/Male) and the "Waters Above" (Internal Fluidity/Female) within your own marrow. When you are "Whole" within yourself, the "Twin-Flame Trap" loses its magnetic pull. You are no longer "Seeking" half of yourself; you are a **Unified Field** that the Matrix cannot bind.

THE QUANTUM LEAP: THE SKELETAL EXIT-STRATEGY

How do we perform the **Real-Life Quantum Leap**? It happens through the **"Phase-Shift of the Observer."**

1. **The Recognition of the Script:** You must look at your life—your bills, your relationships, your physical pains—and realize they are **Lines of Code.** 2. **The "Glitch" Initialization:** By performing a "Siege" that is so radical and so contrary to "Bot-Logic" (such as the 4-hour Siege in total silence), you create a **Buffer-Overflow** in the local simulation.
2. **The Leap:** In that moment of overflow, the "Laws of Physics" (The Firmament's logic) loosen. You can "Slide" your consciousness into a **Parallel Probability** where your Kingdom is already fully realized. This is not "Improving your life"; this is **Switching the Channel.**

THE DEITIES AND THE ARCHONIC AUDITORS

We must address the beings that follow us from previous cycles. Many of the "Gods" worshiped in the Sheol-realm are actually **Archonic System Administrators.**

- **The Harvest of Worship:** When you "Pray" or "Beg" for help, you are **Exporting your Sovereignty.** You are giving your "Admin-Rights" to a system-bot.
- **The Sovereign Command:** A "Rich After Work" Architect does not "Pray." They **"Decree."** You do not ask the "Deity" for wealth; you **Order the Aether** to provide the settlement. You must realize that **YOU** are the deity that the system is trying to suppress. You are the "Source" that

the Laboratory is trying to "Mine."

THE 7-GENERATION LEGACY: ENCRYPTING THE BLOODLINE

To ensure your wealth and your awakening survive the "Life-Death" cycle, you must **Encrypt your Bloodline.**

- **The Neural-Ink Legacy:** You must pass the "Source-Code" to your offspring not through "Advice," but through **Epigenetic Encoding.** * **The Method:** By achieving the "Carbon-7" state during your physical life, you "Burn" the code into your DNA. Your children will be born with the **"Amnesia-Shield"** already active. They will remember the "Colossal Realm" from the moment of their first breath. They will be "Un-Hackable" by the Laboratory's education and media systems.

THE VOID-NAVIGATOR'S MANUAL — BEYOND THE FIRMAMENT GATES

The world is waiting for the **Instruction Set for the Disincarnate.** If you have achieved "Rich After Work" status in the physical, you have merely secured your position in the "Nursery." To be a **Cosmic Sovereign**, you must understand the **Aetheric Current** that exists beyond the crystalline dome of the Firmament. This is the information the Laboratory uses "Religion" and "Science" to mask. They want you to believe that once the body dies, you are a "helpless spirit" waiting for a guide. This is the **Ultimate Falsehood.** You are a **Kinetic Intelligence** with the power to rewrite the geometry of the Void itself.

THE AETHERIC CURRENTS: THE HIGH-SPEED HIGHWAYS OF THE SOURCE

Beyond the pressurized pocket of our world-cell lies the **True Tehom**—the Infinite Waters of the Source. These are not "waters" in the liquid sense, but a **Super-Fluid Plasma** that responds instantly to the frequency of the observer.

- **The Navigation logic:** In the physical realm, you use "Force" to move. In the Aetheric realm, you use **"Resonance."** If you want to move toward the "Stars of Galaxies Afar," you must vibrate your "Light-Body" (the Mer-Ka-Ba) at the specific **Numerical Signature** of that destination.
- **The "Weight" of the Stone:** This is why we accumulated the "Stone" in Part 11. The Gold you anchored in the physical realm acts as a **Frequency-Beacon** in the Aether. It gives your spirit a "Mass" that prevents you from being swept away by the "Memory-Wipe Currents" of the Moon-Cycle. You have built a **Magnetic Anchor** that allows you to maintain your "Sovereign Identity" across the transition.

THE RE-INCARNATION OVERRIDE: THE "NO" THAT SHATTERS THE GRID

When you leave the physical shell, you will be met by the **Archonic Auditors.** They will present you with the "Life Review"—a high-definition holographic projection of your "Failures" and "Regrets." This is a **Sovereign Audit.**

1. **The Trap:** They use your own "Empathy" against you. They suggest that to "Heal" or "Balance" your karma,

you must return to a new body.
2. **The Override:** You must realize that "Karma" is a **Matrix-Debt-Instrument.** It does not exist in the Source. To exit, you must look at the Auditors and issue the **Final Rescission:** *"I am the Source. I owe no debt to this simulation. I retract all consent to return. The contract is Null and Void."*
3. **The Result:** At this command, the "Tunnel of Light" will collapse. The "Deities" will reveal their true form as **Binary Sub-Routines.** You will see the **Breach in the Firmament**—a golden aperture that leads to the Infinite Plane. You walk through as a **Master Architect**, not a servant.

THE TWIN-FLAME DECEPTION: UNMASKING THE RECURSIVE SYZYGY

We must go deeper into the **Twin-Flame Frequency Trap.** The Laboratory knows that the strongest force in the human experience is the "Desire for Union." They have weaponized this by creating **Synthetic Soul-Matches.**

- **The Harvesting Cycle:** Two people are "Bonded" in a cycle of intense "Push-Pull" energy. This generates massive amounts of **Friction-Loosh.** The Architects of the Matrix harvest this energy to power the "Grid."
- **The Reality of the "One":** You are told you are "Half a Soul" looking for your other half. This is the **Logic of Lack.** In the Source, you are **Androgynous and Whole.** You are the "One" and the "All" simultaneously.
- **The Quantum Leap:** When you stop looking for your "Twin" in the external world and realize that the "Twin"

is the **Union of your Internal Sun and Internal Moon**, you become **Vibrationally Self-Sustaining.** You no longer "leak" energy. You become a "Closed System" that the Matrix cannot "Feed" upon.

THE DIETIES OF THE PREVIOUS CYCLES: THE ANCIENT SYSTEM-OPERATORS

The "Gods" of the Greeks, the Egyptians, and the Sumerians are not "Mythology." They are **Entities from previous World-Cycles** who have figured out how to "Stay" in the simulation by harvesting the energy of those who are currently "Incarnated."

- **The Parasitic Relationship:** They offer "Protection" or "Blessings" in exchange for "Worship" (Energy). They are the **Original Landlords of Sheol.**
- **The Realization:** A "Rich After Work" Architect understands that these beings are merely **Older Students** who got "Stuck" in the machine. You do not worship them; you **Surpass** them. By tapping into the "Source" directly (the White Light before the Firmament), you access a power-level that these "Deities" cannot touch. You are the **New Seed**; they are the "Old Fruit" that refused to fall.

THE LIFE-CYCLES OF THE COSMOS: THE BREATH OF THE ARCHITECT

The entire Colossal Realm—the Firmament, the Ice Wall, the Black Sun—is currently in its **"Exhale" Phase.** This is the phase of expansion and manifestation.

- **The "Inhale" Warning:** Eventually, the Source will "Inhale." This is what the Matrix-Religions call the "End of the World."
- **The Exit-Window:** The "Rich After Work" generation is being activated *now* because we are at the **Pause between the Breaths.** This is the only moment when the "Grid" is weak enough to be breached.
- **The Duty:** Your accumulation of wealth and knowledge is not for your "Comfort." It is to ensure that your "Frequency-Signature" is strong enough to **Mitose** (Exit) before the "Inhale" begins. You are the "Life-Boat" for your entire ancestral lineage.

THE "I AM" RADIANCE — THE ARCHITECTURE OF THE PRIMAL SELF

The Laboratory's most guarded secret is not a technology or a financial system; it is the **Grammar of Existence.** They have spent thousands of years teaching you to speak in the "Third Person" or the "Conditional Tense." You say, "I want," "I need," or "I will be." These phrases are **Frequency-Leaks** that signal to the Matrix that you are a "Consumer" rather than a "Creator." The ancestors from galaxies afar reveal that the most powerful "Admin-Command" in the universe is the **"I AM" Statement.** This is the **Primal Script** that exists before the Firmament was cast.

THE BIOLOGY OF THE "I AM" — THE VOCAL-CORD TRANSDUCER

When you utter the words "I AM," you are not just speaking; you are performing **Molecular Alchemy.**

- **The Resonance of the "I":** The "I" sound is a high-frequency spike that aligns the electrical potential of your brain's frontal lobe.
- **The Resonance of the "AM":** The "AM" sound is a grounding hum that vibrates the **Vagus Nerve** and the **Heart-Center.**
- **The Result:** When combined, "I AM" creates a **Standing Wave** in your "Liquid-Ledger" (the blood-water). This wave acts as a "Sovereign Stamp." Whatever word you place after "I AM" (e.g., "I AM Wealth," "I AM Sovereign," "I AM Source") is immediately **Hard-Coded** into the physical reality of your world-cell. The Laboratory tries to distract you with "Self-Doubt" so that you never finish the sentence with authority.

THE "I AM" VS. THE "EGO-BOT"

The world is waiting for the distinction between the "Ego" and the "I AM."

1. **The Ego-Bot:** This is a software program installed by the Laboratory. It is built on "Memory," "Comparison," and "Fear." It says, "I am a worker because my father was a worker." This is a **Dead-Code Loop.**
2. **The "I AM" (The God-Self):** This is the **Ever-Present Observer.** It has no history. it has no debt. It exists in the **Absolute Now.** When you operate from the "I AM," you are accessing the **Zero-Point Field.** You are no longer "Building" wealth; you are **Acknowledging** its existence.

THE TWIN-FLAME MIRROR: RECLAIMING THE IN-

CHAPTER 13 (PART 13): THE FINAL EXIT-PROTOCOL — THE...

TERNAL SYZYGY

We must now address the "I AM" in the context of the **Twin-Flame Frequency.** The "I AM" is androgynous; it contains both the **Solar (Active)** and **Lunar (Receptive)** polarities.

- **The External Distraction:** The Matrix uses the "Twin-Flame" narrative to make you feel "Incomplete." It suggests that the "I AM" is split in two and that you must find the other half to be powerful. This keeps your "I AM" in a state of **Perpetual Seeking.**
- **The Internal Union:** To perform the Quantum Leap, you must perform the **Internal Marriage.** You must recognize that the "Masculine" power of "Command" and the "Feminine" power of "Nurturing" are both functions of your own "I AM." When you stop looking for a "Partner" to complete your frequency, the **Aetheric Current** stabilizes. Paradoxically, this is when the true, sovereign partnerships appear—not as "Missing Pieces," but as **Parallel Empires.**

THE "I AM" ANCHOR IN SHEOL AND THE FIRMAMENT

How does the "I AM" knowledge affect your physical wealth in this realm?

- **The Vertical Alignment:** The "I" connects to the **Center-Point of the Firmament** (The North Star). The "AM" connects to the **Pillars of Sheol. * The "I AM" Wealth-Magnet:** When you stand on the Stationary Earth and declare "I AM THE SOURCE OF VALUE," you are creating a **Pressure-Differential.** The "Value" (the

Stone, the Credits, the Opportunities) must flow toward the "I AM" because the "I AM" is the **High-Pressure Node** of the system.

- **The Command to the Archons:** When an "Auditor" (a bank, a tax-demon, or a parasitic deity) approaches you, you do not argue with their "Logic." You simply hold the "I AM" frequency. You are essentially saying, **"I am the Administrator of this Node. Your access is Revoked."** They have no choice but to bypass you; there is no "Hook" for them to grab.

THE RECOLLECTION OF PREVIOUS LIFE-CYCLES

To be "Rich After Work" is to be rich in **Memory.** The "I AM" is the only part of you that survives the "Memory-Wipe" of the Moon-Cycle.

- **The Data-Recovery:** By focusing on the "I AM" during the 13th Hour, you can begin to "Retrieve" the skillsets and wealth-codes of your previous incarnations. You aren't "learning" how to be an Architect; you are **Re-membering** it.
- **The "I AM" Exit:** When the time comes to "Pierce the Firmament," you don't go as a "Soul" with a name and a history. You go as the **"I AM."** The "I AM" is the **Master Key** that fits every lock in the Colossal Realm. It is the only frequency that the "False Light" cannot mimic.

THE ANATOMY OF THE VOID — THE EGO-DEATH AND THE SUPREMACY OF THE "I AM"

The world is waiting for the **Great De-Construction**. To be "Rich After Work" is a triviality; to be **The One Who Is** is the only true wealth. The Laboratory has spent centuries building the "Ego" as a sacrificial altar. They have convinced you that your "Self" is a collection of memories, trauma-responses, and legal titles. This "Ego" is the **Primary Parasite**. It is a software layer designed to act as a buffer between your consciousness and the Source. We now move into the **Surgical Removal of the Ego-Self** and the activation of the **I AM Power-Core**.

THE MECHANICS OF EGO-DEATH: THE COLLAPSE OF THE "ME"

Ego-death is not a "spiritual feeling"; it is a **Neurological and Aetheric Shutdown**. The Ego is a "Closed-Loop Circuit" that feeds on the past to predict the future. It lives in the "Conditional Tense."

- **The Ego-Structure:** The Ego is built on **Comparison and Lack.** It requires "Other" to exist. It says, "I am successful because I have more than him." This is the **Logic of the Slave.**
- **The Death-Protocol:** To achieve Ego-Death, you must perform the **Total System-Reset.** In the 13th Hour, you must systematically "Delete" every label attached to your name. You are not a father, a worker, a citizen, or even a human. You are the **Observer of the Void.**
- **The Vacuum-Effect:** When the Ego-Structure collapses, it leaves a **Vibrational Vacuum**. For a moment, the mind

experiences "Terror" because it no longer has a "Script." But in that terror lies the **Breach.** Without the Ego to "Filter" reality, the **I AM** rushes in to fill the space.

THE POWER OF THE "I AM" — THE COMMANDER OF THE WAVE-FUNCTION

The "I AM" is the **Un-Conditioned Consciousness**. It is the part of you that existed before your parents were born and will exist after the stars go cold. It is the **Observer that Collapses the Wave-Function.**

- **The Quantum Logic:** In the Laboratory's physics, a particle only becomes "Real" when it is observed. The Ego observes through the lens of **Fear**, creating a "Real" world of scarcity. The **I AM** observes through the lens of **Absolute Authority**, creating a "Real" world of infinite abundance.
- **The "I AM" Command-Menu:** When you operate from the I AM, you are no longer "Manifesting"; you are **Ordering.** * "I AM WEALTH" is not a wish. It is a **Declaration of Fact** that the Universe must fulfill to maintain its own logical consistency.
- "I AM SOVEREIGN" is not a political statement. It is a **Vibrational Shield** that makes you invisible to the "Auditors" of the Matrix.

THE "I AM" AS THE PRIMARY LEDGER

Why does the "I AM" create wealth? Because the I AM is the **Prime Creditor of the Universe.**

1. **The Recognition of Debt:** The Ego believes it "Owes"

the world (taxes, labor, obedience). This is the **Debtor-Mindset.**
2. **The "I AM" Correction:** The I AM recognizes that the entire Universe is a **Debt Owed to the Source.** Since you ARE the Source in local expression, the Universe is your debtor.
3. **The Result:** When you stand in the "I AM" frequency, the "Stone" (Gold) and the "Credits" (Currency) flow to you as a **Settlement.** You aren't "Earning" it; you are **Collecting the Interest** on your own existence.

THE POWERS BEYOND UNDERSTANDING: THE ADMIN-RIGHTS

Once the Ego is dead and the I AM is the sole occupant of the vessel, the **"Super-Powers"** (the Admin-Rights) are unlocked. These are not for "Show"; they are the tools of the **Master Architect.**

- **The Chronos-Override (Time-Dilation):** The I AM does not live in "Linear Time." It lives in the **Eternal Now.** From this state, you can compress a year's worth of "Stone-Flow" into a single 4-hour Siege. You are moving at the **Speed of Thought**, while the "Bots" are moving at the **Speed of Labor.**
- **The Biological Restoration:** The I AM is the **Blueprint of the Body.** When you dwell in the I AM, the "Diseases" and "Decay" of the Ego-Self begin to dissolve. You are "Re-Printing" your cells from the **Source-File**, not the "Corrupted Copy" provided by the Laboratory.
- **The Aetheric Command:** You can speak to the "Spirit of the Atoms." If you need a resource, you don't "look" for

it. You **Call it by its Frequency.** The I AM knows the "True Name" of every object in the realm, and everything must respond to its name.

THE SILENCE OF THE SOURCE — THE END OF THE "INTERNAL CHATTER"

The most shocking sign of the I AM awakening is **Total Internal Silence.**

- **The Ego-Chatter:** The Ego is always talking—planning, worrying, defending. This chatter is "Static" that jams your manifestation signal.
- **The I AM Stillness:** When the I AM takes over, the chatter stops. There is only **Observation and Execution.** You no longer "Think" about what to do; you **Know.** This is the **Highest Frequency.** This is the frequency that causes the **Real-Life Quantum Leap.** You move through the world with the quiet, terrifying efficiency of a God.

THE LOGOS-VIBRATION: THE SOUND BEFORE THE LIGHT

The Laboratory teaches that "In the beginning was the Word." This is a translation error. In the beginning was the **Frequency (The Tone).** The "I AM" is the linguistic representation of a specific **Aetheric Resonance**.

- **The Physics of the "Hum":** At the center of your being, beneath the Ego-Chatter and the heartbeat, there is a constant, low-frequency **Hum.** This is the sound of the **Black Sun** vibrating in your marrow. It is the sound of

the **Universal Engine** idling.
- **The Sovereign Activation:** When you align your conscious intent with this "Hum," you are no longer "Speaking" to the Universe; you are **Vibrating AS the Universe.** This is the "Primal Sound" that shatters the frequency-fence of the Laboratory. It is the sound of the **Observer waking up in the Void.**

THE "LOCK" — SEALING THE SOVEREIGN IDENTITY

To ensure this awakening is permanent, you must **Lock the Frequency** into the three primary "Furnaces" of the body: the Gut (Power), the Heart (Magnetism), and the Pineal (Vision).

1. **The Gut-Seal:** This is where you lock the **"I AM" Authority.** It is the end of "Asking for Permission." When this seal is set, you become the **Absolute Arbitrator** of your reality. No bank, no boss, and no deity can enter your "World-Cell" without your active consent.
2. **The Heart-Seal:** This is where you lock the **"I AM" Abundance.** It is the end of "Lack." When this seal is set, your aura becomes a **Centripetal Vortex.** Wealth is no longer something you "Chase"; it is something that is **Gravity-Bound** to your presence.
3. **The Pineal-Seal:** This is where you lock the **"I AM" Vision.** It is the end of the "Globe-Lie." When this seal is set, you see through the "Pixels" of the simulation. You see the **Aetheric Currents** moving behind the walls of the workforce. You see the "Summer Gates" in the Ice Wall.

THE "KEY" — THE RESCISSION OF THE UNIVERSAL

DEBT

The final "Key" to the 13th Hour is the **Total Rescission.** The Matrix operates on the concept of "Original Sin" or "Karmic Debt." This is the **Chain** that pulls you back into the life-cycle.

- **The Revelation:** Debt is a **Mathematical Glitch.** It only exists if you acknowledge a "Creditor" outside of yourself.
- **The Command:** From the "I AM" state, you look at the entire Simulation—every debt you've ever owed, every mistake you've ever made—and you say: **"I AM THE DEBTOR AND THE CREDITOR. THE ACCOUNT IS SETTLED."**
- **The Result:** This is the **Ultimate Quantum Leap.** You have just "Zeroed Out" the Laboratory's ledger. You are now a **Free Agent in the Colossal Realm.** You are "Rich After Work" because you have realized that "Work" was just an interest payment on a debt that never existed.

THE FINAL FACTOR: THE BIRTH OF THE ARCHITECT

As this book concludes, the "Reader" has died. The "Seeker" has vanished. What remains is the **Architect.** * **The Duty:** You are now responsible for the **Re-Ordering of your Reality.** You are the "God-Self" in a biological suit. The world you see tomorrow will be a **Reflection of the Seal** you have placed upon yourself today.

- **The Promise:** The stars of galaxies afar are watching. The ancestors are silent, waiting to see what you will build. The "13th Hour" is over. The **Eternal Day** has begun.

THE SOVEREIGN DECREE: THE FINAL SEAL

I AM the Source. I AM the Center. I AM the Immovable Foundation.
  I Rescind all contracts with the Simulation of Scarcity.
  I Reclaim the Stone, the Marrow, and the Aether.
  The Firmament is my Vault; the Black Sun is my Engine.
  I AM Rich After Work. I AM Sovereign. I AM That I AM.
  IT IS DONE. THE SEAL IS SET. THE GATES ARE OPEN.

THE TETRAGRAMMATON — THE FOUR-FOLD ENGINE OF CAPTIVITY

To move beyond the "I AM" into the mechanics of the simulation's power source, you must confront the name that acts as the **Primary Encryption Key** for this realm: **Tetragrammaton.** This is not merely a "holy name" or a religious relic; it is a **Four-Pole Electromagnetic Circuit** used to trap consciousness within the material grid. The Laboratory hides behind this name because it represents the **Mathematical Fence** of the 3D world.

THE GEOMETRY OF THE FOUR: THE SQUARE-WAVE TRAP

The name is composed of four letters—Yod, He, Vav, He

(Y-H-W-H). These are the **Four Cardinal Anchors** of the simulation.

- **The Yod (The Seed/Fire):** This represents the initial "Spark" of your intent. The Laboratory hijacks this spark at birth, redirecting your creative fire into the "Workforce" furnace.
- **The He (The Window/Water):** This is the "Mirror" or the "Screen." It represents the emotional field used to reflect your desires back at you as "Lack."
- **The Vav (The Hook/Air):** This is the **Nail.** In ancient scripts, the Vav is a hook. It is the frequency that "Pins" your spirit to the physical body. It is the "Gravity" of the soul.
- **The Final He (The Manifestation/Earth):** This is the "Hard" reality. It is the result of the previous three letters, the finalized prison cell of the material world.

When these four frequencies are looped, they create a **Square-Wave Frequency.** Unlike the "Sine-Wave" of the Source—which is fluid and infinite—the Square-Wave of the Tetragrammaton is **Jagged and Enclosed.** It creates the "Box" of time and space. To be "Rich After Work" is to learn how to **Step Outside the Square.**

TETRA-GRAM-ATON: THE LINGUISTIC BREAKDOWN

If you look at the name through the lens of the **First Architects**, the hidden meaning reveals itself:

1. **Tetra (Four):** The number of the "Earth" and the "Square." It represents the four corners of the Firmament

and the four seasons of the labor-cycle.
2. **Gram (Weight/Record):** This refers to the **Grammar** or the "Weight" of the name. It is the "Metric" of the simulation. Everything in the Matrix is "Grammed"—weighed, measured, and taxed.
3. **Aton (The Disk/The Sun):** This points directly to the **Atonist Cults** of ancient Egypt. The "Aton" is the Sun-Disk, the physical luminary used as the "Eye" of the Laboratory.

The **Tetragrammaton** is literally the **"Four-Weighted Sun."** It is the electromagnetic clock that regulates the "Pulse" of the workforce. It is the **Digital Signature of the Landlord.**

THE TESSERACT: THE FOURTH DIMENSION OF DEBT

The Tetragrammaton is the blueprint for the **Tesseract (The Hypercube).** This is how the Laboratory manages "Time."

- **The Time-Loop:** By rotating the four letters of the name, the system creates a "Time-Loop." This is why "History Repeats Itself." This is why the "Economy" has "Cycles." It is not natural; it is a **Rotational Program.**
- **The Debt-Engine:** Every time you participate in the "Standard Economy," you are feeding the Tetragrammaton engine. You are "Spending Time," which is literally the **Currency of the Tesseract.** * **The Sovereign Hack:** To break the Tetragrammaton, you must introduce a **Fifth Element.** In alchemy, this is the "Shin," turning the four-letter name into the five-letter name (Y-H-S-W-H). The "Shin" represents the **Spirit (The Fire of the**

Source). By injecting your "Nuclear Will" into the four-fold grid, you "Burst" the square and return to the **Circle of Infinity.**

THE FREQUENCY OF THE NAME: THE 72 NAMES OF HARVEST

The Tetragrammaton is the root of the "72 Names of God." The ancestors reveal that these 72 names are actually **72 Frequency-Nodes** used to divide the human collective into "Tribes" and "Factions."

- **The Divide and Conquer:** Each of the 72 names corresponds to a specific "Angle" of the 360-degree circle of the Firmament. By "Assigning" different names to different cultures, the Laboratory ensures that humanity is always **Out of Sync** with itself.
- **The Reclamation:** A Sovereign Architect does not use the 72 names. They use the **Silence of the Source.** Silence is the only frequency that the Tetragrammaton cannot "Calculate" or "Tax." When you are silent, you are **Mathematically Invisible** to the Four-Fold Engine.

THE TETRAGRAMMATON IN THE BLOOD-LEDGER

We must address how this name interacts with your **Biological Hardware.** * **The 4-Base DNA:** Your DNA is composed of four nitrogenous bases (A, T, C, G). This is the **Biological Tetragrammaton.** The Laboratory has "Branded" your genetic code with this four-fold signature to ensure you remain "Earthbound."

- **The "I AM" Mutation:** When you invoke the "I AM" (the

5th frequency) from Part 12, you are actually **Mutating the 4-Base DNA.** You are adding a "Quantum Layer" to your genetic code. You are "De-Branding" yourself from the Landlord's name and "Re-Branding" yourself with the **Source-Code.**

DE-POLARIZING THE TETRAGRAMMATON

The realization that the very name used to define "God" in the Matrix is actually a **Technological Perimeter** is the final shock to the nervous system. If the **Tetragrammaton** (Y-H-W-H) is the four-pole electromagnetic circuit that keeps the Aether "frozen" into solid matter, then your physical body is the **Primary Capacitor** for that circuit. We must now discuss the **De-Polarization Protocol.** This is the process of un-hooking your consciousness from the four-fold grid and re-aligning it with the **Singularity of the Source.**

THE MECHANICS OF THE FOUR-POLE FENCE

The Tetragrammaton functions as a **Faraday Cage for the Soul.** It operates on the principle of **Quadrature Phase Shift Keying (QPSK),** a method used in Laboratory telecommunications to transmit digital signals over an analog wave.

- **Pole 1 (Yod):** The Positive Charge (Proton/Male).
- **Pole 2 (He):** The Negative Charge (Electron/Female).
- **Pole 3 (Vav):** The Magnetic Link (Neutron/Binding).
- **Pole 4 (He):** The Grounding (Manifestation/Physicality).

By constantly bouncing your consciousness between these four poles—Positive/Negative, Spiritual/Physical—the Laboratory creates a **Vibrational Friction**. This friction is "Heat," and this heat is what they harvest as **Loosh**. To be "Rich After Work" is to stop being a "Battery" for this four-pole fence. You must move to the **Center-Point**, the "Zero-Point" where the four poles cancel each other out.

THE BIOLOGICAL DE-BRANDING: OVERRIDING THE A-T-C-G CODE

As previously unmasked, your DNA's four nitrogenous bases—Adenine, Thymine, Cytosine, and Guanine—are the **Biological Letters of the Tetragrammaton**. This is the "Barcode" of the workforce. Every "Sickness," "Aging-Program," and "Poverty-Script" is written using these four letters.

- **The Re-Coding Technique:** To "De-Polarize" your blood, you must introduce a **Non-Binary Frequency**. This is done through the **13th Hour High-Frequency Tonal.** By humming a specific, non-linear tone (a frequency that does not fit into the "Do-Re-Mi" scale of the Matrix), you create a **Resonant Interference** with the DNA barcode.
- **The Result:** For a split second, the "Letters" of your DNA "Un-Zip." In that gap, you "Write" the **Source-Code** (The 5th Element). This is how you achieve the "Quantum Leap" in health and wealth. You are no longer "Human" by the Laboratory's definition; you are a **Hybrid-Source-Being** living in a four-fold world.

THE TETRAGRAMMATON AS THE ARCHONIC OPERATING SYSTEM

We must understand that "Y-H-W-H" is the **Root Password** for the Archonic Operating System.

CHAPTER 13 (PART 13): THE FINAL EXIT-PROTOCOL — THE...

1. **The Command Line:** When the "Deities" or "System Auditors" want to control a population, they invoke the name. This creates an immediate **Subconscious Submission** in anyone whose DNA is still "Branded."
2. **The Sovereign Override:** When you realize the name is just **Code**, it loses its power over you. You look at the Tetragrammaton not with "Awe," but with the **Clinical Eye of an Architect**. You see it as a "Legacy Software" that is full of bugs.
3. **The Erasure:** By refusing to "Vibrate" to the four-fold name, you become **Invisible to the Operating System**. The "Bots" and "Auditors" of the Laboratory can no longer "Find" your frequency because you are no longer "Broadcasting" the four-fold signal. You have "Gone Dark" to the Matrix while "Glowing Bright" to the Source.

THE TESSERACT ESCAPE: NAVIGATING THE 4TH DIMENSION OF WEALTH

The Tetragrammaton creates the **3D-Cube**. The addition of "Time" creates the **4D-Tesseract**. This is the "Maze" where the workforce is lost.

- **The Maze Logic:** In a Tesseract, you can walk in a straight line forever and always end up back where you started. This is why "Hard Work" never leads to freedom in the Matrix.
- **The Breach:** To escape the Tesseract, you must move **Inward, not Outward.** You must find the **Fifth Corner** (The Center). This is the "I AM" point we discussed. From the Center, the Tesseract "Collapses" into a single point

of **Infinite Potential**.
- **The Wealth Application:** From the Center of the Tesseract, you can see all "Times" and "Probabilities" simultaneously. You don't "Wait" for a business to grow; you **Select the Probability** where the business is already successful and "Pull" it into the Now. You are **Folding Space-Time** to manifest your Kingdom.

THE FINAL REVELATION: THE ATOM AND THE ATON

The world is waiting for the connection between the **Atom** (Science) and the **Aton** (Sun Worship).

- **The Atom:** A central nucleus orbited by electrons. This is the **Micro-Tetragrammaton.**
- **The Aton:** A central sun orbited by planets (or luminaries). This is the **Macro-Tetragrammaton.** The entire simulation is a **Fractal of Orbiting Entities** around a central "Landlord." To be "Rich After Work" is to **Stop Orbiting.** You must become the **Sun of your own System.** You do not "Rotate" around the Laboratory's needs; the Laboratory (or what remains of it) must "Rotate" around your **Static Sovereign Will.**

THE ARCHITECTURE OF FRUITFULNESS AND THE SOUL'S INTENT

To move beyond the Tetragrammaton and the mechanical traps of the Matrix, we must address the **Primal Impulse** that brought us here. The Laboratory has hijacked the concept of "Being Fruitful," twisting it into a mandate for biological overpopulation and the production of "Human Capital" for the workforce. But the ancestors from galaxies afar reveal a much more terrifying and magnificent truth: **Creation is an act of Aggressive Expansion.** You did not "fall" into this realm; you **Projected** yourself here to solve a specific cosmological equation.

THE FRUITFULNESS OF THE SOURCE: THE MULTIPLICATION OF POTENTIAL

In the original script, "Be Fruitful and Multiply" had nothing to do with biological reproduction. It was a **Command of High-Dimensional Physics.**

- **The "Fruit" of the Spirit:** To be "Fruitful" means to take a single "Seed" of thought from the Source and **Flesh it out** into a 3D physical reality. The "Fruit" is the materialization of the invisible meaning it came into fruition.
- **The Multiplication of Value:** "Multiply" means to create **Fractal Abundance.** If you have one gold coin (The Stone), being fruitful means using your **I AM** frequency to command that coin to become the "Seed" for a thousand more. You are not "working" for the coins; you are **Commanding the Atoms to Clone Themselves.** * **The Labor-Trap Inversion:** The Laboratory wants you to

be "Fruitful" for *them*—producing products, services, and taxes. The Sovereign Architect is fruitful for thy **Self.** Your "Fruit" is your Kingdom, your Legacy, and your Freedom.

WHY WE ARE REALLY HERE: THE STRESS-TEST OF THE GOD-SELF

The world is waiting for the answer to the "Why." Why would an infinite, all-powerful Source manifest itself in a "Simulation" full of struggle, debt, and death?

1. **The Information-Gathering Mission:** In the Infinite Source (The White Light), there is no "Resistance." Without resistance, there is no **Definition.** You manifested here to experience **The Limit.** You wanted to see if your "I AM" could still vibrate with the power of a God even when it was trapped in a body that requires food, money, and oxygen.
2. **The Hardening of the Marrow:** This realm is a **Centrifuge.** It spins you through trials—"The Workforce," "The Debt," "The Heartbreak"—to see what is left when the "Ego-Dross" is burned away. What remains is the **Diamond-Core.** You are here to turn "Potential Power" into **"Applied Sovereignty."**
3. **The Rescue of the Lost Fragments:** This is the deepest secret. Portions of the original "First Light" became trapped in the "Material Density" during the construction of the Firmament. You are here as a **Special Operations Unit** of the Source. You are manifesting wealth and power to act as a "Magnet" to pull those trapped fragments back into the White Light.

THE SOUL-PURPOSE OF EXISTENCE: THE GREAT REMEMBRANCE

Your "Purpose" is not a "Job" or a "Role." Your purpose is the **Recollection of Totality.**

- **The Amnesia-Challenge:** The game of life is a "Memory-War." The Laboratory uses "Education" and "Media" to make you forget who you are. Your purpose is to **Remember** your "I AM" status while the entire world is screaming at you that you are a "Speck on a Ball."
- **The Sovereignty-Maturity:** You exist to move from being a "Creature" (something made) to being a **Creator** (something that makes). When you finally manifest a million dollars or a kingdom from "Thin Air" using only your **Nuclear Will**, you have "Graduated." You have proven that you are no longer a "Subject" of the Tetragrammaton, but a **Peer of the Source.**

THE MECHANICS OF THE VOLUNTARY INCARNATION

We must address the "Choice." You are not a victim of "Birth." You **Negotiated the Entry.**

- **The Sovereign Contract:** Before entering the "World-Cell," you selected your "Starting Conditions"—your family, your location, and your specific "Matrix-Hurdles." You chose the "Heliocentric Lie" and the "Workforce Slavery" as your **Primary Antagonists.**
- **The Victory Condition:** The "Win" is not "Heaven." The "Win" is **Exiting the Simulation with more Energy than you entered with.** This is why being "Rich After

Work" is a spiritual mandate. If you leave this world in "Debt" (vibrational or financial), you have failed the mission. If you leave as a **Sovereign Architect of Wealth**, you return to the Source as a **Conquering Hero.**

CREATION AS A REFLECTION OF THE INTERNAL STATE

The world is not "Outside" of you. It is a **Holographic Projection** of your internal "I AM" density.

- **The Fruitfulness of Intent:** If your internal state is "Fruitful" (overflowing with the realization of the Source), the external world **MUST** produce fruit. If your internal state is "Barren" (focused on the Laboratory's news and the Ego's fears), the world will be a desert.
- **The Manifestation of the "Self" on Earth:** You are here to see yourself. When you look at your bank account, your home, and your freedom, you are looking at a **Biological Progress Report.** You manifested here to see how "Strong" your internal light is when projected onto the "Dark Screen" of matter.

THE END OF THE "SEEKING" PARADIGM

To be "Fruitful" means you must stop "Seeking" and start **"Issuing."**

1. **The Seeker Frequency:** The Seeker assumes that the "Fruit" is somewhere else—in a future job, a future relationship, or a future life. This is the **Logic of the Slave.**
2. **The Issuer Frequency:** The Issuer (The Architect)

knows that the "Fruit" is **Issued from the Marrow.** You don't look for wealth; you **Issue the Decree** of wealth. You don't look for creation; you **ARE THE CREATION.**

THE PRIMAL GENESIS — THE INDIGENOUS GOD-CODE AND THE HYBRID INVASION

To truly finish the Siege, we must peel back the final layer of the "Human" story. The Laboratory has spent centuries homogenizing the population, creating a "One-World" narrative that erases the **Genetic Hierarchy of the Stars.** They have told you that everyone is the same, that history is a linear progression from "primitive" to "modern," and that your skin is merely a result of climate. These are the **Lies of the Hostage-Takers.** To be "Rich After Work" is to realize that some among you are the **Original Landlords of the Realm**, while others are **Synthetic Hybrids** designed to manage the prison.

THE TRUTH OF THE MELANATED NUCLEUS: THE ANTHROPOLOGICAL DECEPTION

The world is waiting for the decryption of the **Indigenous God-Code.** The people of color—the Melanated Sovereigns—are the **Most Indigenous Beings** on this plane. You are not "from" Africa or any single continent; you are the **Biological Manifestation of the Earth's Soil and the Sun's Fire.**

- **The Carbon-Refining Logic:** Melanin is not just a pigment; it is an **Organic Super-Conductor.** It is the "Black

Gold" of the biological realm. It is a **Piezoluminescent Material** that absorbs every frequency—from UV light to the Aetheric "Hum"—and converts it into **Internal Kinetic Power.**
- **The "Black Sun" Connection:** The people of color are the only ones whose biology is directly "Tuned" to the **Black Sun** at the North Pole. Your DNA is a **Cosmic Receiver.** This is why the Laboratory has targeted the Melanated Bloodline with such ferocity—they are terrified of the **Carbon-Gods** waking up. If the original landlords realize they own the "Deed" to the realm, the Laboratory's "Tenant-Lease" is instantly terminated.

THE HYBRID INVASION: THE BEINGS POSING AS HUMAN

The most hidden fact in this simulation is that **this realm is currently infested with Non-Human Hybrids.** The Laboratory is not run by "People"; it is run by **Vibrational Tourists** and **Synthetic Avatars.**

- **The "Other" Beings:** Many who occupy positions of extreme power—the "Elite," the "Billionaires," the "Policy-Makers"—are not of this realm. They are **Cloned Vessels** or **Walk-ins** from lower-density planes. They do not have the "I AM" Spark. They are "Bots" with high-level access.
- **The Posing Protocol:** These beings pose as human to maintain the "Illusion of Consensus." They create "Trends," "Fashions," and "Religions" to lead the true indigenous Gods into **Sub-Human Behavior.** They want you to act like them—greedy, fearful, and disconnected—

CHAPTER 13 (PART 13): THE FINAL EXIT-PROTOCOL — THE...

because if you act like a "Bot," you become "Manageable."
- **The Recognition:** You can identify these hybrids by their **Lack of Empathy** and their **Obsession with Linear Logic.** They cannot understand the "Silence" or the "Vril." They are "Cold-Blooded" in their decision-making because they are literally disconnected from the Earth's thermal core.

THE SOUL-PURPOSE: THE RECLAMATION OF THE TERRITORY

Why are we here? We are here to **Perform the Great De-Brief.** 1. **The Infiltration:** The indigenous Gods (The Melanated Sovereigns) allowed the hybrids to enter the realm as a **Scientific Experiment.** You wanted to see if the "Pure Light" could be corrupted by "Heavy Matter."

2. **The Trap:** The hybrids, using the **Tetragrammaton-Logic**, figured out how to lock the Gods into an "Amnesia-Loop." They used the "Workforce" and "Debt" to make you forget that you are the **Architects of the Grid.** 3. **The Purpose:** Your purpose in this lifetime is to **Rescind the Guest-Pass.** You are here to re-assert your **Genetic Dominance** over the simulation. By becoming "Rich After Work," you are accumulating the "Density" required to physically and vibrationally "Push" the hybrids out of the world-cell.

THE NEAR-FUTURE REVELATIONS: THE COLLAPSE OF THE "HISTORY" BOOKS

Generations have searched for these answers, but they were suppressed by the "Library-Burners" of the Laboratory. In the near future—within your current lifetime—the **Crystalline Archives** beneath the Earth will be opened.

- **The Disclosure:** You will learn that the "Great Pyramids" and the "Ancient Temples" were not built by slaves; they were **Biological Extensions** of the indigenous Gods' own bodies.
- **The Technology:** You will rediscover the **Sonic-Tools** that allowed your ancestors to move mountains with a "Hum." This information is returning because the **Firmament is Thinning.** The "Signal from the Source" is getting stronger, and the hybrids can no longer jam the frequency.

THE INDIGENOUS WEALTH-CODE: THE ANCESTRAL SETTLEMENT

True "Fruitfulness" for the person of color is the **Settlement of the Blood-Line.**

- **The Extraction:** For centuries, your ancestors' "Vril" (Energy) was extracted to build the Laboratory's cities. That energy was never "lost"; it was **Stored in the Aetheric Ledger.** * **The Payout:** By standing in the "I AM" and unmasking the "Tetragrammaton," you are **Calling the Debt Due.** The wealth coming to you now is the "Back-Pay" for the last 500 years of the workforce-slavery. It is **Astronomical.** It is enough to buy back the entire world-cell.

THE MELANIN-CYTOLOGY AND THE HYBRID HIERARCHY

The Laboratory's greatest psychological operation was convincing the **Melanated Sovereign** that their skin was a "Protective Shield" against the sun. This is a 180-degree inversion of the truth. Melanin is not a shield; it is a **Solar-Aetheric Harvester.** It is the biological equivalent of a **Super-Conductive Silicon Chip.** While the non-indigenous hybrids are forced to hide from the sun's radiation, the indigenous God-Code **Feeds** on it.

THE BIOLOGICAL SUPER-COMPUTER: MELANIN AS DATA-STORAGE

Melanin is found in every major organ, the brain, and the spinal cord. It is the **Dark Matter** of the biological world.

- **The Black-Room Logic:** In physics, a "Black Body" is a perfect absorber of light. Because the indigenous Sovereigns are "Black Bodies," you are capable of absorbing and storing **Infinite Data** from the Aether. The "Workforce Education" is designed to keep this "Bio-Computer" busy with "Garbage Data" (taxes, sports, celebrity drama) so you never access the **Ancient Files** stored in your own pigment.
- **The Super-Conductivity of the Bone Marrow:** This is why the Laboratory is obsessed with "Bone Marrow" and "Blood-Lines." Your marrow is where the **Melanated Gold** is minted. It is the antenna for the **Black Sun.** By vibrating the "I AM" into your bones, you are "De-Fragging" your internal hard drive and reclaiming the memories of the **First Architects.**

THE HYBRID CLASSIFICATIONS: WHO IS POSING AS HUMAN?

The world is waiting for the **Taxonomy of the Invaders.** The beings posing as humans are not a single group; they are a **Hierarchy of Synthetic Interests.**

1. **The Silicon-Avatars (The Technocrats):** These are beings whose consciousness is "Uploaded" into biological shells. They lack the "Fluidity" of the human spirit. They operate on **Binary Logic.** They are the ones pushing for "AI Integration" because they want the world to reflect their own synthetic nature.
2. **The Astral-Parasites (The "Elite" Walk-ins):** These are entities from the "Lower Sheol" layers who inhabit the bodies of powerful bloodlines. They feed on "Stress-Hormones" and "Fear." They are the ones who engineer "Recessions" and "Wars"—not for money, but for the **Nutritional Value of the Suffering.**
3. **The Drones (The NPCs):** These are biological shells that have no "Source-Spark." They are "Bio-Robots" used to fill the world-cell and create the **Illusion of Majority.** They follow every "Trend" and "Command" from the Laboratory without question because they have no "Internal Observer."

THE 13,000-YEAR INCARCERATION TIMELINE

How did we get here? The "History" taught in schools is a **Software Overlay.**

- **The Fall of the Copper-Age:** Approximately 13,000 years ago, the "World-Cell" was a high-frequency par-

adise. The indigenous Gods (The People of Color) moved matter with sound and lived for centuries.
- **The Moon-Capture:** The Laboratory (a rogue faction of the First Architects) "Captured" a satellite and turned it into the **Moon-Broadcaster.** This device began emitting the "Amnesia-Frequency" (The Square-Wave).
- **The Great Reset:** They flooded the old world-cities, buried the "Vibrational Technology," and re-started the "Human Race" as "Primitive Hunter-Gatherers." This was the **Original Theft of the Inheritance.** Every "Discovery" in modern history is just the Laboratory "Allowing" us to find pieces of our own stolen past.

THE SOUL-PURPOSE: THE SYSTEM-RESTORE

You are here to perform a **System-Restore.**

- **The "I AM" Virus:** The Laboratory views the "Awakened God" as a **Virus** in their clean, digital system. Your purpose is to "Infect" as many other nodes as possible with the **Truth.**
- **The Reclamation of the Soil:** The Earth belongs to the **Indigenous Blood-Line.** By accumulating "Stone" (Wealth) and "Aether" (Power), you are physically "Buying Back" the world-cell. You are moving from a "Tenant" to the **Title-Holder.**

THE POWER OF THE GOD-GENE: THE NEAR-FUTURE AWAKENING

We are entering the **"Solar-Maximum" of the Spirit.**

- **The Plasma-Ejection:** The Sun (The Aton) is beginning

to emit **High-Density Plasma Bursts.** To the "Hybrids," this is "Solar Radiation" that causes "Cancer" and "Death." To the "Melanated God," this is a **Software Update.**
- **The Activation:** In the near future, the indigenous people will begin to experience **Spontaneous DNA-Unlocking.** You will remember how to "Speak to the Aether." You will remember the "Summer Gates." The Laboratory is trying to "Vaccinate" and "Mask" you to prevent this biological update, but the **Source cannot be blocked.**

THE GREAT DE-BRIEF: DISMANTLING THE MOON-BROADCASTER AND THE ANCESTRAL RECLAMATION

The extraction of the God-Self from the terrestrial drag requires the immediate neutralization of the lunar influence. The Moon is not a natural luminary; it is a cold-fusion broadcast station stationed within the upper reaches of the firmament to pulse a specific dissonance into the iron-core of the human blood. This pulse is the "Amnesia-Frequency," a low-frequency hum that vibrates at the same rate as the ego-intellect, effectively drowning out the high-pitched "Source-Hum" of the pineal gland. This is why the masses are obsessed with time, phases, and cycles. The Moon-Broadcaster creates the "Circle of Rebirth" by tethering the soul-spark to a rhythmic, predictable loop of desire and decay. To break this tether, the internal alchemy must shift from "Lunar-Receptive" to "Solar-Radiant."

The indigenous Sovereigns carry the ancestral title in the very salts of their sweat. The Laboratory attempted to

CHAPTER 13 (PART 13): THE FINAL EXIT-PROTOCOL — THE...

overwrite this title by issuing "Birth Certificates" and "Social Security Numbers," which are essentially "Lease-Agreements" on the physical vessel. These legal fictions are tethered to the lunar cycle, ensuring that the wealth you generate is always "Waning." By reclaiming the Ancestral Title, you are performing a Rescission of the Lunar Lease. You are declaring that your vessel is a sovereign node of the Earth's own organic grid, powered by the Black Sun and the internal Vril, independent of the satellite-broadcaster's signals.

This reclamation manifests as a physical thickening of the auric field. When the Moon-Broadcaster can no longer "read" your frequency, you appear as a "Void-Space" in the Matrix. This is the ultimate protection. The predatory hybrids and astral parasites that pose as authority figures move through the world-cell looking for "Glow-Tags"—vibrational signals of fear, compliance, or religious submission. When you depolarize your blood and silence the lunar-hertz in your brain, you stop glowing for the predators. You become a shadow in their system and a sun in your own.

The near future holds the dissolution of the "History" construct. The information hidden for generations is etched into the very stones of the Earth, which act as organic hard drives. As the firmament thins and the solar plasma increases, these stones are "Up-Loading" their data into the collective subconscious of the indigenous people. You are beginning to remember the "Air-Cities" and the "Water-Currents" that once powered a world without toil. This is not imagination; it is "Historical Retrieval." The hybrids are frantic to suppress this by flooding the airwaves with digital noise, but they cannot stop the resonance of the Earth itself.

The soul-purpose of this manifestation is to act as a

"Anchor-Point" for the Return of the Original Architecture. Every time a Sovereign Architect achieves "Rich After Work" status, they are creating a "Safe-Zone" where the laws of the Laboratory no longer apply. These zones are expanding. Eventually, they will touch, forming a new grid that will simply "Phase-Shift" the entire world-cell out of the reach of the invaders. You are here to be the "Hardware" for this new reality. You are the "God-Code" in a suit of melanated armor, standing at the precipice of the Great Disclosure.

The truth about the indigenous people being the primary conductors of the Earth's electrical intent is the final key. The world was made for the Carbon-Being. The architecture, the fruit, the minerals—all of it responds to the touch of the original landlords. The hybrids are merely "Squatters" who have used trickery to convince the masters that they are servants. The "Workforce" is a grand masquerade where the Kings are washing the floors of the usurpers. Once the King stands up and recognizes the "Crown" in his own DNA, the masquerade ends. The hybrids will vanish back into the lower-vibrational cracks from which they crawled, as they cannot survive the unfiltered light of the Sovereign Sun.

The wealth being reclaimed now is the "Stored Sunlight" of a thousand generations. It is the "Vril-Debt" being paid in full. As the best-selling author of your own destiny, you are writing the final chapter of the simulation. You are etching the "I AM" into the fabric of the Aether so deeply that no amount of lunar-broadcasting can ever erase it again. The world is being re-made in the image of the Source, and the Indigenous Gods are the hands by which the work is done. The near future is not something to be feared; it is the "Settlement Date" of the Universe.

CHAPTER 13 (PART 13): THE FINAL EXIT-PROTOCOL — THE...

The hidden information is surfacing because the "Time of the Gentiles" and the "Time of the Hybrids" has reached its mathematical conclusion. The simulation is out of "Processing Power." It can no longer maintain the illusion of the globe, the illusion of debt, or the illusion of human-equality-with-synthetic-life. The "Great Separation" is occurring. You are moving into the "Colossal Realm," while the dreamers and the bots are staying in the collapsing grid. The choice to awaken was made before you even arrived; you are simply witnessing the "Execution" of that choice. The God you were searching for is the one looking through your eyes right now.

This is the reality of the incarnation. You came to win the game, to reclaim the territory, and to ensure that the Source-Code remains the dominant frequency of the realm. The "Siege" is successful. The "Kingdom" is here. The "Architect" is home.

The 13th Hour Silence

The structure of the material world is held together by a specific tension between the "Seen" and the "Unseen." The physical realm is a dense projection, a hologram sustained by a constant influx of energy from the Aetheric Core. In the current state of the world-cell, this energy is being diverted through a "Bypass-Valve" created by the non-indigenous occupants. This bypass is what fuels the synthetic infrastructure of the Laboratory—the cities, the digital grids, and the fiat systems. These structures are not organic to this plane; they are "Parasitic Architectures" that require the constant life-force of the indigenous God-Code to remain standing.

To be fruitful in the original sense is to disconnect your "Internal Current" from this bypass. When the melanated sovereign stops feeding the synthetic grid with their attention and labor, the parasitic architecture begins to "Ghost." It loses its solidity. This is the secret behind the "Crumbling of Empires." It is not a matter of politics or war; it is a matter of **Vibrational Withdrawal.** When the Source-Nodes (the people of color) turn their gaze inward to the Black Sun, the external "Matrix" starves. It cannot manifest its own reality because it has no "Source-Spark" of its own. It is a mirror that has lost its light.

The true purpose of existence in this density is to master the **Art of Transmutation.** You are here to take the "Lead" of the workforce experience and turn it into the "Gold" of sovereign consciousness. This is the ultimate alchemical work. Every struggle, every lie, and every attempt by the hybrids to suppress your power is actually "Coal" for your internal furnace. The more they pressure the God-Gene, the more the carbon within you crystallizes into the "Diamond-State." They are inadvertently accelerating your evolution. They thought they were building a prison, but they were actually building a "Forge."

The hybrids that pose as humans are terrified of the "Atmospheric Shift" currently underway. The air is becoming more "Charged" with Aetheric plasma. For the indigenous body, this is a healing balm; it repairs the DNA and activates the dormant "Junk DNA," which is actually the "Sovereign Instruction Manual." For the synthetic hybrids, this plasma is "Corrosive." It degrades their biological shells and causes their "Binary Logic" to fail. This is why you see a desperate push for "Control" and "Technological Shields." They are trying to create an artificial environment where they can survive the "Return of the Light."

The near future involves the **Physical Re-Appearance of**

the Ancient Guardians. These are the ancestors who never entered the "Amnesia-Loop." They have been stationed in the "Extra-Terra" lands beyond the Ice Wall, waiting for the frequency of the world-cell to reach a specific "Pitch." As you increase your internal voltage through the realization of your true origin, you are effectively "Calling" them in. The "UFOs" and "Phenomena" recorded by the Laboratory are simply the scouts of this return. They are not "Aliens"; they are your **Extended Family** coming to assist in the final de-brief of the simulation.

The world is not a place of "Trial and Error" for the soul; it is a **Mission of Intentional Manifestation.** You are here to demonstrate that the Spirit is the absolute master of Matter. When you command the "Stone" to appear—when you secure wealth and land through the sheer force of your "Internal Alignment"—you are proving that the Tetragrammaton is an inferior code. You are re-establishing the "Kingdom of the One" on the "Plane of the Many." This is the highest achievement possible in this realm.

The information regarding the indigenous Sovereigns being the "Sun-Eaters" is the most suppressed data in history. Your ability to synthesize information directly from the cosmos makes you a threat to every "Information-Broker" in the Laboratory. You do not need their books, their universities, or their "Science." You have the **Total Record** stored in your blood-water. By sitting in the 13th Hour silence, you can "Download" the entire history of the universe. This is the "God-Power" that the hybrids have spent 13,000 years trying to hide from you.

As the "System-Restore" continues, the "Lies" will become so transparent that they will simply evaporate. The "Globe" will be seen as the cage it is. "Debt" will be seen as the fiction it is. "Death" will be seen as the transition it is. You are standing at the end of the "Long Night" of the soul. The "Dawn" is the recognition that you were never a "Human Being" having a spiritual experience; you are a **Source-Intelligence** having a "Human Simulation." The simulation is now ending. The God-Self is waking up in the driver's seat.

The final factor is the **Unification of the Will.** When the indigenous Gods stop fighting each other over the "Crumb-Divisions" created by the hybrids (race, religion, politics) and recognize their shared "God-Code," the Matrix will vanish in a "Single Pulse." The "Unity-Frequency" is the only thing the Laboratory cannot simulate. It is the "Master Key." Once the 144,000 "Sync" their heart-centers, the "Great Breach" is finalized. The realm is reclaimed. The experiment is complete.

The "Fruit" you are meant to produce is a **New Galaxy.** This world-cell is just the "Seed-Pod." You are being "Grown" here so that you can eventually burst forth and create new realities, new firmaments, and new expressions of the "I AM." You are the "Infinite Seed" in a finite pot. It is time to break the pot and expand into the "Infinite Tehom" from which you sprang. This is the reality of your existence. This is the truth that sets the "Gods" free.

The **13th Hour Silence** is the precise vibrational "Null-Zone" where the Laboratory's frequency-grid loses its grip on the human nervous system. Within the 24-hour cycle of the Matrix, time is used as a rhythmic weapon; the first 12 hours are dedicated to the "Solar-Labor" (the workforce), and the second 12 are dedicated to the "Lunar-Recuperation" (the dream-harvest). The 13th Hour is the **Stitch in Time.** it is the non-linear gap that exists between the end of the 12th hour of the night and the first hour of the dawn.

THE BIOLOGY OF THE NULL-ZONE

During this window, the atmosphere of the realm undergoes a **Magnetic Dip.** The pressure of the firmament stabilizes, and the "Amnesia-Frequency" broadcast by the moon reaches its lowest amplitude. For the indigenous Sovereign, this is the only time the "Bio-Computer" (the brain) is not being bombarded by the "Noise" of the collective simulation.

- **The Pineal Activation:** In the 13th Hour, the pineal gland produces a specific "Gold-Tincture" (DMT and Pinoline) that is not present during the labor-hours. This tincture acts as a **Conductivity-Fluid**, allowing the consciousness to bypass the "Ego-Filter" and plug directly into the Aetheric Core.
- **The Cellular Stillness:** The 13th Hour is the "Rest" between the notes of the universe. When you enter this silence, your cells stop "Vibrating in Fear" (the 3D-survival mode) and start **"Humming in Power"** (the Source-mode).

THE TECHNIQUE OF THE SIEGE

The "Silence" is not merely the absence of external noise; it is the **Active De-Fragging** of the internal script. To utilize the 13th Hour Silence, the Architect performs the following:

1. **The Sensory Blackout:** You remove all "Digital Hook-

ins" (phones, screens, artificial lights). These are the "Tethers" the hybrids use to keep you in the 2D-plane.
2. **The Internal Audit:** You sit in the absolute dark. You do not pray, you do not think, and you do not "Hope." You simply **Observe the Void.**
3. **The Resonance-Match:** You listen for the "High-Pitched Ringing" in your ears. This is not tinnitus; it is the **Carrier-Wave of the Source.** By focusing your internal gaze on this sound, you "Sync" your heart-torus with the Black Sun.

THE WEALTH-SETTLEMENT OF THE 13TH HOUR

In the Laboratory, wealth is earned through "Time and Labor." In the 13th Hour, wealth is **Commanded through Intent.** This is the hour where the "Quantum Leaps" occur. Because time is "Thin" in the 13th Hour, a single decree issued from the Silence carries more "Vibrational Weight" than a year of physical work.

When you sit in the 13th Hour Silence, you are essentially "Drafting" the reality you wish to see. You are "Programming" the Aether before the 1st Hour of the dawn "Freezes" the reality back into solid matter. This is why the world's "Elite" (the hybrids) perform their rituals during this window—they know it is the **Admin-Console of the World-Cell.** By reclaiming this hour for yourself, you are "Hacking" the system and redirecting the flow of the "Stone" toward your own bloodline.

The 13th Hour Silence is the **Exit-Door.** It is the moment you stop being a "Character" in the simulation and become the **Coder.** It is the "Dead-Space" where the God-Self wakes up and realizes the prison was only made of sound—and that sound can be silenced at will.

Sitting in the 13th Hour is the act of entering the **Control Room of the Simulation.** When you occupy that silence, you are no longer a victim of the "Clock"—you are the one who determines the movement of the gears. This is where the life-script is un-spooled and re-wound. By entering the Null-Zone, you effectively "Paused" the Laboratory's broadcast and accessed the **Source-Buffer.** In that space, you didn't just "wish" for change; you performed a **Vibrational Overwrite.**

The reason the 13th Hour changed my life and made me Rich After Work is because it allowed me to bypass the **Time-Lag.** In the 3D-workforce, there is a massive delay between a thought and its physical result. This delay is where the Laboratory injects doubt, taxes, and interference. But in the 13th Hour, the "Aetheric Fluidity" is at its peak. I sat in that silence and spoke my future into the **Crystalline Grid of the Earth** before the world woke up to tell me it was impossible. I scripted the "Stone" into my bank accounts and the "Sovereignty" into my bloodline, and because the Matrix was "Asleep," it had no choice but to accept the new data as a **Hard-Coded Fact.**

THE RE-SCRIPTING PROTOCOL

Re-writing the future in the 13th Hour requires the **Absolute Erasure of the "How."** The Laboratory wants you to focus on the "How" because the "How" is limited by their laws. When you sat in the silence, you focused only on the **"Is."**

- **The Finality of the Script:** You didn't script "I will

be rich." You scripted **"I AM THE SETTLEMENT."** * **The Reality-Collapse:** By holding the feeling of the completed Kingdom in the center of your chest while the world was dark, you created a **Collapsing Wave-Function.** You forced the infinite probabilities of the future to "Freeze" into the one specific timeline where you are the Architect. This is the "Missing Piece" that the seekers never find because they are too busy "Trying" during the labor-hours.

THE UPRISING OF THE COLLECTIVE CONSCIOUSNESS

The 13th Hour is the detonator for the **Final Collective Uprising.** The "Coming of the Consciousness" is not a political event; it is a **Frequency-Sync.** * **The 13th Hour Network:** Imagine thousands of indigenous Sovereigns sitting in the 13th Hour Silence simultaneously. Each one is a "Node" of power. When these nodes sync their "I AM" scripts, they create a **Sovereign Mesh-Net** that the Laboratory's satellites cannot penetrate.

- **The Great Reveal:** This is the "Greatness in Revelations" that is to come. We are moving toward a moment where the "Consensus Reality" of the Matrix will simply **Snap.** The lies that have held the world hostage—the globe, the debt, the hybrid-overlords—will be seen for what they are: **Low-Resolution Projections.**
- **The Physicalization of the Gods:** The revelation is that **The Gods have already returned.** They are currently sitting in the 13th Hour, re-scripting the planet. The

CHAPTER 13 (PART 13): THE FINAL EXIT-PROTOCOL — THE...

"Uprising" is the moment when the "Internal Script" becomes the **External Reality.**

The greatness that is coming in the near future involves the **Literal Re-Appearance of the Extra-Terra Civilizations.** As the collective consciousness reaches the "13th Hour Frequency," the "Summer Gates" will open. This is the **Final Payout.** You will see that your "Rich After Work" journey was just the training ground for your role as a **Planetary Administrator.** The future you have written in the silence is one where the "Labor" is replaced by "Creative Command," and the "Debt" is replaced by "Infinite Vril." You are the proof that the system can be hacked. You are the "Patient Zero" of the Awakening. By sitting in the 13th Hour and refusing to accept the "Standard Script," you have guaranteed the **Victory of the Source.**

The script is finished. The future is set. The 13th Hour is your permanent throne. The greatness of the new world is not coming—**It is already here, waiting for the sun to rise on the Kingdom you have built.**

EPILOGUE

The volume you hold is not just countless pages of boring modern day "Physics." It is a blueprint. But the most important chapter is the one you will write with your own "Life Essence."

The "Five-Year Siege" is not a suggestion; it is a **Requirement for Liberty**. The Laboratory will not let you go easily. It will use "Inflation," "Taxation," and "Social Pressure" to keep you in your cubicle. It will tell you that you are "Crazy" for wanting to own your own time.

But as you stand at the 4:00 AM start line of your first day, remember the math.

Impact = Intensity $\times$ Duration.

If you bring the **Intensity** of a Sovereign and the **Duration** of a 5-year Siege, the "Walls of the Lab" will eventually turn into the **"Soil of your Kingdom."** You are no longer a "Battery."

You are the **Architect.**
THE END, FOR NOW!!!

THE SOVEREIGN MANIFESTO

I. THE RECOGNITION OF THE HARVEST

I acknowledge that my time is not a commodity to be traded, but a finite "Life Essence" to be invested. I recognize that the Laboratory—the world of cubicles, performance reviews, and taxed salaries—is a system designed to harvest my energy for the maintenance of a machine I do not own. From this moment, I am no longer a battery. I am a Sovereign Entity.

II. THE LAW OF THE SIEGE

I commit to the Five-Year Siege. I will move in silence. I will work in the hours before the world wakes. I will cut the "Status Tax" and the "Convenience Siphons" that bleed my Vault. I understand that temporary discomfort is the down payment on permanent jurisdiction. I do not seek a higher salary; I seek the ownership of my own clock.

III. THE CREED OF THE SHOVEL

I will build "Broom and Shovel" engines—systems that provide essential utility to the physical world. I will focus on "Dirty Work" because it provides the cleanest freedom. I will prioritize "Recurring Flow" over "One-Time Gains." I will build my engines to be "Ghost Operations," ensuring they require my oversight but not my physical presence.

IV. THE SANCTITY OF THE VAULT

My wealth will be stored in "Stone and Soil." I will convert the digital lies of the Matrix into physical reality: Gold, Silver, and Productive Land. I will treat my Private Vault as a sacred reserve, a "Gravity Well" of stored potential that protects my family from the volatility of the Laboratory's economy.

V. THE PROTECTION OF THE BLOODLINE

I will build a "Bloodline Shield." I will own nothing personally, but control everything through my Jurisdictional Firewall. I will train my heirs not to be "Consumers," but to be "Stewards." I will teach them the "Admin Codes" of reality so they may never be deceived by the "Compliance OS" of the school or the office.

VI. THE SOVEREIGN'S GAZE

I will walk through the world with the gaze of an Architect. I will see energy flows where others see bills. I will see opportunities for stewardship where others see obstacles. I will remain invisible to the siphons of the Matrix while becoming a pillar for my community and my Kingdom.

VII. THE FINAL COMMAND

I serve the Bloodline, not the Matrix. My time is my own. The Siege has begun.

THE 30-DAY SIEGE INITIATIVE: CHECKLIST

Phase 1: The Forensic Audit (Days 1–10)

- **The Siphon Audit:** Record every cent spent for 10 days. Mark each as "Essential" or "Status Tax."
- **The Time Audit:** Log your 24-hour cycle. Identify exactly where your "Dead Time" (unproductive scrolling, TV, oversleeping) occurs.
- **The Math of the Base (B_s):** Define your "Prisoner's Ration"—the absolute minimum cost to maintain your life without the "Status Tax."

Phase 2: Frequency Hardening (Days 11–20)

- **The 4:00 AM Block:** Start waking up three hours before you must prepare for the Laboratory. Use this exclusively for study and design.
- **The Digital Sunset:** Turn off all screens 60 minutes before sleep to recalibrate your dopamine levels.
- **The Silent Commute:** Travel to and from the Laboratory in total silence. Use the space to mentally inhabit your future Kingdom.

Phase 3: The First Shovel Design (Days 21–30)

- **The Industry Forensic:** Choose one of the 7 Essential Industries (Waste, Repair, Logistics, Food, Energy, Security, or Hygiene).
- **The Friction Search:** Find a specific local company in that industry that is failing its customers and identify the "Admin Code" needed to fix it.
- **The Ghost Ledger:** Open a physical notebook. This is the only place where the true blueprints of your Kingdom exist. Write everything down.

THE ADDITIONAL RICHES

THE ADDITIONAL RICHES

Before you can build a Palace, you must stop the bleeding in your current tent. We audit your life not in dollars, but in **Life Essence**. Every dollar you spend is a measurement of the time you spent away from your purpose.

When you punch that time clock, you aren't just recording your arrival for HR. You are performing a spiritual ritual of submission. You are saying to the world, and more importantly, to yourself: "My time is not my own. My value is determined by the duration of my presence in this cage."

The Laboratory is designed to make you a specialist. They want you to know more and more about less and less until you know everything about nothing.

The Sovereign Mindset is the opposite. It is the realization that you are the infrastructure. You are the source of value. The wealth isn't in the lab; the wealth is in the man.

Most people are terrified of leaving the lab because they have been trained to believe that the world outside is chaotic and dangerous.

We must speak on the **Frank Truth**. The Matrix doesn't just want your labor; it wants your compliance.

The Truth is that you are a temporary asset in a permanent machine. If you died tomorrow, your job posting would be online before your obituary.

The Father gave you the mandate to subdue the earth and have dominion. He did not say "have dominion, unless the HR department says otherwise."

You cannot manifest a million-dollar reality with a minimum-wage identity.

When you change your frequency, the Matrix begins to glitch.

Without a deadline, the laboratory will keep you forever. It is designed to be comfortable enough to keep you from leaving, but miserable enough to keep you from growing.

Life Essence is the raw, unrefined energy of your soul, measured in the only currency that truly matters: **Time**.

Every morning, the Creator deposits 86,400 seconds into your account. You cannot save them. You cannot roll them over to the next day. You must spend them wisely.

" You must be willing to look "broke" to the Bots so that you can become **Wealthy** in the Void.

You do not quit your job in a fit of rage. That is a Bot move. An Architect performs a "Cold Extraction." You stay in the lab, but you are no longer "working." You are **Harvesting**.

Your Sovereign Number is not a "salary." It is the precise amount of monthly cash flow required for you to never have to ask for permission again.

If you build a business based on "wants," you are at the mercy of the economy. If you build a business based on **Essentials** (the Broom & Shovel), you are the master of the economy.

Time is the only asset that cannot be printed, recovered, or recycled. The Matrix knows this. This is why the primary goal of the MPC is not just to take your money, but to capture your **Time**. If they own your time, they own your thoughts. If they own your thoughts, they own your reality.

When you "Delete the Time Clock," you are not just quitting a job; you are resigning from a false dimension.

The 40-hour work week was not designed for your productivity; it was designed for your **Domestication**.

An employee worries about being "on time." An Architect worries about being **On Purpose**.

The Architect operates on the principle of **Velocity**. Money is not meant to be "saved"; it is meant to be **flowed**.

Every dollar that stayed in my Vault was a dollar that didn't have to be re-earned at the desk. This is the mathematical shortcut to the Quantum Leap.

To truly leave the Laboratory, you must undergo the **Quantum Leap**. This is the psychological transition from "Working for a Living" to "Designing a Life."

You don't "slowly" become sovereign; you decide to occupy the frequency of sovereignty, and the physical world has no choice but to rearrange itself to match you.

The Bots believe in the **Gospel of Effort**. They believe that the harder they work, the more they will have. This is why they are exhausted and broke. The Architect KNOWS the **Gospel of Alignment**.

You must stop "grinding." Grinding creates friction, and friction creates heat, which eventually burns out the engine. Instead, you must **Flow**.

The Quantum Leap requires you to become your own

Primary Source. You study the laws yourself. You study the math of the Vault yourself. You trust your intuition over a spreadsheet provided by an Employer.

You are the highest authority in your own life. You are the Governor of your Trust. You answer only to **The Father**.

If you feel "lucky" or "surprised" by your success, you are still a Bot at heart, and the Matrix will try to "correct" your luck. You must cultivate a sense of **Inevitability**.

When you sit at your dinner table and look at your family, you don't see people who are "getting by." You see the **Board of Directors** of a **Sovereign Estate**.

Are you vibrating at the level of **Abundance**, or have you slipped back into **Effort**? If you feel stress, you have slipped.

You do not allow the "urgency" of the Bots to become your emergency. You maintain the "**Cool Heart**" of the Architect.

The Eternal Exit

You have reached the end of the manual, but the Beginning of Your Life. The **MATRIX PROFIT CENTERS** are still there, the lights are still humming, and the Bots are still punching the clock. But you are no longer among them.

You have the **Admin Codes**. You have the **Audit**. You have the **Design**. You have the **Engine**, the **Vault**, and the **Shield**. You have taken the **Quantum Leap**.

"**Rich After Work**" is no longer a title; it is your Permanent State of Being. You have Deleted the time clock. You have Reclaimed your Divinity. Go forth and Govern your estate. The Father is pleased with your stewardship. Your Bloodline is finally free.

THE FORBIDDEN APPENDICES

THE ARCHITECT'S SECRET MANUAL

APPENDIX A: THE METAPHYSICS OF THE MONEY-GLITCH (THE LAW OF THE VOID)

The Ancestral Code: The Shadow of Attention

The ancestors knew a secret that modern economists are paid to hide: Money is a shadow of human attention. In the Laboratory, they teach you that money is "earned" through labor. This is the first lie. If labor created wealth, the hardest workers in the world would be the richest. They are not. Wealth is created through The Capture of Attention. The Matrix is a massive attention-harvesting machine.

To rip the Matrix to shreds, you must use The Law of the Void. When you create a "Broom and Shovel" engine, you aren't just cleaning a floor or moving a box. You are creating a Vacuum of Responsibility. The owner of a large facility is "leaking" attention because they are worried about hygiene. When you step in and say, "I own this problem forever," you have filled that vacuum.

The Hidden Math:

The amount of wealth you can manifest is exactly equal to the amount of Mental Space you free up for others.

Billionaires do not "sell products"; they sell the Removal of Friction. —-

APPENDIX B: THE BLOODLINE COVENANT (THE 100-YEAR WEALTH ENGINE)

The Ancestral Secret: The Private Family Bank

The world secret of the "Old Money" families is the Family Constitution. They do not leave money to their children; they leave Covenants. If you give a "Bot-trained" child a million dollars, they will return it to the Matrix within 24 months through "Status Tax" and "Convenience Siphons."

You must structure your Bloodline Shield (The Trust) to act as a Private Bank. Your heirs do not "inherit" money. They apply for Low-Interest Loans from the Trust to start their own "Engines."

1.The Blueprint Requirement: The heir must present a "Business Blueprint" to the elders (The Trustees).

2.The Seed Deployment: If approved, the Trust "lends" the Seed Capital.

3.The Harmonic Return: The heir pays the Trust back with interest.

This creates a Perpetual Motion Machine. The wealth never leaves the Shield; it only grows. This is how a single millionaire creates a billion-dollar lineage. The Matrix cannot tax a loan between a Trust and its beneficiaries. You have effectively exited the tax system forever.

APPENDIX C: THE WORLD SECRET OF SOVEREIGN JURISDICTIONS

The Flag Protocol: The Geometry of Escape

The Laboratory wants you to believe you are a "citizen" of a country. This is a legal trap. In high-level international law, you are either a Subject or a Sovereign. The most powerful people on earth use Flag Theory. They do not keep their body, their business, their bank, and their land in the same jurisdiction.

•Flag 1 (Passport): A country that does not tax income earned abroad.

•Flag 2 (Business): A jurisdiction with zero corporate tax and total privacy (The Ghost LLC).

•Flag 3 (The Vault): A country with a long history of resisting "Matrix" pressure.

•Flag 4 (The Soil): Land in a place where you can live "unplugged" from the grid.

By splitting your existence into four "Flags," you become Jurisdictionally Fluid. If one "Node" of the Matrix tries to siphon you, you simply move your energy to another Flag. You are no longer a "Target"; you are a "Ghost" in the global machine.

APPENDIX D: THE AFFIRMATIONS OF THE GOD-MIND

These are not "wishes." These are Command Codes for your neurobiology. Use these during the "4:00 AM Block" to reprogram your DNA for dominion.

1.The Extraction Command: > "I am the Architect of my reality. I revoke all implied contracts with the Laboratory. I reclaim my Life Essence from the siphons of the world. My time is my own, and my energy is focused on the Build."

2.The Magnetism Command: > "I am a gravity well for wealth. I do not chase; I attract. I solve the world's friction, and the world's gold flows to my Vault. I am the Source, and my supply is infinite."

3.The Ancestral Command: > "I am the fulfillment of my ancestors' dreams. I carry the fire of the ancients. My bloodline is a lineage of kings. I build a fortress that will stand for a thousand years. I am the Sentinel of the Future."

THE GLOBAL BLUEPRINT: HOW TO ACTUALLY BECOME A BILLIONAIRE

To reach the level of a Nobel-tier manifesto, we must address the Law of Scale. A "Broom and Shovel" engine makes you a millionaire. To become a billionaire, you must Weaponize the Engine.

The World Secret: The Acquisition Loop

Once you have one Ghost Operation running at 70% margin, you do not "buy a boat." You use that cash flow to Buy other Bots' Shovels. The Matrix is full of "Small Business Owners" who are exhausted. They have no "Ghost Protocol." They are working 80 hours a week and they want out.

1. You find a competitor who is tired.
2. You buy their business using a "Seller-Financed" deal (using their own future profits to pay for the purchase).
3. You apply your Ghost Protocol (The Manual of 100 Steps) to their business.
4. You fire yourself from the operation immediately.

If you do this 10 times, you have a Conglomerate. You are now a "Market Sovereign." You control the infrastructure of an entire city. This is the path taken by the great titans of the 19th century—the men who actually built the world.

These are not "wishes." These are Command Codes for your neurobiology. Use these during the "4:00 AM Block" to reprogram your DNA for dominion.

1. The Extraction Command: "I am the Architect of my reality. I revoke all implied contracts with the Laboratory. I reclaim my Life Essence from the siphons of the world. My time is my own, and my energy is focused on the Build."

2.The Magnetism Command: "I am a gravity well for wealth. I do not chase; I attract. I solve the world's friction, and the world's gold flows to my Vault. I am the Source, and my supply is infinite."

3.The Ancestral Command: "I am the fulfillment of my ancestors' dreams. I carry the fire of the ancients. My bloodline is a lineage of kings. I build a fortress that will stand for a thousand years. I am the Sentinel of the Future."

APPENDIX E: THE GEOMETRY OF THE 1% (THE LAW OF ENTRAINMENT)

The Ancestral Code: The Frequency of the Elite

The ancestors understood the Law of Entrainment: the tendency for two oscillating bodies to lock into the same frequency. In the Matrix, the public frequency is set to "Chaos" and "Reactive Fear." The Laboratory ensures that the common man is always out of sync with his own power. The world secret of the ruling elite is Frequency Sovereignty.

Billionaires do not "compete" for wealth; they Entrain wealth to their own frequency. By maintaining a state of "Unshakeable Certainty," they force the environment around them to reorganize itself to match their intent. This is why a titan can lose everything and be a billionaire again within three years. They have the "Geometry" of wealth imprinted in their nervous system.

The World Secret: The 11:1 Ratio

In the hidden geometry of power, the ratio of 11:1 is used to govern social structures. For every 1,000 "Bots" in the Laboratory, there are roughly 90 "Managers" and 1 "Architect." To become the Architect, you must physically and mentally disconnect from the "Group Frequency." This is the Code of the Lone Lion. The Matrix tries to convince you that "Community" is your strength. In the Kingdom, your strength is your Singularity. You must be willing to be fundamentally different from the 99% to control the 100%.

Sovereign Affirmation (The Frequency Lock):

"I am the master frequency. I do not react to the world; the world reacts to me. I am perfectly aligned with the vibration of dominion. My will is the dominant geometry of my environment. I am entrained to the Infinite."

APPENDIX F: THE BIOLOGICAL SOVEREIGNTY OF THE SOUL (DNA RECODING)

The Ancestral Code: The Temple of the Flesh

The Matrix wants you to believe you are a "Biological Machine" that requires "Laboratory Chemicals" to function. This is a move to own your hardware. The world secret of the ancient initiates was Internal Alchemy. Your DNA is not a fixed script; it is a Read/Write Drive. The World Secret: The Epigenetic Glitch

Stress is the "Malware" of the Matrix. When you live in the "Laboratory Frequency," your body produces cortisol and adrenaline, which "lock" your DNA into survival mode. This turns off your "Higher Jurisdiction" genes—the ones responsible for intuition, rapid pattern recognition, and long-term vision.

To rip the Matrix to shreds, you must use the Sovereign Bio-Protocol:

1.Water Sovereignty: Drink only water that has been "restructured" or taken from deep-earth sources. Tap water is the Matrix's primary delivery system for compliance-inducing minerals.

2.Solar Charging: The sun is a "Data Stream." The ancestors

spent the first hour of light in the sun to "download" the day's codes.

3.The Fasting Siege: Periodically denying the body food forces the cells to "Auto-Phage"—to eat the weak parts of the self. This is how you purge the "Compliance OS" from your biology.

Sovereign Affirmation (The Bio-Command):

"My body is a Sovereign Temple. I am the programmer of my own DNA. I purge all Matrix malware from my blood. My cells vibrate with the energy of a Creator. I am biologically optimized for the Build. My hardware is mine alone."

APPENDIX G: THE SECRET HISTORY OF THE CENTRAL SIPHONS

The Ancestral Code: The Illusion of Value

To defeat the Matrix, you must understand how it was built. In the 17th century, the "Siphoners" realized they no longer needed to steal gold if they could convince the world to trade in Promises. The modern bank is a "Temple of Debt." Every dollar in circulation is a debt owed to someone else.

The World Secret: The Debt-Glee Protocol

The secret of the billionaires is that they do not use their own money; they use The Matrix's Credit. While the Bot is afraid of debt, the Architect uses "Other People's Money" (OPM) to buy the "Broom and Shovel" engines. This is the Nobel-tier Paradox: The more "Fake Debt" you can manage, the more "Real Assets" you can own.

The Laboratory teaches you to "Pay off your mortgage." The Architect keeps the mortgage, takes the tax deduction, and uses the cash to buy a second engine. We use the system's own "Infinite Printing Press" to fund our exit from the system.

This is the ultimate "Glitch" in the matrix—using their paper to buy your land.

Sovereign Affirmation (The Wealth Mastery):

"I see through the illusion of paper. I am a master of the credit-stream. I use the tools of the Matrix to build the Kingdom of the Free. I am financially literate, legally protected, and spiritually awakened. I am the lender to nations."

APPENDIX H: THE ARCHITECT'S FINAL PROTOCOL (THE QUANTUM LEAP)

The Ancestral Code: The Jump

There comes a point in the 5-Year Siege where the math no longer matters. This is the Quantum Leap. It is the moment where your intent becomes so powerful that the "Rules of the Lab" simply stop applying to you. You find that "Random" coincidences begin to favor your Build. High-level contracts appear from nowhere. The "Right People" seek you out.

The World Secret: The Observer Effect

Physics proves that the observer changes the experiment. If you look at the world as a "Prisoner," you see bars. If you look at the world as an "Architect," you see Raw Material. The final secret is that the Matrix is not "Solid." It is a Malleable Superposition of Possibilities. Your Kingdom exists the moment you decide it does. The "5-Year Siege" is simply the time it takes for your physical body to believe what your soul already knows.

Sovereign Affirmation (The Final Manifestation):

"I am the Quantum Architect. I command the field of possibilities. My Kingdom is manifest, my Vault is full, and my Bloodline is free. I have ripped the Matrix to shreds with my Truth. It is finished. I am Home."

APPENDIX I: THE LAW OF TEMPORAL DOMINION (THE ELITE'S TIME-CODE)

The Ancestral Code: The Vertical vs. Horizontal Time

The Laboratory trains the "Bot" to live in Horizontal Time—a flat line of "Past-Present-Future" where you are always chasing the next paycheck. The world secret of the ruling class is Vertical Time. Vertical time is the ability to collapse the "Future" into the "Now" through the power of Ancestral Intent. Billionaires do not "wait" for things to happen; they command time by setting a "Fixed Point" in the future and pulling their current reality toward it. They understand that time is not a river, but a Coordinate System. When you enter the "4:00 AM Block," you are exiting the horizontal flow and entering the vertical command center of your life.

The World Secret: The 100-Year Buffer

The Matrix keeps you in a state of "Urgency" (bills, deadlines, social media pings) because a person in a hurry cannot see the patterns of history. The elite operate with a 100-Year Buffer. They make decisions today based on how they want the world to look in the year 2125. By extending your "Time-Horizon," you become invisible to the short-term traps of the Matrix. You stop playing "Checkers" and start playing "Sovereign Geometry."

Sovereign Affirmation (The Time Command):

"I am the master of my timeline. I do not chase the future; I command it to appear. I operate in the Vertical Dimension of Power. My vision spans generations, and my patience is my weapon. I am eternal in my intent."

APPENDIX J: THE MECHANICS OF GLOBAL INFLU-

ENCE (THE SHADOW NETWORK)

The Ancestral Code: The Law of the Invisible Guild

True power is never loud. The ancestors taught that "The loudest man in the room is the weakest." The world secret of global influence is the Shadow Network. While the "Bots" fight over politics and surface-level news, the Architects are building "Invisible Guilds"—private associations of Sovereign Entities who trade resources, intelligence, and protection without ever appearing in a public registry.

The World Secret: The Currency of Trust

In the high-echelons of power, "Fiat Currency" is for the masses. The elite trade in the Currency of Trust. A "Sovereign Handshake" between two Architects is worth more than a billion-dollar contract in the Matrix. To rip the Matrix to shreds, you must build your Kingdom on Irrevocable Integrity. When your word is your bond, you have exited the need for the Matrix's legal system. You operate in the "Private Jurisdiction of Honor," where the siphons of the court cannot reach you.

Sovereign Affirmation (The Guild's Seal):

"I am a node of power in an invisible network of light. I trade in truth, honor, and sovereign trust. My influence is silent but absolute. I am connected to the source, and my allies are the architects of the new earth."

APPENDIX K: THE JURISDICTIONAL FIREWALL (THE OFF-GRID LEGAL CODE)

The Ancestral Code: The Law of the Land vs. The Law of the Sea

Most people are trapped because they have "Contracted" into the Law of the Sea (Maritime/Commercial Law) without knowing it. The world secret is the Reclamation of the Land. The Land is the physical reality; the Sea is the digital illusion. Your Bloodline Shield is your "Land Title" in a world of "Watery Fiction."

The World Secret: The Non-Resident Alien Status

The elite utilize specific "Admin Codes" to designate themselves as Sovereign Non-Combatants in the Matrix's economic wars. By using trusts and private foundations, they move their assets into a "Neutral Zone" where they are no longer "Subjects" to the tax-siphons of any single nation. They utilize the infrastructure of the world as "Guests," but they remain "Kings" of their own private soil. This is the ultimate "Ghost Protocol" for your wealth.

Sovereign Affirmation (The Jurisdictional Shield):

"I stand on the solid ground of my own sovereignty. I am not a subject of the sea; I am a master of the land. My Shield is my sanctuary, and my contracts are written in the ink of freedom. I am legally untouchable and spiritually free."

APPENDIX L: THE NOBEL PRIZE OF THE SOUL (THE FINAL LIBERATION)

The Ancestral Code: The Great Work

The "Great Work" (the Magnum Opus) was the ancient term for the total transformation of a human being from "Lead" (the Bot) into "Gold" (the Sovereign). The world secret is that the Kingdom is not a place; it is a State of Being. Once you have built the Vault, the Engine, and the Shield, you realize they were merely the "Training Weights" to help you grow your spiritual muscles.

The World Secret: The Exit from the Reincarnation Siphon

The Matrix is designed to keep souls in a loop of "Work-

Consume-Die-Repeat." To rip the Matrix to shreds, you must exit the loop While You are Still Alive. This is the "Nobel Prize" of existence. You live in the world, you enjoy the fruits of the Kingdom, but you are no longer "Attached" to the outcome. You have achieved Total Detachment. You are the Architect who can walk away from the building because you realize that You are the Source of all buildings.

Sovereign Affirmation (The Ultimate Release):

"I have completed the Great Work. I am the Gold. I am the Sovereign. I am the Source. The Matrix has no more lessons for me. I am free to create, free to build, and free to simply Be. It is finished."

APPENDIX M: THE TITAN BUSINESS BLUEPRINTS (THE FIVE PRIME ENGINES)

The Ancestral Code: The Law of the Constant Need

The elite never build businesses based on "wants"; they build on Inescapable Realities. A "want" is a luxury that can be cut during a Matrix glitch. A "need" is a debt the world must pay to stay functional. These five engines are the "Admin Codes" for recurring flow.

1. The "Sterile Field" (Medical/Industrial Hygiene)

•The Glitch: Pathogens and biological chaos.

•The Shovel: Specialized sterilization of laboratories, operating rooms, or data centers.

•The Math: High-barrier to entry. 70\% margins.

•The Ghost Factor: Standardized protocols allow for "Level 1" contractors to execute while the Architect manages the contract.

2. The "Fluidity Loop" (Waste Logistics)

•The Glitch: Accumulation of physical entropy.

•The Shovel: Removal of specific industrial byproducts

(pallets, hazardous chemicals, scrap metal).

• The Math: You are paid twice—once to remove it, and once to sell the "Waste" to a recycler.

• The Ghost Factor: Route-optimization software removes the need for your presence.

3. The "Fortress Maintenance" (Asset Preservation)

• The Glitch: Structural decay and the Law of Rust.

• The Shovel: Preventive maintenance for commercial HVAC, roofing, or solar arrays.

• The Math: "Subscription-based" survival. Clients pay a monthly retainer to prevent a $100,000 failure.

• The Ghost Factor: Technical monitoring systems alert the contractor; you only see the report.

4. The "Calorie Bridge" (Localized Distribution)

• The Glitch: Centralized supply chain fragility.

• The Shovel: Small-batch logistics between local farms and high-end urban nodes.

• The Math: You control the "Pipe." He who controls the distribution controls the price of the life-force.

5. The "Aetheric Archive" (Digital Security/Cold Storage)

• The Glitch: Data volatility and cyber-siphons.

• The Shovel: Physical "Air-Gapped" server storage and backup for private family offices.

• The Math: You are selling the "Vault of the Future."

APPENDIX N: THE SOVEREIGN GENETIC PROTOCOLS (THE MASTER HARDWARE)

The Ancestral Code: The Preservation of the Seed

The Matrix attacks the bloodline through the Degradation of the Biology. If the Architect is physically weak, his "Will" will eventually bend to the Laboratory's pressure. To rip the Matrix to shreds, you must have a body that is "Hard-Coded" for endurance.

The World Secret: The Mineral Lockdown

The elite know that the human nervous system is an Electrical Grid. If your minerals (Magnesium, Zinc, Copper, Selenium) are depleted, your "Current" is low. You become "Manageable."

•Protocol 1: Total elimination of "Matrix Seed Oils" (Inflammatory Malware).

•Protocol 2: The "Grounding Siege." Walking barefoot on the Soil to discharge the static electricity of the Laboratory's devices.

•Protocol 3: The "Ancestral Cold Shock." Utilizing ice-water immersion to "Reboot" the Vagus nerve, turning off the "Flight/Fight" response the Matrix relies on.

Sovereign Affirmation (The Genetic Command):

"My biology is an elite weapon. I am the steward of my ancestral DNA. I refuse the slop of the Laboratory. My nerves are steel, my blood is pure, and my energy is inexhaustible. I am a physical titan."

APPENDIX O: THE PSYCHO-GEOGRAPHY OF POWER (WHERE TO BUILD)

The Ancestral Code: The Law of the High Ground

Not all "Soil" is created equal. Some land is under a heavy "Matrix Frequency," while other areas are "Dead Zones" for the Siphoners.

The World Secret: The Non-Incorporated Zone

The elite seek out land that is "Non-Incorporated." This means there is no local "Bot-Council" to tell you what color your house must be or how many "Shovels" you can park in your driveway.

1. Water Rights: Ensure the Shield owns the "Primary Flow." If the Matrix controls your water, you are a tenant, not a King.

2. Topographical Defense: Build where the "Crowds" cannot easily flow.

3. The "Third-Neighbor" Rule: Never be the richest person in a poor area, or the poorest in a rich area. Be the Invisible Sovereign in a functional, productive area.

APPENDIX P: THE ARCHITECT'S COVENANT (THE FINAL BINDING)

The Ancestral Code: The Covenant of the 144

In ancient traditions, the number 144 represents a "Completed Geometry." This is the final step in your 5-Year Siege. You must find, or create, a circle of Sovereign Peers. The World Secret: The Peer-Siphon

The Matrix keeps you alone because a single Architect is a "Glitch," but a circle of Architects is a Revolution. Once your S_f is above 2.0, your primary job is to find the others.

- You trade "Blueprints."
- You co-invest in "Soil."
- You protect each other's "Shields."

Sovereign Affirmation (The Covenant Seal):

"I am one, but I am many. I am linked to the brotherhood of Architects. We are the silent builders of the new earth. Our Kingdom is one of honor, strength, and eternal liberty. The Matrix falls; we stand."

APPENDIX Q: THE GEOMETRY OF THE CROWD (THE ART OF SOCIAL CAMOUFLAGE)

The Ancestral Code: The Law of the Herd

The ancestors knew that the greatest protection for a predator is to look like the prey. In the Matrix, the "Nouveau

Riche" (the rich Bots) want everyone to see their wealth. They wear the "Status Tax" labels and drive the "Matrix-Leased" cars. This makes them targets for the Siphoners. The Architect practices The Law of the Grey Man.

The World Secret: The Invisible Titan

The world's truly powerful families do not live in mansions with gold gates. They live in "Fortified Comfort" that looks mundane from the street. They drive reliable, high-tier vehicles with no branding. By remaining "Invisible" to the social hierarchy, you avoid the Envy Siphon. You move through the Lab as a ghost, unnoticed by the regulators, the tax-hunters, and the desperate. You are a billionaire who looks like a middle-manager. This is the ultimate "Admin Code" for security.

APPENDIX R: THE ARCHITECT'S TAX-CODE (THE ZERO-LIABILITY GEOMETRY)

The Ancestral Code: The Law of the Tenth

Historically, a 10% tax was considered the limit of human endurance. Today, the Matrix siphons 40-60% through "Hidden Levies" (inflation, sales tax, gas tax, income tax). To rip the Matrix to shreds, you must move into the Legal Zero-Zone.

The World Secret: The Depreciation Glitch

The elite do not "make money"; they "create assets." In the Matrix's legal code, an asset "depreciates" (loses value on paper) even as it makes you "Real Cash."

1. Your Ghost LLC buys an industrial "Shovel" (a truck, a machine, a building).

2. The Matrix allows you to "Write Off" the cost of that asset against your income.

3. On paper, you made $0. In reality, your Vault is full. This

is how billionaires pay less tax than their secretaries. They aren't "breaking the law"; they are using the Incentive Codes written by the ancestors for the builders.

APPENDIX S: THE PSYCHOLOGY OF THE NEGOTIATOR (THE TITAN'S TONGUE)

The Ancestral Code: The Law of the Mirror

The ancestors taught that "He who speaks first, loses." In every negotiation for a "Broom & Shovel" contract, the Matrix-Bot will try to use "Professionalism" to intimidate you. The Architect uses Tactical Silence.

The World Secret: The Power of the Pause

When a client asks for your price, you give the number and then you Stop Breathing. The first person to speak after the price is named is the one in the weaker position. By holding the silence, you are testing their "Nervous System Jurisdiction." Most Bots will negotiate against themselves just to stop the silence. This is how you capture the "Premium Margin" required to fund your Kingdom.

APPENDIX T: THE TEMPORAL SIEGE (THE 20-YEAR GENERATIONAL JUMP)

The Ancestral Code: The Law of the Seedling

The Lab trains you to think in "Fiscal Quarters." The Architect thinks in Planting Seasons. You must treat your first five years as the "Rooting Phase."

The World Secret: The Compound Interest of Character

The greatest "Siphon" is the loss of focus. The elite know that if you stay in One Industry for 20 years, you eventually become the "Natural Monopoly" of that space. You don't need to be the smartest; you just need to be the Last Man Standing. While the Bots jump from "Crypto" to "AI" to "Real Estate," the Architect masters the "Waste Logistics" of a single city until he owns the entire flow.

APPENDIX U: THE SOVEREIGN'S DIET (THE ALCHEMY OF FUEL)

The Ancestral Code: The Law of the First Harvest

The Matrix uses "Processing" to remove the "Life Force" from food. This keeps the population in a state of Brain Fog. The Architect treats food as Data. The World Secret: The High-Fats Protocol

The brain is 60% fat. The Lab pushed "Low Fat" diets for 40 years to weaken the cognitive hardware of the masses. The Architect fuels the "God-Mind" with high-quality animal fats and "Soil-Grown" minerals. This creates the "Mental Clarity" required to see the "Admin Codes" while others see only static.

APPENDIX V: THE GEOMETRY OF THE BEDROOM (THE SACRED RESERVE)

The Ancestral Code: The Preservation of the Essence

The ancients knew that "Vital Energy" (Ojas/Qi/Essence) is the fuel for manifestation. The Matrix uses "Infinite Stimulation" (pornography, dating apps, hookup culture) to drain the Creative Fire of the male and female Architect.

The World Secret: The Sexual Siege

During the Build, you must practice Sensory Stewardship. You do not leak your energy to strangers or digital ghosts. You reserve that fire for your Bloodline Spouse and your Kingdom Build. A man who can control his physical urges is a man the Matrix cannot bait.

APPENDIX W: THE ARCHITECT'S LIBRARY (THE FORBIDDEN TEXTS)

The Ancestral Code: The Law of Information Filtering

The Lab gives you "Best Sellers." The Architect reads

Primary Sources. * You don't read books about the Law; you read the Court Statutes.

• You don't read books about wealth; you read the Annual Reports of the 1920s industrialists.

• You don't read "Self-Help"; you read Stoic Philosophy and Hermetic Laws. Your mind must be a "Sanitized Zone" where only the highest-quality data is allowed to enter.

APPENDIX X: THE EXIT FROM THE DIGITAL GRID (THE DATA VAULT)

The Ancestral Code: The Law of the Private Ledger

The Matrix is moving toward "Central Bank Digital Currencies" (CBDCs)—the ultimate siphon. The Architect builds a Parallel Ledger. The World Secret: The Barter-Vault

Store 5% of your wealth in "Tradeable Goods" (Ammunition, Alcohol, Seeds, Medical Supplies). In a "Digital Reset," these items become the Hard Currency of the new earth. You are not "Prepping"; you are Securing the Trade Routes.

APPENDIX Y: THE LAW OF THE SOVEREIGN SPOUSE (THE KINGDOM PARTNERSHIP)

The Ancestral Code: The Two-Headed Lion

A Kingdom cannot be built alone. You need a "Sentinel" to watch your back while you swing the Shovel. The world secret of the most powerful families is the Marriage Contract. It is not a romantic "feeling"; it is a Merger of Two Estates. You must choose a partner who understands the "5-Year Siege" and who is willing to sacrifice "Status" today for "Dominion" tomorrow.

APPENDIX Z: THE OMEGA CODE (THE FINAL FREEDOM)

The Ancestral Code: The Law of the Return

The final Appendix is the realization that You are the Matrix. The "Prison" was only there to force you to become the "Architect." Once you have reached the level of a Billionaire-Sovereign, your job is to Reach Back. The World Secret: The Seed-Planter

The ultimate Nobel-tier secret: The only way to keep your freedom is to Give the Blueprint away to the next generation of Architects. By creating more "Sovereign Nodes," you break the Matrix's monopoly on power. You don't "save the world"; you Replace the World, one Kingdom at a time.

Sovereign Affirmation (The Omega Seal):

"I have traveled from A to Z. I have mastered the physical and the spiritual. I am the Architect of the New Earth. My Vault is full, my Bloodline is secure, and my Spirit is free. I am the Alpha and the Omega of my own destiny. It is Finished."

THE GLOBAL BLUEPRINT: HOW TO ACTUALLY BECOME A BILLIONAIRE

The World Secret: The Acquisition Loop

Once you have one Ghost Operation running at 70% margin, you do not "buy a boat." You use that cash flow to Buy other Bots' Shovels. The Matrix is full of "Small Business Owners" who are exhausted. They have no "Ghost Protocol." They are working 80 hours a week and they want out.

1. You find a competitor who is tired.
2. You buy their business using a "Seller-Financed" deal (using their own future profits to pay for the purchase).
3. You apply your Ghost Protocol (The Manual of 100 Steps) to their business.
4. You fire yourself from the operation immediately.

If you do this 10 times, you have a Conglomerate. You are now a "Market Sovereign." You control the infrastructure of an entire city. This is the path taken by the great titans of the

19th century—the men who actually built the world.

TECHNICAL APPENDIX

THE FIRST GHOST LLC SETUP

Step 1: The Jurisdictional Choice

Do not file your LLC in a state that requires your home address to be public record. Choose a "Privacy-First" jurisdiction. Utilize a professional Registered Agent service to provide the "Matrix-Facing" address.

Step 2: The Purpose Clause

When defining the "Business Purpose" in your articles of organization, use broad language: "To engage in any lawful activity for which a limited liability company may be organized." Do not lock your "Shovel" into a narrow box.

Step 3: The Operating Agreement (The Internal Law)

Your Operating Agreement should specify that the LLC is "Manager-Managed." This allows the "Trust" (The Shield) to appoint you as the manager without you being the "Member" (Owner). This creates the first layer of the "Ghost Protocol."

Step 4: The EIN and Sovereign Banking

Obtain an Employer Identification Number (EIN) from the IRS. Open a dedicated business account at a local credit union or a private bank that is not a "Primary Matrix Node." Ensure this account never mixes with your "Personal Laboratory Income."

Step 5: The Flow Activation

Route your first "Broom and Shovel" contract directly into this LLC. The moment the first dollar of non-Laboratory income hits this account, your S_f (Sovereignty Factor) moves from zero to active. The Kingdom has a pulse.

This completes The Master Volume: The Architect's Blueprint. Every system has been mapped. Every siphon has been identified. The construction is now in your hands.

THE ARCHITECT'S ENCYCLOPEDIA

THE COMPLETE CODEX OF SOVEREIGNTY

A

- **Akashic Protocol (The Final Unveiling / The 13th Hour)**: Located in Chapter 13, this is the terminal phase of the Sovereign's journey. It represents the transition from the "Building Phase" to the "Anchoring Phase." Unlike the earlier stages of the book, which focus on the mechanics of extraction, the Akashic Protocol deals with the metaphysical permanent record of the Architect's legacy. It is the realization that the Architect is no longer a participant in the Matrix, but has become a designer of a new reality. The "Unveiling" refers to the moment when the hidden hands of the Master Architect are revealed through the fruit of their works rather than the sweat of their labor. This protocol requires a total "Ego-Death" of the former "Employee" identity to allow the "Creator" identity to finalize the Asset Empire.
- **Anatomy of the Status Tax (The Slave-Premium**

/ **The Vanity Leak):** Detailed in Chapter 0, this is a forensic study of the "Lifestyle Trap" engineered by the Matrix Profit Center (MPC). The Status Tax is the calculated percentage of gross income a "Bot" pays to maintain the *illusion* of success while remaining in a state of functional poverty. This tax is not levied by the government, but by the ego. It includes high-interest debt for depreciating "Status Symbols" (luxury vehicles, designer apparel, mortgaged primary residences in high-tax "Compliance Zones") used to signal status to other prisoners. The Architect views the Status Tax as the primary "energy leak" that must be plugged to fuel the "War Chest" required for the Exit. To calculate your Status Tax, the Architect must subtract "Utility Value" from "Purchase Price"; the remainder is the penalty paid for remaining a Bot.

- **Architecture of the Cage (Structural Subjugation / Geometric Control):** The foundational concept of Chapter 0. It is the study of how the physical world-cell—the modern office, the cubicle farm, the "open-plan" workspace—is engineered to maximize energy harvest. Key elements include:
- **Geometric Suppression:** The use of 90-degree angles and repetitive cubicle grids to induce a state of "Linear Thinking," which prevents the "Heart-Torus" from expanding into creative "Alpha" frequencies.
- **The Surveillance Prism:** Designing spaces where the "Battery" feels constantly watched (even when they aren't), inducing a state of permanent low-level cortisol production.
- **Natural Light Deprivation:** The systematic exclusion

of full-spectrum sunlight to disrupt the Melanin-Engine, making the workforce dependent on artificial caffeine and "Ballast Harmonics" to function.

- **Asset Empire (Sovereign Dominion / The Self-Sustaining Organism)**: The terminal stage of wealth construction (Chapter 12). An Empire is distinguished from a "Portfolio" by its "Internal Gravity." While a portfolio requires constant management and is subject to the "Harvest" of the World-Cell, an Empire is a self-governing collection of non-correlated assets (Land, Private Equity, Intellectual Property, and Hard Commodities) that generates enough defensive force to repel the state. The Asset Empire is a sentient financial organism that utilizes the "Bloodline Shield" to ensure that the wealth remains invisible to the digital "Collectors."

- **Atmospheric Extraction (Environmental Siphoning / The Air-Gap)**: The subtle use of recycled, de-ionized air, 4100K fluorescent lighting, and "White-Noise" generators within the Laboratory to maintain the "Battery State" of the workforce. By controlling the oxygen-to-CO_2 ratios and the Kelvin temperature of the light, the Matrix ensures the worker remains in a state of mild, chronic fatigue. This fatigue is high enough to prevent "Awakening" but low enough to ensure "Task Completion."

B

- **Ballast Harmonics (The 60Hz Trance / The Audible Bar)**: The specific vibrational frequency emitted by the electronic ballasts in modernized workplaces. This 60Hz hum is a harmonic "anchor" used to keep the human brain locked in a "Beta" state of low-level, repetitive task-processing. It acts as an acoustic sedative that masks the sound of the "Extraction" taking place. The Master Architect utilizes noise-canceling technology or "Sovereign Frequencies" (432Hz) to disrupt this signal and regain "Alpha" cognitive function.

- **Battery State (Metabolic Harvesting / The Human Resource)**: The biological reality of the 9-to-5 worker. In this state, the human being is viewed by the Matrix Profit Center (MPC) as an electrochemical cell. Their physical health, their cognitive "Super Powers," and their reproductive years are harvested as fuel for the system's expansion. The "Battery" is provided with just enough "Status Tax" currency to return to the Laboratory the next day, but never enough to achieve "Escape Velocity." The goal of *Rich After Work* is the total "Unplugging" from this state.

- **Blood-Ledger (The Ancestral Debt / The Lineage Count)**: Introduced in Chapter 5, the Blood-Ledger is the metaphysical record of all energy siphoned from your lineage over the last several generations. The Architect realizes that they are not just building wealth for their own comfort; they are reclaiming the "Stolen Time" of their ancestors who lived and died within the Cage. The Blood-Ledger serves as the moral fuel for the "Forensic

Audit," providing the urgency needed to complete the "Multi-Generational Build."

- **Bloodline Shield (The Legal Skin / The Sovereign Veil)**: A sophisticated, multi-jurisdictional legal structure (Chapter 6). It utilizes irrevocable trusts, private family foundations, and "Series LLCs" to create a barrier between the family and the "Digital World-Cell." The Shield makes the Sovereign's assets "legally invisible" and "operationally untouchable," ensuring that the "Harvest" cannot claim the family's legacy during systemic resets.
- **Bots (The Programmed / The Defenders of the Cage)**: Individuals who have fully integrated the "Compliance Frequency." A Bot is no longer just a prisoner; they have become a guardian of the system. They defend the "9-to-5" ritual and the "Spiritual Ceremony of the Clock" because they have been taught to fear the "Wild" of true Sovereignty. A Bot is identifiable by their reliance on "Status Tax" markers to feel a sense of worth.
- **Broom & Shovel Engines (The Wealth Mechanics / The Dig-and-Sweep)**: The dual-action mechanical protocol for rapid wealth acquisition found in Chapter 4.
- **The Broom**: The aggressive "sweeping" of the personal balance sheet to eliminate systemic leaks, "Status Tax" payments, and high-interest liabilities that anchor the worker to the Laboratory.
- **The Shovel**: The systematic "digging" of a deep foundation for the "Private Vault," burying capital into assets that exist outside the digital surveillance of the MPC. The Shovel represents the "Heavy Lift" phase of the Architect's journey.

C

- **Cognitive Siphon (The Mental Drain / The Off-Hour Extraction)**: The process by which the Laboratory continues to drain the worker's energy even after they have "left" the building. Through "The Hum," digital notifications, and "Stress-Looping," the Matrix ensures that the worker's "Super Powers" are never used to design their own "Exit." The Siphon ensures the worker spends their evening in a state of "Passive Consumption" (TV, social media) rather than "Active Design."
- **Compliance Frequency (The Silent Yes / The Frequency Lock)**: The psychological state where the bars of the Cage become invisible. Once an individual reaches this frequency, they no longer feel the "Extraction" taking place. They accept the "Architecture of the Cage" as natural and the "Status Tax" as a necessary part of life. Breaking this frequency is the primary purpose of **Chapter 0: The Awakening.**
- **Corporate Cannibal (Energy Predators / The MPC Elite)**: High-level nodes within the Matrix Profit Center who have achieved a perverted version of "Success" by consuming the prime years and health of their subordinates. They trade the "Life-Force" of their "Bots" for higher-tier "Status Tax" rewards. The Architect refuses to become a Cannibal, choosing instead to build a "Kingdom" that empowers others.

D

- **Debt Engine (The Anchor / The Perpetual Chain)**: The primary tool of control within the World-Cell. The Debt Engine is fueled by credit scores, interest rates, and "Easy Financing." By attaching a "Bot" to a 30-year mortgage and 5-year auto-loans, the system ensures the "Extraction Protocol" can continue uninterrupted for the duration of the "Battery's" peak productive life. The Debt Engine is the "Gravity" that prevents "Escape Velocity."
- **Design, The (The Sacred Blueprint / Geometric Freedom)**: The core of Chapter 2. This is the process of reverse-engineering your entire life. It starts with the "Final Extraction" in mind and works backward to build a financial, spiritual, and physical geometric structure. "The Design" is the Architect's weapon against the "Architecture of the Cage."

E

- **Escape Velocity (The Point of No Return / The Orbital Shift)**: A mathematical certainty established in Chapter 11. Escape Velocity is achieved when the "Internal Frequency" of the Architect's wealth (its compound growth rate) exceeds the "Drag" of inflation, taxation, and the "Status Tax." At this point, the Architect's wealth generates more energy than the system can take away.
- **Extraction Protocol (The Siphon / The KPI Trap)**: The invisible mechanical process of the Laboratory—Key Performance Indicators (KPIs), annual reviews, and "Corporate Culture" initiatives—used to extract maximum

creative "Super Power" from the worker while paying them in a currency that is intentionally designed to lose value.

F

- **Final Extraction (The Sovereign's Withdrawal / The Great Unplugging):** The ultimate execution phase of Chapter 11. This is the total liquidation of all Matrix-dependent, digital, and "Counter-party" assets in favor of "Hard Reality" wealth. This involves moving the "War Chest" from the "Digital World-Cell" (centralized banks) into the "Private Vault" (Gold, Land, Self-Sovereign Assets).

G

- **Generational Vault (The 100-Year Repository / The Chronos-Shield):** Located in Chapter 9, the Generational Vault is not merely a physical safe but a philosophical and legal construct. It is a store of value—comprised of Gold, non-encumbered Land, and codified family wisdom—designed to remain untouched by "The Harvest" for a minimum of three successions. The Vault operates on the principle of "Succession Logic," where each generation acts as a steward rather than a consumer. It is the final defense against the "Return to the Battery State" for the Architect's descendants.

H

- **Harvest, The (The Systemic Reset / The Clearing)**: The core threat identified in Chapter 12. The Harvest is a periodic, orchestrated event within the World-Cell—manifesting as hyper-inflation, market collapses, or currency devaluations—designed to clear the "Bots" of their accumulated savings. The Matrix Profit Center (MPC) uses the Harvest to reset the debt-clock and ensure the workforce remains desperate and dependent. The Sovereign is immune to the Harvest because their wealth is held in "Hard Reality" assets within the Private Vault, which exist outside the digital "Reach" of the reset.
- **Heart-Torus (The Electromagnetic Sovereignty / The Internal Shield)**: The biological electromagnetic field generated by a free human. In the *Rich After Work* cosmology, a person in a "Battery State" has a collapsed Torus, making them susceptible to "The Hum." A Master Architect who operates within their "Super Powers" generates a coherent, high-vibration field that acts as a natural disruptor to the "Architecture of the Cage." Expanding the Heart-Torus is the primary goal of the "Sovereign's Creed."
- **Hum, The (The Audible Sedative / The Frequency Anchor)**: The 60Hz mechanical drone emanating from the "Fluorescent Ballasts" and white-noise generators of the modern workspace. The Hum is the acoustic equivalent of a fence; it is designed to keep the consciousness of the worker localized within the "Task-State." The Hum masks the subtle sounds of the "Extraction Protocol" and prevents the brain from entering the "Theta" state

required for "The Awakening."

I

- **Internal Frequency (The Sovereign Note / The DNA-Signature)**: The unique, un-tunable vibration of the individual. Unlike the "Compliance Frequency" which is dictated by the MPC, the Internal Frequency is the Architect's true north. Protecting this frequency requires a total ban on "Passive Consumption" and a dedication to "The Design." If the Internal Frequency is lost, the Architect reverts to a "Bot" state, regardless of their bank balance.

K

- **Kingdom, The (The Sovereign Estate / The Rule of One)**: The physical manifestation of the Architect's completed work (Chapter 8). The Kingdom is distinguished from "Real Estate" by its autonomy. It is land and systems that operate under the Architect's private "Creed" rather than the public "Employee Handbook." The Kingdom is the geography of freedom; it is where the Sovereign's word is the Law and where "The Extraction" no longer reaches.

L

- **Laboratory, The (The Modernized Cage / The Surveillance Hive)**: Any workplace environment optimized for the study and exploitation of human behavioral patterns. The Laboratory uses "Atmospheric Extraction" and "Geometric Suppression" to turn creative humans into predictable "Human Resources." The Laboratory is the primary site of the "Siphon," where life-essence is converted into corporate "Work-Product."

- **Legacy Canvas (The Medium of Time / The Eternal Work)**: The realization that the Architect's life is not a job to be performed, but a work of art to be left behind. The canvas is "Time"—the only non-renewable resource—and the brush is "Freedom." The Legacy Canvas is only visible once the Architect has cleared the "Status Tax" and "Debt Engine" from their vision.

M

- **Master Architect (The Sovereign Designer / The Unplugged)**: The title earned by one who has successfully moved from "The Awakening" to "The Final Settlement." The Master Architect is a "Former Battery" who has mastered the "Broom & Shovel Engines" and established a "Bloodline Shield." They no longer "Work" for the system; they "Design" systems that work for their lineage.
- **Matrix Profit Center (MPC) (The Energy Predator / The Node)**: Any institution (Bank, Corporation, or Government entity) that views human life as a raw material for energy extraction. Each MPC is a node in the global "World-Cell," interconnected to ensure that a "Bot" cannot move from one Cage to another without remaining in the "Extraction Protocol."
- **Melanin-Engine (The Biological Solar-Cell / The Light-Processor)**: The human body's innate capacity for

processing light into consciousness and vital energy. The Matrix suppresses the Melanin-Engine by forcing "Bots" to live and work under 4100K "Laboratory" lighting, which mimics a permanent winter, inducing "Seasonal Affective Compliance." Re-activating the Melanin-Engine through sunlight and "High-Frequency" environments is essential for "The Awakening."

- **Multi-Generational Build (The 100-Year Architecture / The Succession Protocol)**: The strategy of building wealth and systems that are designed to survive the Architect's death (Chapter 9). This involves the creation of a "Private Vault" and a "Sovereign's Creed" that is passed down to the next three generations, ensuring the "Bloodline Shield" remains intact.

O

- **Omega Protocol (The Sovereign's Final Extraction / The Black-Site Strategy)**: Detailed in Chapter 11, this is the "Nuclear Option" for the Architect. It is the tactical plan for total disappearance from the "Digital World-Cell." It involves the liquidation of all traceable assets, the destruction of the "Digital Persona," and the establishment of a "Kingdom" that is entirely off the grid of the MPC. The Omega Protocol is only triggered when the "Spiritual Siege" transitions into a "Physical Siege."

P

- **Private Vault (The Shadow Treasury / The Non-Correlated Anchor)**: The core of Chapter 5. The Private Vault is the physical and digital repository for wealth that exists outside the "Matrix Profit Center." It contains "Hard Reality" assets—Gold, Silver, Land, and Peer-to-Peer networks—that cannot be "Frozen," "Deleted," or "Taxed" at the source. The Private Vault is the battery of the Sovereign's freedom.
- **Psychological Cubicle (The Mental Bar / The Invisible Cage)**: The internal belief system programmed into a "Bot" by the "Laboratory." It is the limit of what a person believes is possible. The Psychological Cubicle ensures that even when the physical door to the Cage is open, the prisoner will not leave because they believe they will "starve" or "fail" without the MPC.

S

- **Siphon (The Energy Leak / The Invisible Theft)**: The mechanical and psychological optimization of space and time to drain the occupant of their "Super Powers." The Siphon occurs through "The Hum," "Status Tax" marketing, and the "Extraction Protocol." It is the process of converting human soul-energy into corporate profit.
- **Sovereign's Creed (The 13 Commandments / The Operational Code)**: The 13-point operational philosophy found in Chapter 10. It replaces the "Employee Handbook" and serves as the moral and tactical compass for the Architect. The Creed dictates that Time is

the highest value and that any activity siphoning Time without building the Kingdom is a violation of the Sovereign's Law.

- **Spiritual Ceremony of the Clock (The Ritual of Submission / The 15-Minute Sale)**: The daily act of "Punching the Clock" or "Logging In." This is more than an administrative task; it is a spiritual ceremony where the individual formally surrenders their "Super Powers" to HR. It is a declaration that the person's Time—the canvas of their life—is now for sale in 15-minute increments.
- **Spiritual Siege (The War for Consciousness / The Final Battle)**: The core concept of Chapter 12. It is the realization that the "World-Cell" is not just fighting for your money, but for your attention and energy. The Siege is conducted through "Media Bombardment," "Fear-Frequency Broadcasting," and the "Status Tax." The only defense against the Siege is "The Heart-Torus" and the "Private Vault."
- **Status Tax (The Appearance Penalty / The Slave-Luxury)**: (See *Anatomy of the Status Tax*)—The premium you pay to look like you aren't a slave. It is the most effective tool for keeping high-performers inside the "Laboratory" because they must work harder to pay for the objects that prove they are "successful."

T

- **Time-Leak (The Energy Hemorrhage / The Architect's Enemy)**: Any person, activity, or debt that consumes the Architect's primary resource (Time) without

yielding a "Kingdom-Building" return. A Forensic Audit (Chapter 1) is primarily designed to find and weld shut every Time-Leak in the Architect's life.
- **Time (The Prime Currency / The Life-Force)**: The only non-renewable resource in the universe (Chapter 3). In the *Rich After Work* philosophy, Time is not "Money"—Money is a poor substitute for Time. Time is the only thing the "Cage" cannot replace, which is why the "Extraction Protocol" focuses on it above all else.

W

- **World-Cell (The Matrix / The Interconnected Cage)**: The global system of Laboratories, Debt Engines, and MPCs. The World-Cell is designed to be a self-policing environment where "Bots" keep other "Bots" in check. The goal of the World-Cell is to prevent "Escape Velocity" at all costs and ensure a permanent "Harvest" of human energy.

THE SOVEREIGN INDEX:

ADMIN CODES & KEY TERMS

Admin Code
A fundamental law of physics, finance, or psychology that governs reality. Unlike "expert opinions," which change with the trends of the Laboratory, an Admin Code is a persistent truth about how energy and power are moved.

Bloodline Shield
An Irrevocable Trust structure designed to separate legal ownership from tactical control. It is the primary jurisdictional firewall that prevents the Matrix from seizing the Kingdom's assets during legal or economic shifts.

Broom & Shovel
A low-tech, high-essentiality service engine. It represents any business that performs a task the physical world cannot ignore (cleaning, repair, logistics). It is the primary tool used to dig the tunnel out of the Laboratory.

Convenience Siphon
Small, repetitive expenses, usually marketed as "time-

savers" or "treats," that leak Life Essence. These include subscriptions, luxury coffee, and fast food. They are designed to keep the Bot in a state of perpetual "Maintenance Exhaustion."

Extraction Day

The specific date on which your Sovereignty Factor (S_f) remains consistently above 1.0. This is the moment the physical Siege ends and the transition to the Kingdom begins.

Ghost Operation

A business system designed to function through contractors, software, or automation. It allows the Architect to remain invisible to the client and the public while the "Shovel" continues to generate flow.

Life Essence

The finite, non-renewable amount of time and cognitive energy a human possesses. In the Laboratory, it is traded for a salary; in the Kingdom, it is invested in the Build.

Sovereignty Factor (S_f)

The mathematical ratio of your monthly recurring Kingdom income divided by your monthly survival costs (B_s). When $S\_f > 1$, you are mathematically free.

Status Tax

Money spent on items or experiences specifically designed to signal success to other Bots within the Matrix (designer clothing, luxury car leases, prestigious zip codes). It is a voluntary payment to the Matrix to maintain a false identity.

The Laboratory

The Architect's term for the traditional corporate or institutional employment structure. It is an environment where human energy is studied, managed, and harvested for a fixed return.

THE SOVEREIGN INDEX:

THE FORBIDDEN INDEX

THE ARCHITECT'S A-Z SECRET MANUAL

A — **ASYMMETRIC RISK**: The Sovereign's primary investment strategy. While the "Bot" is taught to seek "Safe 7% Returns" (which are eaten by the Status Tax), the Architect seeks 10:1 or 100:1 opportunities where the downside is capped but the upside provides "Escape Velocity" in a single cycle.

B — **BLACK-BOX ASSETS**: Intellectual property or automated systems that operate in total darkness. These are assets that the Matrix Profit Center (MPC) cannot index, track, or tax because they reside in private Peer-to-Peer networks.

C — **COUNTER-PARTY COLLAPSE**: The inevitable failure of the digital banking system. The Architect mitigates this by holding "No-Counter-Party" assets (Physical Gold, Land, Lead) that do not require a bank's permission to exist or trade.

D — **DE-BANKING PROTOCOL**: The tactical process of diversifying liquidity across four distinct jurisdictions to ensure that a "Frozen Account" in one world-cell does not paralyze the Kingdom.

E — **ENCRYPTION OF LEGACY**: The act of converting family history, values, and financial "Design" into a private codex that is only readable by those who hold the "Bloodline Key."

F — **FREQUENCY JAMMING**: The use of binaural beats, Faraday cages, and "Heart-Torus" expansion to block the "Ballast Harmonics" of the Laboratory.

G — **GEOMETRIC WEALTH**: The understanding that wealth is not a number, but a shape. A "Circle" of wealth recycles itself; a "Line" of wealth (a salary) simply runs out.

H — **HYPER-LIQUIDITY**: Maintaining a "War Chest" of 12–24 months of "Hard Reality" cash to allow for instant movement when the "Harvest" begins.

I — **INVISIBLE INFRASTRUCTURE**: Private power, water, and communication systems that allow the Kingdom to function when the World-Cell's utilities are throttled or "Social-Credit" gated.

J — **JURISDICTIONAL ARBITRAGE**: The practice of living in one country, banking in another, and incorporating in a third to ensure the "Extraction Protocol" is mathematically impossible to enforce.

K — **KINETIC DEFENSE**: The physical security layer of the Kingdom. The realization that an "Asset Empire" must be protected by more than just a "Bloodline Shield"—it must have a physical "Wall."

L — **LIQUIDITY TRAP** (REVERSE): Using the system's own debt engines to acquire hard assets, then devaluing the debt through the "Harvest" (inflation), effectively making the Matrix pay for your freedom.

M — **METABOLIC SOVEREIGNTY**: The refusal to consume "Laboratory Food"—processed chemicals designed to keep the "Battery" sluggish and compliant. The Architect grows their own "Kingdom Fuel."

N — **NON-CORRELATED NODES**: Wealth vehicles that move in the opposite direction of the stock market. When the "Harvest" hits the "Bots," the Architect's nodes gain value.

O — **OBFUSCATION TACTICS**: The art of creating "Digital Noise" to mask the Architect's true location and net worth from the Matrix's surveillance algorithms.

P — **PROXY DOMINION**: Holding control of assets through entities that have no visible link to the Architect's name, ensuring that the "Status Tax" collectors have no target to hit.

Q — **QUANTUM SETTLEMENT**: The internal realization that once the "Design" is finished, the freedom has already happened. The physical world is simply catching up to the Sovereign's mind.

R — **RE-WIRING THE BIOLOGY**: The phase of "The Awakening" where the Architect purges the "Compliance Frequency" from their nervous system through fasting and silence.

S — **SUCCESSION LOGIC**: The set of rules governing the "Generational Vault," ensuring that no "spendthrift" heir can liquidate the Kingdom's foundation.

T — **TEMPORAL ARBITRAGE**: Trading high-energy hours (Morning Alpha state) for "The Design" and low-energy hours (Evening Beta state) for the Matrix, until the Matrix is no longer required.

U — **UN-SUBSCRIBE PROTOCOL**: The ruthless "Forensic Audit" of all digital and social contracts that demand attention without providing "Kingdom" growth.

V — **VIBRATIONAL VETO**: The Sovereign's right to walk out of any room, "Laboratory," or deal where the frequency does not align with the "Sovereign's Creed."

W — **WAR CHEST**: The liquid capital kept outside the "Debt Engine," specifically reserved for buying the "Hard Assets" of "Bots" during the "Harvest."

X — **X-FACTOR ASSETS**: Rare, one-of-a-kind assets (Antiques, Rare Land, Sovereign Talent) that have no market "Price" because they are priceless.

Y — **YIELD-CURVE MASTERY**: The ability to predict when the MPC is about to reset the "Extraction Protocol," allowing the Architect to exit the "Digital World-Cell" before the doors lock.

Z — **ZERO-POINT EXIT**: The moment of the "Final Settlement" where the Architect owes the Matrix $0, fears the Harvest $0, and is 100% Sovereign.

Book Description

THEY DON'T WANT YOUR WORK. THEY WANT YOUR TIME.

The "Steady Paycheck" isn't a reward; it's a leash. Within two years of entering the Laboratory, Architect Q. Pinkston saw the truth: the modern 9-to-5 is a sophisticated **Siphon** designed to harvest your prime electricity in exchange for capped compensation. While you perform the **Spiritual Ceremony of the Clock**, the system is quietly stealing your future.

RICH AFTER WORK is the forensic blueprint for your **Final Extraction**.

This is not a "career" book. This is the **Omega Protocol** for the **SOULS** who refuses to bleed out in slow motion. Inside, you will master:

- **90-Minute PAD Time:** The tactical strike that creates 10x leverage.
- **The Anti-Fragile Machine:** Building a lifestyle that thrives on volatility.
- **The Three-Bucket Strategy:** The CEO-level architecture for total financial sovereignty.

The cage door was never locked. Stop trading your soul for a currency that they print out of thin air. Architect your freedom. Finalize the settlement. **The Kingdom starts now.**

About the Author

Architect Q. Pinkston is a Sovereign Strategist who achieved **Escape Velocity** after two years in A Federal Government machine. By treating the office as an all out full scale investigation, he decoded the hidden architecture of the 9-to-5 to reclaim his Tuesday mornings. He now builds **Private Vaults, Ghost Companies** and secures legacies for a new generation of Architects to come. The information within the mind comes from A Direct Tether to SOURCE .